TABLE OF CONTENTS

TABLE OF CONTENTS *continued*

THE
SYSTEM

MARCHING BAND
METHODS

GARY E. SMITH

Cat# G-9277
Copyright © 2016 **GIA Publications, Inc.**
7404 S. Mason Ave.—Chicago, IL 60638
GIAmusic.com

AUTHOR'S PREFACE

Outstanding marching bands and drum corps are established from a solid foundation of fundamentals. Performance improves in direct proportion with the maturation of the basic principles. Therefore, developing a process of continuous learning and development is imperative for the chosen leaders of any band.

Marching bands and drum corps have been evolving for decades—from providing entertainment at sporting events and parades, to performing at competitions and festivals. The diversity of these organizations makes it challenging to establish a "one size fits all" approach to every situation.

It is not surprising then, that there is no standardization of terminology, teaching methods or drill design techniques that can be universally applied. To compensate, some organizations fill this void by developing their own methods to achieve consistency in their performances.

The System, is the quintessential resource for augmenting an existing marching band program or developing a new one from the ground up. It is my hope that the directors and leaders responsible for teaching or administering any marching organization, value the significance of creating and refining a system to attain their highest level of performance.

–Gary E. Smith

Associate Director of Bands and
Director of the Marching Illini, Emeritus
University of Illinois, Urbana-Champaign
President of the American Bandmasters Association (ABA)—2017

I. LEADERSHIP

Principles

Simply defined, *a leader is someone who has the ability to affect the behavior of others, mentally and/or physically.* Although someone may be authoritative and knowledgeable on a subject, it does not necessarily equate to effective leadership. Leadership is more than titles. It must also include the combination of in-depth knowledge of a subject with motivational, disciplinary, and organizational skills to affect behavior, and to influence an organization or a group of people.

One's leadership style is how a leader applies his/her skills and knowledge to lead others. Leadership styles can be positive or negative, constructive or destructive, progressive or regressive. Regardless of approach used, a successful leader must possess an appropriate background of skills and knowledge related to the organization involved.

People seek leadership roles for a wide range of reasons, from personal recognition to a passionate desire to help others. Potential leadership tendencies are present in everyone, and can be developed to various levels.

> A LEADER IS SOMEONE WHO HAS THE ABILITY TO AFFECT THE BEHAVIOR OF OTHERS, MENTALLY AND/OR PHYSICALLY.

Motivation in a Group Effort

Motivation represents how people choose to behave and function within an activity. A leader cannot motivate others; people motivate themselves based upon the experiences and environment provided by the leadership elements of the group. Therefore, leaders should concentrate their efforts on finding methods to achieve group success, because it is success that causes people to motivate themselves in a positive manner. "Bi-products" of success, include determination, hard work, pride, enthusiasm, responsibility, and healthy attitudes.

Respect and Purpose

The biggest challenge with leadership is gaining the respect and rapport needed to maintain a healthy working relationship within the group. All successful leaders have two characteristics in common: they possess specialized skills and knowledge related to their activity, and they have the ability to effectively transfer that expertise to benefit the group.

Leading by Example

Leaders must function as role models, demonstrating enthusiasm, and resolute high standards. They should consistently apply a positive approach when working with group participants. Leaders must also work harder than others, setting an example in all aspects of the ensemble's mode of operation, never expecting anything from others that they do not demand of themselves.

Self Improvement

People who are admired by others demonstrate many positive qualities. A leader must be the type of person that others respect. Good leaders make self-improvement an ongoing process, continually assessing their weaknesses, and working hard to strengthen them. Group participants are perceptive, and recognize personal growth and maturation in their leaders. Although a leader might never achieve perfection, it should be the goal.

Problem Solving

As problems arise, leaders are faced with the challenge of finding solutions. Leaders must examine possible causes of each problem, and determine the most appropriate solution. Careless decisions, misunderstandings, or poor communication usually cause conflicts. Good leaders are sensitive to other people's feelings, and are cautious to not prejudge motives for undesirable behavior. Anyone can identify problems, but only prudent leaders can solve them.

Discipline and Attitude

Dealing with discipline and attitude problems are perhaps the most perplexing challenges a leader faces.

Before deciding how to deal with a discipline problem, gather all the facts. Always give troublemakers the benefit of the doubt before passing judgment. They are more likely to respond positively to people who are compassionate, patient, and helpful. Do not make false or hasty assumptions about a discipline problem's underlying causes. Look for every possible solution, and determine the most appropriate action for each situation, realizing that answers are not always obvious. There are no standard formulas for solving problems—each situation is unique, and must be treated independently.

ABOVE ALL, REMAIN OBJECTIVE, RESPONSIVE, COMPASSIONATE, POSITIVE, AND PATIENT.

Student leaders need to be careful not to overstep their authority or to get involved in critical situations, such as interpreting policies or determining penalties. Serious problems should be referred to the director immediately. The focus for student leaders ought to be on efforts to improve the group's morale while remaining helpful, and supportive. The responsibilities of student leaders must be clearly defined by the director, and conveyed to the group participants.

Positive Versus Negative Reinforcement

Groups of individuals can be encouraged to behave in certain ways by using either positive or negative reinforcement. The negative approach uses tactics such as fear, stress, threats, and unreasonable demands. Often this includes some form of punishment when behavior is not appropriate. Leaders who use positive reinforcement encourage participants to succeed by being helpful, patient, compassionate, enthusiastic, sincere, and dedicated. Participants are more likely to respect leaders who use positive methods.

Although it is possible to achieve success with either approach, the positive method will produce individuals who are self-motivated with good attitudes, self-discipline, and work ethics. They tend to have an inner desire to contribute to the group's efforts and ultimate achievements. Participants learn to develop good attitudes because they want to achieve success. Success breeds success, and failure breeds bad attitudes.

SUCCESS BREEDS SUCCESS, AND FAILURE BREEDS BAD ATTITUDES.

IMPORTANT FACTORS WHEN CONSIDERING HUMAN BEHAVIOR:

- Many times leaders seek solutions to solve symptoms of problems rather than seeking their root causes
- Discipline problems are usually a result of inefficiency, disorganization, misunderstandings, a lack of communication, or a breakdown in the system
- Leaders must look at their own behavior when identifying potential causes of discipline problems
- Evaluating the entire problematic situation before making decisions is a more effective tactic than jumping to conclusions and passing judgment before understanding all of the facts
- Negative behavior of individuals does not always signify a bad attitude or a lack of desire
- Pride, enthusiasm, and good mental discipline cannot be achieved with demands only. These qualities are the result of positive and successful experiences to which all participants contribute
- Some problems are simply beyond a leader's control, and must be solved by someone else
- Not all problems can be solved

Instructions for Using Self-Evaluation Chart

The attributes listed on the **Self-Evaluation Chart** itemize important leadership qualities as they relate to marching ensembles. Use the guide at the top of the scale to establish a general standard when evaluating.

- Evaluate each attribute by placing a dot in the box directly below the appropriate score. Be completely honest.
- When finished, connect the dots with straight lines. This will produce a graph that visually illustrates strengths and weaknesses.
- Total the points, and divide by 20 to get an overall average. Use the scale at the top to determine a numerical evaluation in each category.
- Have friends fill out an evaluation to compare their perceptions with your own personal evaluation.
- To measure progress, do another evaluation at a later date on the same form, using a different colored pen or pencil to illustrate comparisons.

The results will reveal a breakdown of leadership characteristics, as related to marching ensembles. The chart also provides a graphic representation of which qualities need improvement. Since these leadership qualities can be improved, it is helpful to identify deficiencies, and concentrate on strengthening those areas. This type of chart can be used to evaluate other subject matter by changing the criteria listed in the left column.

SELF-EVALUATION CHART OF LEADERSHIP QUALITIES

NEVER ——→ SOMETIMES ·——→ AVERAGE ·——→ USUALLY ·——→ ALWAYS

ATTRIBUTES	0	5	10	15	20	25	30	35	40	45	50	55	60	65	70	75	80	85	90	100
Knowledgeable																				
Skilful																				
Compassionate																				
Industrious																				
Organized																				
Positive																				
Patient																				
Honest																				
Confident																				
Disciplined																				
Responsible																				
Creative																				
Emotionally stable																				
Flexible																				
Friendly																				
Helpful																				
Healthy																				
Personable																				
Enthusiastic																				
Perceptive																				

Student Leadership

A student leader's role is dual in capacity, serving the ensemble, and director in a leadership role while simultaneously functioning as a participant in the ensemble. In a sense, student leaders bridge the gap between participants, and the director. Student leaders can assume many responsibilities that do not require the specialized and extensive professional education their directors have acquired. With minimal training, they can assist with organizational duties such as taking attendance, planning trips, preparing the drill field and rehearsal room for rehearsals, issuing or collecting music, and equipment, etc. During rehearsals they can help teach, refine drill, or work with individuals who need special help. Student leaders can also learn how to assist with writing drills, selecting music, and planning the performances. The possibilities are infinite, and all contribute to the ultimate success of the organization.

There is however, an important message to convey—**a student leader should never "boss" their peers.** Student leaders should not be placed in a position were they "give orders" to their peers, make policy decisions, or discipline fellow students. Participants will resent student leaders who go beyond the boundary of authority as defined by their directors. To clarify this with the ensemble, directors must clearly define the responsibilities of the student leaders.

Remember that students do not want to be "bossed around" by people their age, nor will they respect fellow students who perceive themselves to be superior. Student leaders should work hard to earn the trust and respect of their peers; it cannot be demanded.

IT IS IMPORTANT TO REMEMBER THAT EVERYONE IN THE GROUP IS EQUAL, AND MAKES A SIGNIFICANT CONTRIBUTION TO THE TOTAL SUCCESS OF THE ENSEMBLE'S ACHIEVEMENTS.

Student leaders must support the philosophies and goals of their director, and prove by their actions that they deserve leadership roles. Becoming an effective leader demands hard work, and an ongoing commitment to acquiring a command of basic fundamentals and knowledge, related to the marching ensemble. The greatest challenge, is to develop the ability to share your expertise with others in such a manner, that the entire group benefits. Furthermore, it is important to remember that everyone in the group is equal, and makes a significant contribution to the ensemble's success.

5 Ideal Qualities of a Student Leader

1. A Teacher
Fine marching ensembles are built on a strong base of music, and marching fundamentals. Good teachers contribute to the success of this process by sharing their knowledge and skills with the ensemble during large group rehearsals or individual instruction. An effective teacher is one who can promote good performance skills, facilitate appropriate behavior in students, set high goals, and develop the methods to achieve those goals.

Good teaching techniques and knowledge of subject matter are two of the most important attributes of an effective teacher. As authorities in the medium of marching and music, good teachers should be able to build upon a strong base of fundamentals. The entire ensemble benefits, and is highly motivated when its teachers provide an environment conducive to a constant process of progress and maturation.

2. A Leader
The most successful leader is one who has earned the respect of his or her peers. Respect is achieved over a period of time, after displaying such virtues as patience, honesty, enthusiasm, maturity, industry, responsibility, integrity, compassion, organization, and competence. Once a leader obtains adequate knowledge and skills pertaining to marching methods, he or she must be able to convey this information effectively to others. Success is measured by the progress the ensemble makes resulting from the guidance provided by its leaders. Leaders should not view themselves as superior, but rather as authorities whose goal is to help others improve in their marching and musical abilities.

3. An Administrator
Organizing trips, fundraising projects, concerts, libraries, distributing equipment and uniforms, and maintaining records are just a few examples of how leaders can help improve the organizational structure. When the organization of an ensemble breaks down, every aspect of the group's operation is affected. These responsibilities are so enormous that they must be shared by several people, such as members of parent

organizations, student leaders, or other members of the ensemble. Delegation of responsibilities is an essential skill when dealing with the complexities of organization within the music department.

4. A Musician

Superior musicians can make significant contributions toward the musical growth of the ensemble by transferring their own musical talent and knowledge to others. Essential musical qualifications include conducting skills, knowledge of music literature, and advanced musical training on their particular instruments. It also includes the ability to administer effective and productive rehearsals that result in constant musical progress. Teachers of auxiliary groups who are good musicians are more likely to choreograph artistic movements, which are visually enhancing, and dramatize the music.

5. A Marching Specialist

Every marching ensemble strives to achieve precision and uniformity, both musically, and visually. This can only be accomplished with methodical attention to detail. A great leader identifies and solves musical, and marching problems. Knowledge about drill design, field measurements, various types of marching steps, choreography, conducting, and music style is essential. Someone who is knowledgeable in marching techniques should be able to write, teach, and perfect drills. He or she should also be able to instruct the group on how the fundamentals relate to the success of a performance.

Basic Considerations for Selecting and Training Student Leaders

1. To begin, the director should make a list of student leadership positions that would be an asset to the administration of the total program. It is imperative that a detailed description of the responsibilities for each position be clearly defined, and published for reference and efficiency. This makes it easier for individuals to choose positions that fit their interests and abilities.

SOME TYPICAL CHOICES:

- Drum Majors
- Music Section Leaders
- Marching Section Leaders
- Uniform Managers
- Drill Designers
- Music Arrangers
- Office Managers
- Marketing Staffers
- Equipment Managers
- Librarians
- Rehearsal Organizers
- Public Relations Personnel
- Record Keepers
- Recruiters
- Student Conductors

2. Determine the best process for selection of student leaders for each position. It is essential that the responsibilities of each position are compatible with the qualifications of the candidates. The selection process must be fair and open to all interested, and qualified participants. Publish the process in detail with dates, deadlines, and desired qualifications. Document the entire process. Consider including other qualified staff people in the selection process.

SOME PROCEDURES FOR SELECTION MIGHT CONSIST OF THE FOLLOWING:

- Auditions
- Written Applications
- Submitted Essays
- Interviews
- Elections
- Appointments by the Director
- Volunteer
- Combinations of Processes

3. Train student leaders to fulfill their duties effectively. Do not assume they will automatically perform in a desired manner. Make sure they know what their limitations of authority include. Never allow students to make administrative or policy decisions. They should never be involved with disciplinary situations or in reprimanding fellow participants. Student leaders must be fully supportive of the director's goals, philosophies, procedures, and decisions.

METHODS USED IN TRAINING STUDENT LEADERS:

- Workshops
- Manuals
- Individual Conferences
- Attending Specialized Clinics
- Seminars
- Conventions
- Conferences
- Student Mentoring

4. Teach the student leaders how to identify problems when they are small, and how to solve them. Small problems are usually easy to solve. If they are not resolved when they are small, they can become bigger problems that are difficult to solve.

5. Observe and evaluate constantly the performance of the student leaders. Meet with them frequently to offer critiques, and give them suggestions for improvement. Keep the lines of communication open at all times. The student leaders are an ideal resource for monitoring the morale, attitude, and reaction to the process of progress.

6. Directors should seek input and suggestions from the student leaders for professional improvement. They will respect their directors more when they realize constructive input is a two-way street.

7. Thoroughly inform the ensemble about the responsibilities of each student leader. The "chain of command" should also be defined to make communication more streamlined. This will help eliminate the barrage of questions that can be answered by the student leaders, saving the director time, and minimize confusion.

8. Utilize the veterans as assistant leaders. Even though they do not have student leader titles, they are critical as positive role models. They can contribute in the training of younger participants, and assist the directors and student leaders by giving individual attention to those who might need extra help.

9. Student leaders are valuable for breaking down divisions within the various factions of the group. Discourage cliques and activities that divide the group's overall bonding. Cleverly planned social activities can help eliminate these barriers. During rehearsals, various sections should organize themselves into different combinations of personnel to encourage friendships from outside their own section—resulting in strong moral and unity.

10. It must be understood that the student leaders are not "bosses", and no more important than anyone else in the group. All participants must be treated as equals. Student leaders have defined responsibilities which have nothing to do with being superior to, or more important than their peers.

11. Student leaders should avoid negative responses to stress, confusion, disagreement, or tension within the group. They must consistently remain positive, supportive, enthusiastic, responsible, compassionate, and patient. They must transcend the temptation to become despondent when things are not going smoothly.

12. Respect must be earned. Student leaders can only gain respect from their peers with their actions, and behavior. It cannot be demanded or given by the director. Effective leaders can make significant contributions to the progress of the group only when they have the respect of their peers.

> *GOOD LEADERS DO WELL WHEN THINGS ARE GOING WELL. GREAT LEADERS DO WELL WHEN THINGS ARE NOT GOING WELL.*

The Selection & Development Of Student Leaders

by **Dr. Tim Lautzenheiser**

"You cannot teach a man anything. You can only help him discover it within himself."

—Galileo

Over the past three decades I have enjoyed the tremendous opportunity to present leadership seminars to students, teachers, administrators, and business professionals throughout the nation. Leadership, unlike many disciplines, is constantly shifting, evolving, changing, and becoming. In fact the more we learn about the art of leadership, the more puzzling and mysterious it becomes. Modern day leadership experts continue to highlight the importance of developing leadership values along with the understanding of systemic leadership techniques. The shift from people control to group empowerment is a common theme in today's contemporary leadership training. Ultimately, the welfare of the people is the primary concern. The process becomes equally as important as the product.

Bands and music programs are perfect settings for leadership training. The band culture represents a microcosm of the community environment, and requires a cast of leaders to teach, explain, create, and serve the various members of the musical society. Student leaders are not a luxury, but a necessity, therefore the selection, training, and guidance of these young leaders is a crucially important aspect of every band director's daily responsibility. The following chapter is a leadership blueprint, dedicated to helping you and your students develop a positive and productive student leadership curriculum, that will serve the band in achieving excellence in every aspect of the band program.

TOPICS:

1. Character Traits Of A Student Leader
It is a view of the six character traits desirable (and necessary) for the selection of the leader candidate.

2. A Paradigm Shift For Today's Leaders
The emphasis on intrinsic motivation as opposed to extrinsic rewards becomes the charge for every young leader; to this end, the expectations of the leader are outlined in a clear and concise approach.

3. The Personal Values Of A Student Leader
Simply put, *sharing* and *forgiving* are key virtues for creating a safe, encouraging, and challenging environment that fosters the growth of the members of the band.

4. Choosing Leaders: Maturity Is The Key
If there is one absolute in the leader-selection process, it is the measurement of the candidate's maturity. Is he/she prepared to assume the additional responsibilities and assigned tasks?

5. Solution-Driven Leaders: The Ultimate Choice
Many people can recognize the problem, the successful leader is the person who offers the solution. It is vitally important the student leader understands the key to quality is determined by the collective work ethic of his/her followers.

Try reading each topic as a separate template of leadership training. I suggest you have your student leader candidates study these various areas of leadership development as they launch on their leadership journey. Everyone will benefit from this exercise.

Student leaders are no longer a luxury in our educational world, but rather a necessity, particularly in the field of music. Any successful ensemble is made up of a strong director, and a committed group of responsible and dedicated student leaders. We count on these extraordinary young people to offer their

1. Character Traits of a Student Leader

time and energy in the ongoing growth and development of our programs; without them, much of the daily work simply will not be completed.

Students are usually eager to assume the leadership roles, but are they capable of assuming the responsibilities that accompany the real leadership agenda? Do they truly understand the personal price of leadership? The selection process cannot be taken lightly, for the student leaders will often determine the attitude, the atmosphere, and the level of achievement for the entire organization. They are the pace setters for every member of the ensemble.

So many factors enter into this important choice. Are the candidates competent? Are they emotionally secure? Will they assume a leadership posture both in, and out of the rehearsal environment? Can they handle stress and pressure? Are they willing to make decisions that are not self-serving, but focused on their followers? Do they accept criticism and learn from their mistakes? Are they selfless rather than selfish? Ultimately, will they serve as positive role models for each and every band student? These are not easy questions to answer, but they are crucially important inquisitions, for it is unfair to everyone to assign leadership responsibilities to an individual who has not developed the level of maturity needed to assume the added responsibilities associated with productive leadership.

Over the years of teaching the skills and techniques of student leadership I have observed many students who are confident in their abilities, and certain they can do the job and do it quite well; however they have great difficulty turning hopes and visions into reality. The results are devastating to their followers, the program, and the perceived self-worth of the leader him/herself. In truth, everyone loses. How can we, as directors, avoid this dilemma?

In our urgency to have our students become more responsible and productive, we are constantly looking for those opportunities of growth that will allow them to experience the pathway to success. After all, our fundamental mission as educators is to prepare them for the rigors of adulthood. It is exciting and personally gratifying when we see them rise to the occasion, but the penalty of failure has a high price tag in terms of the emotional damage to the student's self-confidence. Unlike many other aspects of education, failure in student leadership means others are at risk of the shortcoming. If a student leader does not accomplish the given task, it can (and often does) have a negative impact on all the followers. The consequences can range from outward hostility to exclusion from the group.

In extreme cases the wounded student leaders will make a decision to never be put in a similar situation where he/she will be subject to such personal pain. They choose to side-step any leadership responsibilities in the future.

Metaphorically, we do not pick a tomato from a garden until it is ripe, for it will be of no value to anyone. It is impossible to place the prematurely picked vegetable back on the mother-plant. Likewise a student leader who is not ready (not ripe) will be incapable of surviving the pressure and stress of leadership if he/she has not grown to the necessary stage of leadership maturity.

There is an art to the selection process, and veteran educators are careful to find the students who are:

Selfless
Watch for the students who are always taking the time to help those around them. You can quickly identify this important trait, "*consideration for others,*" by simply observing their behavior before, and after rehearsals.

Persistent
Tenacity is an attribute necessary for attaining excellence at any discipline. Many people will begin a new endeavor with a sense of positive enthusiasm, but you are interested in the students who complete their assigned responsibilities. We are not measured by what we begin, but by what we complete.

Consistent
Most student leaders are at a time in their lives when they are establishing their personal habits and life-values; they are truly deciding who they are. Dreams, goals, and desires can shift radically from one day to the next. Pinpoint the students who are predictable, and demonstrates emotional stability; those who can "*stay the course*".

Affable
It is often tempting to favor the student leader who is a gifted musician, and this is certainly an important aspect of his/her qualifications. However, it is vital for the student leader to have a healthy rapport with the other members of the organization. Popularity aside, the chosen student leader must be recognized, and respected by the majority of the group.

Honest

Slighting the truth is commonplace. The student who avoids the temptation to exaggerate or embellish the truth, and is willing to accept the consequences that often accompany honesty, is a rare commodity. Everyone will benefit from being in the presence of a person who demonstrates such personal integrity.

Faithful-Loyal

"United we stand, divided we fall." This well-known phrase is still sound advice for every leader. The students who are always tried-and-true loyalists are your best nominees for student leadership positions. At this stage of leadership, commitment to the group is mandatory, and any disagreements or issues should be dealt with behind closed doors, and in strict confidentiality. There must be a sense of unity in front of the ensemble members.

These six personality traits are only a starting point; however they will establish a strong foundation for the selection-qualifications of any student leader. We, as educators, must be sensitive to the overwhelming effects student leadership can have on the development of the individual. We are in a position to help our students create a sense of self-worth that will serve them throughout their lives. We can guide their efforts and energies to ensure a positive experience for all concerned. As their leaders we have an immeasurable influence on their leadership for life.

2. A Paradigm Shift for Today's Leaders

The entire realm of leadership training has taken a dramatic shift over the last three decades. The strong-armed approach to leadership success has given-way to the concept of allowing the follower to become an invested contributor to the overall mission. There is a greater emphasis on intrinsic motivation rather than using extrinsic rewards as a means for individual or group achievement.

The cornerstones of this paradigm shift emphasize a *win-win* concept embracing both the requirements of the project responsibilities and the welfare of the people involved. It diminishes the power struggle often associated with the traditional positioning, turf protection, rank-and-file status, etc. To find success in this modern day blueprint of leadership style, these four laws of leadership must be understood and integrated into every decision made by the assigned leader; they serve as the foundation blocks of contemporary leadership.

People are more important than titles.

The focal point remains on the welfare of the people involved. The leader constantly monitors the overall attitude of the group assuring a sense of mutual understanding and synergistic effort based on individual and group commitment, focused on the agreed objectives.

We can't lead others until we lead ourselves.

Role modeling plays a vital part in the leader's ongoing communication with the members of the organization. While delegation is still an important aspect of the process, the leader sets the pace by demonstrating the expectations and the standards desired to achieve positive results. The most effective form of leadership is positive role modeling.

Leaders are measured by what they give.

Leadership is an opportunity to give to those who are part of the group, organization, ensemble. The position of leadership is a license to help all those who are part of the forum. If there is not a measured contribution to the forward progress of the group, the value of the leader is diminished to the point of being merely a title carrier.

Leaders assume total responsibility.

When something goes awry, the leader immediately assumes the responsibility for the breakdown rather than pointing the finger of blame at anyone else. The welfare of the followers is primary in every facet of the leader's agenda. Adapting this new leadership consciousness to any musical ensemble, offers the individual players a greater opportunity to "own the group", and accept the responsibilities for the positive growth and development of the organization.

Everyone wins.

3. The Personal Values of a Student Leader

When asked, *"Who would like to serve in a leadership role as we continue to move forward with our band program?"* Do the students really comprehend the extended effort, and energy required to fulfill the responsibility/agenda that lies ahead?

All too often an enthusiastic young want-to-be leader will eagerly assume the coveted title only to be quickly disillusioned following several unsuccessful attempts to garner group support while trying to accomplish the given project. Personal discouragement leads to giving up, and (unfortunately) all future leadership opportunities are avoided based on past experiences of perceived failure.

Do we properly prepare our students for "what lies ahead" when they choose to become student leaders? Or do we simply (and randomly) pick this-or-that person to fill the given position? Are your leaders selected via a popularity vote, or are they chosen because of their abilities, skills, talents, and intentions?

LEADERSHIP IS MADE UP OF 2 PHILOSOPHICAL COMPONENTS:

1. Leadership is FOR GIVING.

2. Leadership is forgiving.

Many young people see a leadership position as the chance to be in charge, to tell others what to do, to delegate work, and to put themselves in a posture of authority. Nothing could be further from the truth. The essence of an effective leader lies in the student's ability to serve others, to create success for the people in the organization. It is the opportunity to give, to contribute, to roll-up one's sleeves and begin moving in a positive forward direction. Whether it is straightening the chairs, putting the stands away, creating a colorful bulletin board, or working with someone on a musical passage, the leader is the person who does—what needs to be done, when it needs to be done, whether he/she wants to do it or not, without anybody asking.

The second aspect of leadership centers on the concept of forgiving. When something goes awry (and it will), many young leaders want to react to the situation by reprimanding the followers for their inability to fulfill the leader's suggestions. However, the true leader will forgive the people involved and pro-actively refocus the energies to correct the problem and quickly get back on course. Psychologically (and intellectually) we know, *"People do not get better by making them feel worse."* All too often, there is a tendency for young leaders to chastise those who fall short of the given assignment; nothing could be more detrimental to the trust-relationship necessary for future success in any leader/follower relationship. The solution is simple: forgive, correct, and proceed forward.

When selecting those chosen students who will be working with their peers in a leadership capacity, look beyond their group popularity, their musical gifts, and even their academic standing; begin to observe how they interact with others, and pay special attention to those who always are considerate of their fellow students and willing to serve those by going above and beyond the call of duty. These are the candidates who are most likely to succeed as leaders; they live the values required of every contributing leader by giving and forgiving.

4. Choosing Leaders: Maturity is the Key

How do you choose your student leaders?

Is there a specific criteria that you use in the selection of these crucially important role models?

Do you have a particular standard they must achieve before they are candidates?

What expectations do you have of these people?

After studying and working with countless student leaders over the years, it is clearly apparent; some students are ready for the extra responsibilities student leadership requires, and many are not. What determines this crucial difference? It appears to lie in the area of individual maturity, not chronological age, but personal maturity. Some young folks easily assume (and consume) the added workload while others may buckle under the pressure. As teachers we have an obligation to be sensitive in our selection of student leaders; for we are asking them to give up the privileges of their classmates and enter into a role that will demand their undivided attention, if they are to succeed. As you can quickly see, being a student leader requires the individual to give up much of his or her freedom in return for the opportunity to dedicate more time and energy to the given goal.

While being a student leader is often misinterpreted as a status upgrade, it is in truth, the acquisition of more responsibilities. It is all too easy for the aspiring student leader to be blinded by enthusiasm of the moment, and accept the charge before truly understanding what will be required of him/her. This is where we, as caring educators, must be cautious and realistic in our assessment of their readiness. Once again let us revisit the original questions pertaining to the selection process. It is imperative we begin with this inquiry, "Is the student mature enough to emotionally embrace the tasks at hand in a fashion that will positively add to his/her personal growth and development?" Simply put, can they handle what will be asked of them? Although there is no definitive template to measure something as arbitrary as maturity, there are some guidelines that can help you in identifying those students who are being considered for student leadership positions.

LEVELS OF MATURITY

Level 1—SELFISH

Selfishness focuses on the preoccupation with "self." A student might be a stellar musician, but he/she easily becomes upset unless everything supports his/her personal welfare and opinion. Beware of the student who unconsciously, or by design, makes decisions that supports his or her self-promotion and/or personal agenda. Little will be gained if he/she is given the power to make decisions that will impact others. Inevitably more time will be spent dealing with the problems caused by immature decision-making than will be spent enjoying the benefits of the young leader's efforts. We often rationalize the fact these students might in fact, prosper by putting them "up front" or giving them extra responsibilities. Alas, it is rare they will rise to the occasion. It would be a much kinder and more positive choice to allow them to spend extra time in the growth process before asking them to put others' considerations and personal welfare ahead of their own.

Level 2—INDEPENDENT

We often see independence as a reaction to the lack of results achieved with a selfish attitude. The human mind comes up with a logical reason why others do not respond to our wishes and concludes: "It is easier to just do it myself than to depend on others and be disappointed."

Many people function at this level throughout life, and are quite successful; however they are unto themselves and perfectly satisfied to do their own thing. In fact they may be uncomfortable letting others get involved. Since they produce excellence in their area of interest; we are often deluded into thinking they will transfer a similar standard of achievement to their followers if they are given a leadership position; however the "independent" may become frustrated when the followers do not immediately choose to replicate the his/her personal habits and work patterns. They have a tendency to give-up in disgust when the going gets rough and revert to the, "I'll just do it myself," habit that has served them so well in the past.

Level 3—COOPERATIVE

A student must be at Maturity Level 3 before being considered for any kind of leadership position that involves dealing with other people. Cooperative personalities are aware nothing will be gained without a sense of mutual understanding; all this must be well fueled with a cooperative attitude. Then, and only then, *I-ME* syndrome gives way to a genuine *WE-US* approach to every situation. Satisfying the ego will become secondary to the forward motion and the personal welfare of the group. This student leader understands the benefits of cooperative decision-making are far greater than self-serving independent choices. Granted, it takes a mature individual to see beyond the instant gratification derived from serving oneself before thinking of others. Level III, cooperative, is a transition to the final and most important perspective needed for effective leadership.

Level 4—GIVING

We have many examples of givers, and we all know those who will go the extra mile, but this level of giving does not require any kind of reciprocation. Those who operate from a posture of giving, do so for the pleasure of the process. The payoff for this individual lies totally in the opportunity to serve. While thank yous are appreciated, they are not required. Their payment lies in the process of the giving. So often student leaders will find themselves discouraged because nobody recognizes their dedicated efforts. It is true we all enjoy personal acknowledgment along the pathway of life, but a mature leader is clearly aware the most important affirmation of his/her leadership success is often disguised in the extension of more work and extra responsibilities being added to the leadership agenda. In essence, *"The reward for a job well done is the opportunity to do more."* The student leader who is a genuine giver is a rare commodity; everyone in the group will gain by experiencing the magic created by a **giving leader**. It is his/her **presence** that makes the difference; what greater role model could there possibly be for the followers?

The student leader selection process is certain to affect every aspect of your program. We often make our choices based on everything from age, talent level, attendance, personal favors, etc. In all fairness to everyone we must be honest in assessing the maturity of those students who want to be given the opportunity to serve others through various student leadership positions. Carefully seek the student who wants to improve the conditions for his/her compatriots by unselfishly contributing to the given goal. When you find this individual, you have identified a student leader in action, put this person in charge to take the lead.

5. Solution-Driven Leaders: The Ultimate Choice

How many times have we heard the haunting phrase, *"You are either part of the problem or you are part of the solution."* In choosing our student leaders, it is vitally important to select exemplary role models who are solution-oriented, rather than problem-plagued.

Students who wish to serve in a leadership capacity must first understand true leadership requires an individual to do more than his/her counterparts; it is about serving others. Student leaders are the doers, they are the people who roll up their sleeves, and go to work.

Even after an extensive explanation of the personal and group expectations, I often wonder if the hopeful student leader really understands the level of commitment, dedication, patience, and personal sacrifice needed, required, even demanded? For those students who wish to take on the challenges of leadership, and for those directors who are looking for the student who has the right leadership qualifications, review the following thoughts, for these are the requisites in selecting, and developing the solution-driven leader.

Focus on the solution, not the problem.

A gifted leader will seek an objective/solution, and then begin to move in the direction of the given goal, rather than dwelling on the current status, and all the reasons the organization cannot reach the objective. This comes about by using a clear and concise blueprint of solution-driven, vs. problem-driven plan of action.

The *solution-driven leader* (SDL) spotlights the strengths of the followers, and emphasizes what is already working. Instead of quickly pointing out everything that is wrong, ineffective, inefficient, and preventing forward progress, the leader will first make a point to recognize the various aspects of the project, (including the people) that give it credibility, and make it worth the follower's investment of time and energy. The benefit package must be obvious or there will be no ownership of responsibility by the followers, thus no group cooperation, and lackluster participation.

The solution-driven leader sets the stage for open communication, and personal involvement. To often we look for those we can blame for the present predicaments; such behavior can garner initial agreement and emotional approval, but it has nothing to do with solving the problem. It is, at best, a momentary "feel good," and rarely serves the group or the leader. The *SDL* will create a safe, open forum of communication with everyone, and begin to listen to any and all suggestions in an effort to attain a better outcome. In turn everyone begins to become more involved in the implementation of a plan that reflects the group's thoughts and ideas.

The solution-driven leader keeps everyone focused on the goal. We often sabotage ourselves by dwelling on the opposite of what we want. Noted psychologist/philosopher, *Abraham Maslow* said, *"The mind will lead us in the direction of our dominant thought."*

If we spend our time thinking about why something will not work, we are leading ourselves to a predictable failure. A *SDL* will continue to communicate the desired goal to the members of the group; what the mind can conceive, the person can achieve. We must picture high level achievement in our minds at all times, and be realistic in the assessment of what it will take to reach the goal. This is one of the fundamental responsibilities of every *SDL*, they are to focus the energy of the followers on the anticipated results.

The solution-driven leader creates energy and enthusiasm.

The best way a leader can create energy and enthusiasm for a group is to model positive energy and sincere enthusiasm. This does not necessarily mean assuming the role of a cheerleader, or extending shallow disingenuous compliments. It means demonstrating a genuine care for the people, the goal ,and the welfare of everyone involved. A lethargic, negative leader will drain energy from any group, and he/she will amplify the problems facing the organization. On the other hand an enthusiastic positive leader will infuse the group with the needed energy to move forward and discover the endless possibilities available as a result of group cooperation. A *SDL* understands the secret to all leadership, the one aspect over which he/she has complete control in every situation, the ability to choose one's attitude at every moment of every day.

...THE ABILITY TO CHOOSE ONE'S ATTITUDE AT EVERY MOMENT OF EVERY DAY.

The solution driven leader creates an atmosphere conducive to effective, and efficient problem solving while giving continuous renewal to everyone involved. Being a leader does not mean, having all the answers. Young leaders often think they are responsible for every solution, answer, and resolution; such logic can result in frustration, confusion, and even delusion. A perceptive and effective solution-driven leader will encourage an ongoing exchange of helpful ideas from those who are part of the group. Every suggestion will be met with genuine appreciation, and the communication will be used as an opportunity to confirm the value of the person involved. If we inadvertently or purposefully reject someone's suggestions, we stifle his/her creativity, and create a barrier for further communication. Maintaining an open, honest, safe environment for group problem solving is seen by many as the most important contribution of any solution-driven leader.

Young people are often enamored by the idea of leadership and the personal benefits they perceive to be a part of the leadership position. Choose those who can comprehend the reality of leadership, those who are willing to go the extra mile on behalf of their peers, those who understand the key to quality is determined by the collective work ethic of their followers.

Group Psychology

An ensemble is defined as "*two or more people performing as a group*". Therefore a marching ensemble is a group effort, and should be perceived by its leaders as an organization that can be influenced to behave in various ways. Since success is the ultimate goal, it is also important that the group's leadership understand some basic psychology that is common among all group efforts.

IMPORTANT PRINCIPALS TO AVOID NEGLECTING:

- Group participants should understand that there are no shortcuts to success. Only hard work with clearly defined goals and effective methods to achieve them can result in the success of the entire group.

- Good discipline within a group is the product of the leadership's efficiency, organization, consistency, competence, and communication. Discipline breaks down when there is confusion or frustration.

- People desire to participate in or associate with groups that are successful.

- Participants of successful groups tend to have healthy attitudes, and are willing to sacrifice time and effort to sustain, and build upon future success.

- Individuals in any group activity want to be treated as equals with their peers.

- Members in a group desire to feel that their contribution is significant to the operation of the organization.

- Participants want to feel that they have input and influence on the overall philosophies and policies of their organization.

- Individual participants need to understand that their performance skills are built upon a strong base of fundamentals, continually undergoing a process of maturation.

- No individual should feel that their contribution is more important than anyone else in the group.

- Veterans should use their experience to benefit the group by assisting younger participants with learning new skills.

- In addition to the positive feeling success provides, every group needs to understand the educational, mental, physical, social, and musical benefits of participation.

- Individuals within a group desire to be respected, and feel their efforts are appreciated and recognized.

- Successful groups want to hear the truth at all times.

- Individual participants within a group should never be singled out and reprimanded in a negative manner. Questioning a member's integrity is counter-productive.

- A leader should NEVER pass judgment on what is going on inside someone else's mind or take on the role of the judge, jury, and executioner. The reasons for someone's negative behavior are seldom what they seem to be on the surface.

- Successful groups can learn how to improve by observing the efforts of other groups with similar objectives.

- Individual mistakes should be tolerated with patience, as long as an effort to succeed is being made.

Interesting Facts About Geese

There is an interesting correlation between the following facts about geese, and the type of teamwork and leadership that is prevalent in any type of successful **group effort**. Reading these facts to the group participants might help everyone more easily understand the importance of working together in an unselfish and efficient manner.

FACT 1

As each goose flaps its wings, it creates "uplift" for the birds that follow. By flying in a "V" formation the whole flock increases its flying range by 71% over what each bird could do, if it flew alone.

FACT 2

When a goose falls out of formation, it suddenly feels the drag and resistance of flying alone. It quickly moves back into formation to take advantage of the lifting power of the bird immediately in front of it.

FACT 3

When the head goose tires, it rotates back into the formation and another goose flies to the point position.

FACT 4

The geese flying in formation honk to encourage those up front to keep up the speed.

FACT 5

When a goose gets sick, wounded, or shot down, two geese drop out of formation and follow it down to help and protect it. They stay with it until it dies or is able to fly again. Then they launch out with another formation or catch up with the flock.

LESSON 1

People who share a common direction and sense of community can get where they are going quicker and easier because they are traveling on the momentum of one another.

LESSON 2

If we have as much sense as a goose, we stay in formation with those headed where we want to go. We are willing to accept their help and give help to others.

LESSON 3

It pays to share leadership and take turns doing the hard tasks. As with geese, people are interdependent on each other's skills, capabilities, and unique arrangements of gifts, talents and resources.

LESSON 4

We need to make sure our honking is encouraging. In groups where there is encouragement, the production is much greater. The power of encouragement (to stand by one's heart on core values and encourage the heart and core of others) is the quality of honking we seek.

LESSON 5

If we have as much sense as geese, we will stand by each other in difficult times as well as when we are strong.

System + Spirit = Success: A Guiding Axiom

The two most important attributes of a successful marching ensemble are *system* and *spirit*. *System* is a way of doing things. The *System* is the totality of what the director determines, such as organization, procedures, activities, philosophies, teaching methods, marching and playing style, and policies. *Spirit* represents how the members react to the *system*, it includes good attitudes, and work ethics. When both of these qualities are outstanding, success follows, producing results such as pride, sacrifice, enthusiasm, and dedication.

QUOTES FOR SUCCESS

"You can't lead others until you lead yourself. It's not what you can do; it's what you will do that makes you a leader. Leaders never get finished."
—**Tim Lautzenheiser**

"A total commitment is paramount to reaching the ultimate in performance."
—**Tom Flores,** NFL Coach

"The best preparation for tomorrow is to do today's work superbly well."
—**Sir William Osler**

"The way I see it, if you want the rainbow you gotta put up with the rain."
—**Dolly Parton**

"The road to success is always under construction."
—**D.M. Czarnecki**

"You can't become a Michael Jordan overnight. Even he had to practice."
—Anonymous

"All things are difficult before they are easy."
—**John Norley**

"Genius is the ability to reduce the complicated to the simple."
—**C.W. Ceran**

"Yesterday is history. Tomorrow is mystery. Today is a gift. That is why it is called the present."
—**Anonymous**

"Progress always involves risk; you can't steal second base and keep your foot on first."
—**Anonymous**

"This is not Burger King™. You can't have it your way."
—**Professor Johnny Lane**

"A great pleasure in life is doing what people say you cannot do."
—**Walter Gegehot**

"Shoot for the moon. Even if you miss it you will land among the stars."
—**Anonymous**

"Obstacles are those frightful things you see when you take your eyes off your goal."
—Anonymous

"Excellence means doing your very best in everything, in every way."
—Anonymous

"Teamwork is the ability to work together toward a common vision, or stated differently, the ability to direct individual accomplishment toward organizational objectives. It is the fuel that allows common people to attain uncommon results. Simply stated, it is less me and more we."
—Anonymous

Practice doesn't make perfect. Perfect practice makes perfect.
—Rick Pitino

"The will to win is not what matters. The willingness to pay the price to win is what matters."
—Bobby Knight

"Leadership is the art of accomplishing more than the science of management says is possible."
—General Colin Powell

"Leaders are made, they are not born. They are made by hard effort, which is the price which all of us must pay to achieve any goal that is worthwhile."
—Vince Lombardi

"The quality of a person's life is in direct proportion to their commitment to excellence, regardless of their chosen field of endeavor."
—Vince Lombardi

"It's not whether you get knocked down; it's whether you get up."
—Vince Lombardi

"The difference between a successful person and others is not a lack of strength, not a lack of knowledge, but rather in a lack of will."
—Vince Lombardi

"A leader must be honest with himself and know that as a leader he is just like everybody else. He must identify himself with the group, must back up the group, even at the risk of displeasing superiors. He must believe that the group wants from him a sense of approval. If this feeling prevails, production, discipline, and morale will be high, and in return, you can demand the cooperation to promote the goals of the company."
—Vince Lombardi

"To achieve success, whatever the job we have, we must pay a price for success. It's like anything worthwhile. It has a price. You have to pay the price to win and you have to pay the price to get to the point where success is possible. Most important, you must pay the price to stay there."
—Vince Lombardi

"Winning is a habit. Unfortunately, so is losing."
—Vince Lombardi

"Winning is not everything—but making the effort to win is."
—Anonymous

"We did everything on Lombardi Time. Once, in pre-training camp, a receiver showed up for a meeting five minutes early, which meant he was really ten minutes later than everyone else. Coach Lombardi jumped on him. 'Young man,' he said 'you'll never play for me if you can't be on time.' That fellow didn't make the team either."

—Sonny Jurgensen

"Perfection is our goal. Excellence will be tolerated."

—Gary Smith

"Use what talents you possess to benefit others."

—Gary Smith

"There are no shortcuts to success. Setting high goals then working hard to achieve them is the key."

—Gary Smith

"What you achieve today will not be good enough for tomorrow."

—Gary Smith

"Learning is a lifetime process of maturation."

—Gary Smith

"No matter how good you are, you could be better."

—Gary Smith

"Be affected by those who you admire. Don't copy them."

—Gary Smith

"Concentrate on helping those who are struggling. Strong people will get better without your help."

—Gary Smith

"Success breeds more success. Failure breeds bad attitudes."

—Gary Smith

"Don't disappoint those who chose you to lead."

—Gary Smith

"The best leaders are those who seek to strengthen their weaknesses and capitalize on their strengths."

—Gary Smith

"There is a solution to every problem. Finding it is what leaders do."

—Gary Smith

"Anyone can identify problems. Effective leaders would rather solve them."

—Gary Smith

"Complainers usually create bigger problems than the ones they are complaining about."

—Gary Smith

"If no one likes being around negative people, then why would you choose to be negative?"

—Gary Smith

"Fix small problems before they become big."

—Gary Smith

"Leadership titles are not what gains respect from followers. "

—Gary Smith

"The better you make yourself, the more you have to give to others."
—Gary Smith

"Support the policies and philosophies of your director, even if you don't agree with them."
—Gary Smith

"As a leader, you are no more important than anyone else in the group."
—Gary Smith

"Never take for granted the good things others do for you."
—Gary Smith

"The are no shortcuts to success. Only hard work and persistence is the way."
—Gary Smith

"A becoming a great leader without a plan is merely a wish."
—Gary Smith

"System plus spirit equals success."
—Gary Smith

Losers say, "It may be possible but it's too difficult."

Losers find two or three sand traps near each green.

Losers find problems in every answer.

Losers say, "It's not my job."

Losers develop an excuse.

Winners develop a program.

Winners say "Let me do it for you."

Winners find answers to every problem.

Winners find a green near every sand trap.

Winners say, "It may be difficult but it's possible."

Develop the attitude of a Winner!

Suggested Reading

Listed below are some excellent books related to various concepts of leadership, motivation, and teamwork.

Reach For The Summit—The Definite Dozen System for Succeeding at Whatever You Do
by Pat Summit—*basketball coach at the University of Tennessee; winner of 5 NCAA Championships.*

- Never Wait 'Til Next Year
- Respect Yourself and Others
- Take Full Responsibility
- Develop and Demonstrate Loyalty
- Learn to Be a Great Communicator

- Discipline Yourself So No One Else Has To
- Make Hard Work Your Passion
- Don't Just Work Hard, Work Smart
- Put the Team Before Yourself
- Make Winning an Attitude

- Be a Competitor
- Change Is a Must
- Handle Success Like You Handle Failure

Success Is A Choice—Ten Steps to Overachieving in Business and Life
by Rick Pitino—*basketball coach of the University of Kentucky Wildcats and the Boston Celtics.*

- Deserve Victory
- Always Be Positive
- Learn From Role Models
- Learn From Adversity

- Build Self-Esteem
- Establish Good Habits
- Thrive on Pressure
- Survive Success

- Set Demanding Goals
- Master the Art of Communication
- Be Ferociously Persistent

The Art of Successful Teaching:
A Blend of Content & Context
by Tim Lautzenheiser

The Joy of Inspired Teaching
by Tim Lautzenheiser

The Power of Positive Thinking
by Norman Vincent Peale

How to Win Friends and Influence People
by Andrew Dale Carnegie

The Seven Habits of Highly Effective People
by Stephen R. Covey

See You At The Top
by Zig Ziglar

Teamwork
by Glenn Parker

II. MUSIC

Style

Musical style, or the manner in which music is played, is the key to excellent musicality and interpretation. The slightest deviation from the proper tempo or an articulation might destroy the precision, meaning, and character of the music.

When rehearsing music, make stylistic interpretations clear so that uniformity is achieved within the ensemble. For example, if a note is to be played short, determine how short, and whether it is heavy or light. Vocalizing articulations, pitches, expressive inflections, phrasing, and rhythms are an effective way to refine style while simultaneously conserving the wind players' endurance.

> **MUSICAL STYLE, OR THE MANNER IN WHICH MUSIC IS PLAYED, IS THE KEY TO EXCELLENT MUSICALITY AND INTERPRETATION.**

Teaching Articulations
Players should understand how to play these five basic articulations to achieve uniformity within the ensemble.

1. MARCATO ∧
Heavy attack with space between the notes (not necessarily short). The tempo determines the note length. Use a heavy "T" attack (using the tip of the tongue), with air support in proportion to the strength of the attack. At very fast tempos the notes would be short, but at slower tempos they are detached, not short.

2. STACCATO •
Light attack with space between the notes (not necessarily short). The tempo determines the space between the notes. Use a light 'D' attack (using the soft part of the tongue), with air support in ratio to the attack. At very fast tempos the notes would be short, but at slower tempos they are detached, not short. Depending on the style of music, the intensity of the 'D' articulation can vary from light to heavy.

3. LEGATO —
Smooth and sustained.
The air should flow constantly from note to note with the only interruption on the articulation of the next note. Use a light 'D' attack, keeping the air moving between the notes.

4. ACCENT >
Heavy attack with full note value. The air flows without interruption until the next note is articulated. Use a heavy 'T' attack matching the air velocity. In some older music styles, it is appropriate to slightly space the notes. With contemporary, rock, and jazz music, the accented notes should be played full value.

5. SLUR ⌒
Smooth, connected, and sustained. Move from one note to the next without articulating. Keep the breath flowing between all notes, as indicated by the slur marking.

WHEN VOCALIZING:

- Practice heavy, medium, and light attacks on 'T' for unmarked, *marcato* & *accents*.
- Practice heavy, medium, and light attacks on "D" for *legato* and *staccato*.
- Equalize the attack with the appropriate air velocity.
- Use vowels for tone color: Dark: 'OO'-Neutral: 'AH'-Bright: 'EE'
- Use 'T' following the vowel for short notes, or clipped releases. e.g. 'DAHT' or 'DIT'

Listening to recordings of various professional musicians and ensembles assists the students in learning how to imitate various styles of music. For example, the best way to emulate swing style is to listen to *Count Basie* or *Duke Ellington* recordings. The more students are exposed to models of what they are imitating, the more mature their stylistic interpretations will be.

Expressive Style

Most marching band musicians do not emphasize expressive playing to the extent that occurs when playing concert music. As a result, it is seldom that marching bands achieve lyrical qualities when performing sensitive music. Consider these common stylistic interpretations when teaching lyrical music.

- Stretch and taper ends of phrases. Do not "clip" them, leaving big holes between the old and new phrase
- When playing softly, darken the tone
- Play longer phrases, shaping the dynamics with the contour of the melodic line
- Enrich the tonal balances by decreasing treble voices and increasing lower voices
- Avoid strident sounds when increasing volume especially when playing in the upper registers
- Encourage players to feel the emotional aspects of the music
- Develop a strong sense of inner pulse to avoid rushing or compressing rhythms
- Strive to blend individual sounds within each section, and the total ensemble
- Weigh the longer notes more heavily than the shorter notes

The Basics of Swing Style *(figure 006)*

Marching bands commonly experience stylistic problems when playing in the swing style. This feel is challenging to achieve because wind players have a tendency to articulate too heavily. Rhythms often sound "square" because they are more closely associated with duple patterns rather than with triplet patterns. To develop proper style, begin by learning to articulate lightly, and smoothly, verbally producing triplet-based patterns with the syllables *'DOO DOO DOO DAH'* (or *'DU'*). Use 'OO' or *'U'* vowels for dark sounds. Use *'AH'* for normal textures, and *'EE'* for bright sounds. Use *'T'* attacks for neutral, accented,

and *marcato* articulations. Use a light *'D'* attack for *legato*, and *staccato* articulations. Remember there are various levels of intensity on *'T'* or *'D'* attacks, depending on the style of the music. Sometimes a heavy *'D'* attack is more appropriate than a *'T'* attack (as with some *rock-styled* rhythms).

Once articulations and vowel colors are understood, practice the swing feel first vocally, then instrumentally. The triplet feel is similar to 6/8, 9/8, and 12/8 meters. For example, repeated eighth note patterns in the swing style should be interpreted as quarter-eighth note rhythms in 12/8, 6/8, 3/8, or 9/8 meters.

Verbalizing various swing patterns assists the players in developing uniformity of articulations as an ensemble. Written examples can be extracted from published music, or simple exercises can be created, and used during warm-ups. There are several published swing exercises that can be utilized to teach the swing style. It is important to keep the air moving through the entire phrase.

Rock & Latin Styles *(figure 007)*

The character of most *Latin* and *Rock* styles of music is largely determined by articulations. As in the swing style, vocalizing vowels and consonants helps achieve uniformity of articulations, phrases, and inflections. When the ensemble can sing the phrases with precision, the stylistic uniformity will be improved. The total meaning of a musical phrase is defined by how the articulations are played. This is also true of the tempo, pulse, phrasing, dynamics, balance, and expression.

Some rock style arrangements are not always marked with articulations, and must be interpreted by the director and the ensemble. In most cases repeated eighth notes should be played with a hard *legato* articulation. Accents should be played full value. For syncopated patterns, play on the "back side" of the beat for better style.

Most Latin rhythms should be played with lighter articulations. The pulse should never feel rushed, therefore, establishing a tight groove with the rhythm section. Inflections are not always marked in the music, but they must be played and felt by the ensemble. Vocalizing is the key to uniform articulations, phrasing, and inflections.

figure 006 - Swing Style Exercise

Swing with triplet feel

tah....tut   tut...tu..tah   dudahtdu.....du.du.dah...   du.dah.......du.dah.......dahdudot

tah.................tut   tut   tut tut tut tu.tah.......................................tut   tut   tow...

Swing style

doodoodaht   doodoodaht   doo   daht daht dahtdahtdaht . doodaaaaaaaaah

taaaaah   taaaaah   taaaaah   taht   taht   taht   taht   taht too taaaaaaaaaaaaaaah

figure 007 - Rock and Latin Style Exercise

Rock - straight eighth notes

tah..tah....tah....tah   du.du.du..dah   du.....daht daht..du.daht   du.du.dah.du.du.....dah du.du.du/dah.du.daht

tah du.du.tah.du.du..........tah.du.du.tut tah.tah.tah... tut tut tah..tah.tut   tah.......tut

Latin - straight eighth notes

dit dah..ditdit dah.dahdit   dit   dit dit   dah...   ditdit du du du du dudit   tut tah..tut.tah

5 Basic Elements of Good Musicianship

Music rehearsals should be carefully planned with the specific goals and methods identified. Plan each rehearsal beforehand to assure that the most immediate musical problems will be addressed. Be prepared to demonstrate solutions by singing or playing examples.

Music rehearsals should be carefully planned with the specific goals and methods identified. Plan each rehearsal beforehand to assure that the most immediate musical problems will be addressed. Be prepared to demonstrate solutions by singing or playing examples.

Begin each rehearsal with a warm-up and tuning routine designed to improve the players' musicianship. The warm-ups need to be productive, with defined short and long range objectives. Make sure this routine does not become boring, predictable or disorganized. Whatever methods are used, the results should yield progressive maturity of musicianship.

Well organized and productive rehearsals not only improve musicianship, but also help to develop good attitudes and work habits. If time is wasted, students will begin to lose interest and disruptive behavior may result.

The primary goal of any music rehearsal is to improve the musicality of each performer. The director needs to understand what causes good musicianship and apply proper methods for the improvement of musicality during instruction. The most effective rehearsals are those that emphasize what causes the music to happen, rather than on the music itself. Although these qualities are defined separately, they all affect and are related to each other.

1. Tone
(The quality of sound.)

Each player should strive to produce the best possible characteristic tone. Before this can happen, there must be a mental concept of desirable sound. Demonstrating an example of good tone can be done by an individual in the band, a clinician, an instructor, or with recordings of outstanding musicians.

Students need continual exposure to model examples of good tone quality. Ideally, these characteristic sounds should be uniform within each section. Once the students have an idea of how they should sound, they need to understand the factors that affect their sound, which are proper breathing, embouchure, posture, and equipment.

Developing good tone at all dynamic levels and ranges is a lifelong process. It is important that the musical exercises incorporated in rehearsal allow for a steady progression of this maturation. Students should be discouraged from playing at extreme dynamic levels or in ranges that produce poor tone and pitch.

2. Intonation
(Pitch)

Intonation and tone are inseparable as the same factors affect both aspects alike. When playing in an ensemble, individual players must listen and compare their pitch to that of the ensembles, and then make appropriate adjustments. The goal is to learn how to listen and adjust to the pitch center of the total ensemble.

> **THE PITCH CENTER OF AN ENSEMBLE IS THE AVERAGE OF ALL THE PITCH VARIANCES PRODUCED BY THE TOTAL GROUP.**

If everyone in the ensemble played a *Concert B♭*, some players might be sharp and some flat. If they were asked to sing that pitch, the results would most likely be a matched pitch. This *pitch center* is the average of all the pitches generated by the total group. When playing an instrument, the correct note can easily be produced without playing perfectly in tune, but when singing, the pitch must be mentally conceived, then matched with the voice.

How to find and adjust to the pitch while playing

Sound the tuning pitch, using either a member of the ensemble or a tuning device. This is the reference pitch, or the center pitch everyone needs to match. Have everyone hum the reference pitch because it is easier for students to hear themselves when humming. This forces the students to listen and transfer the pitch to a mental process.

Next, have the students play their instruments while making adjustments to the reference pitch they are humming. This teaches the students to tune to themselves.

Always tune from the lower instruments up. This makes it easier for the students to hear themselves as they enter by building the pitch from the lowest musical sounds. While the ensemble is tuning, individuals should continue humming until they begin playing their instruments.

When tuning outdoors in sections, one player from each section should tune to the pitch reference using this process and transfer that pitch to their sections. Always tune the ensemble in the same climatic conditions and temperature in which they will be performing. When the temperatures are extreme, allow the pitch center to go up or down to avoid extreme adjustments of the instruments.

Ultimately, the wind players must learn to apply this process while playing their instruments. It is a continual process of listening to themselves, making comparisons to the total ensemble, and then making adjustments to eliminate individual differences.

3. Ensemble
(Two or more musicians performing together uniformly)

Ensemble is a multifaceted concept, essentially involving a congruence of sound between various combinations of musical groupings. For example, ensemble issues might include the compatibility of melody to accompaniment, woodwinds to brass, percussion to winds, first parts to second and third parts, etc. Every aspect of music affects ensembles, including rhythm, phrasing, tone, intonation, articulations, volume, and balance.

The key to a good ensemble is attention to relationships and comparisons, or how one musical element affects another. Students should learn to listen for these relationships, and appropriate adjustments to correct incompatibilities.

4. Balance
(The total compatibility of sound)

Balance is determined by relationships. The same factors that affect the ensemble can also affect balance. There is a misconception that volume is the only factor when establishing good balance. Although balance is most commonly affected adversely by improper dynamics, it can also be affected by differences in pitch, tone, instrumentation balances, scoring, articulations, field placement, instrument facing, and style.

THERE ARE THREE BASIC TYPES OF BALANCES:

1. *Tonal Balance*: How various instrumental groupings are balanced (high, middle, and low textures).

2. *Harmonic Balance*: How various chord tones and harmonies are balanced.

3. *Sectional Balance*: How various instrumental groupings within the ensemble are balanced.

Achieving good balance is a process of making constant comparisons and adjustments. Individuals need to listen to themselves comparatively and make adjustments for balances between various groupings. Students should strive for a characteristic sound that is uniform within their section. Each section must strive for the same uniformity within the entire ensemble.

During warm-ups, practice balancing chords with different instrumental groupings, so the students can learn to hear different tonal and harmonic relationships. Also, practice maintaining these balances at all dynamic levels and ranges of *tessituras*.

5. General Musicianship
(All other musical considerations)

This includes additional musical elements such as tempo, phrasing, articulations, expression, technique, and timbres. All of these interpretations are what determine musicality and proper style.

Achieving Uniform Balance

Construct a perfectly balanced *B♭ chord* by individuals, not parts. Go through the entire wind section, assigning concert *B♭—D—F*—equally distributed. For example, assign the trumpets and clarinets their *C—E* and *G* on the staff. Stay in the middle *tessituras* and make sure each section has an equal number of players for each cord tone. Keep the bass instruments on middle *B♭ concert*.

Have everyone play what they determine as *mezzo forte*. Make adjustments until all instruments are balanced with a uniform and desirable *mezzo forte*. Use two arms held chest level, fingertips touching to indicate the dynamic level of *mezzo forte*. Use the arms like a volume control raising and lowering them to standardize a balanced volume level for *pianississimo, pianissimo, piano, mezzo piano, mezzo forte, forte, fortissimo, and fortississimo*. Maintain a consistent balance and timbre at all extreme dynamic levels.

In addition, work to extend the quality of these extreme dynamic levels. Refine balances by holding up the right arm for brasses only and the left arm for woodwinds only. Experiment separating both arms at chest level and changing the balance between the woodwinds and brasses.

Pointing the first finger up or down will indicate moving the pitch up or down by half steps. Continue to utilize the same hand signals used for the scales such as cutting off the winds and having them hum and match pitches within a chord structure.

Maintaining Focus During Rehearsals
One technique to help maintain the focus of an ensemble in rehearsals is to utilize various unison verbal responses from the group to select questions. This requires a much more active level of attention than when passively listening.

Internalization: The Key To Rhythmic Precision

Before beginning the process of teaching fundamentals, it is important the students understand that a solid foundation of fundamentals is what facilitates good marching and playing. The level of execution is directly related to command of the basics.

Begin by defining and illustrating the concepts of *Style* and *Precision*. Introduce the process of *Internalization* and how it is the ultimate key to achieving good precision and timing. Also define and demonstrate *Subdivision* and how it is an integral part of internalization. Explain that subdivision is the process of dividing each beat into two or three equal parts. When a group can mentally subdivide effectively, it will be significantly easier to follow the conductor, especially when the tempos change or are extremely slow. The tempo is established by a reference, either a conductor or an audible time beating device such as a drum tap or amplified metronome. This reference is called an *external pulse*.

Demonstrate subdivision simply by having the group count four beats divided in half while someone conducts various tempo changes ('*one and two and three and four and*'). This is a great illustration of how subdivision makes it easier to maintain a precise tempo as a group, even when the *tempi* change radically or the ensemble is in a spread formation.

Next introduce inner pulse, a mental process. This is demonstrated by having the group count out loud subdividing for four counts, and then do the same mentally—while someone conducts various *tempi*. The process of maintaining a subdivided pulse while following a visual pulse is called internalization. Develop exercises that teach the group internalization to improve precision.

Example Exercise 1: Have the group count four subdivided beats out loud, and then do the same mentally for four counts while someone conducts a consistent tempo. Once this is achieved with precision, start the same exercise, and then stop conducting to determine whether or not the group is able to maintain pulse periodically without an external reference (conductor).

Example Exercise 2: Practice with an external pulse of four subdivided beats counting out loud, followed by four subdivided beats counting internally, and then clapping on the ninth count. If the clapping is together, the internalization is working. Practice this with various tempos. Once this is mastered, the silent counts can be extended.

Example Exercise 3: Have someone conduct a four pattern with a steady tempo while the group counts out loud on count one and on the '*AND*' of count three, internalizing the beats between. Once this is achieved, do the same exercise while changing the *tempi*.

Executing these types of mental exercises with the ensemble teaches individuals to develop a mental process that is synchronized within the larger group. This produces the effect of rhythmic precision, both musically and with marching execution. It is similar to Christmas tree lights all blinking at the same time. The electrical current that flows through the lights is similar to the internalization of beats that flows through the minds of the ensemble members. Try creating additional exercises to improve the process of internalization until it becomes natural for the entire group.

Editing Existing Arrangements

For bands that do not have perfect instrumentation, modifications can be made to existing music arrangements to achieve more desirable results. If the music has not been imputed into a music software program, it would be worthwhile to do so, for making any modifications simply and quickly. The following are typical examples on how to alter an arrangement to solve music problems, customize structure and improve quality.

Saxophones

The saxophone family provides a wealth of doubling possibilities. The alto saxophones have a wide range and can be used to strengthen, or replace second/third trumpets, mellophones/horns, upper trombone parts or other critical woodwind parts that need enhancement. The tenor saxophones can strengthen or replace trombones, mellophones, and baritones (euphoniums). Finally, baritone saxophones can support the basses.

Using Instruments With Rests

Sometimes parts need reenforcement; double them with instruments that have rests. The possibilities are unlimited.

Re-Assign Parts

If there is a section in the band that has ample numbers, re-assign some of them to play a different part where there is a lack of instrumentation. Modern scoring software makes it is easy to transpose a new part from a different line in the score.

Change Keys

If the *tessituras* of an arrangement are too high causing a strained sound, transpose the entire arrangement down to a more comfortable range for the players.

Simplify

Simplify wind and percussion parts when the players are struggling with execution. Change rhythms, alter melodies and cut parts from the music. When it becomes obvious that a particular music passage is not going to improve with rehearsals, do not hesitate to make changes that make the music more accessible for the students. For example, a quick solution to resolve a challenging percussion part is to extract a phrase from a different location in the chart and substitute it for the trouble spot. An advantage to this solution is that the percussion players do not need to learn new music.

Cut & Paste

Do not be afraid to cut and paste various sections of the music to accommodate a better structure for the arrangement. There is nothing wrong with extracting music phrases from different locations in the score to customize the structure of the music. Provide a solution that might be used to strengthen the end of the show, or improve the transitions between various sections in the performance.

Change Octaves

Try taking a phrase up or down an octave to improve the quality of the sound.

Change Articulations

The character and style of the music is largely determined by articulations. Changing articulations to make a phrase more stylistically correct is a simple process. For example, add a *forte piano crescendo* to a long note, insert *accents*, change *staccato* to *slurred,* and etc.

Change Dynamics

Sometimes changing the dynamics can make the music more interesting. Adding a crescendo or decrescendo is an effective way to merge an old phrase into a new one.

Cutting Or Adding Parts

A solo, or even a passage for full band, can be altered to feature a section, or vice versa.

Insert Drum Breaks

Insert short or long drum breaks in appropriate places to heighten the impact of an introduction to a new musical section.

Change Rhythms

Alter rhythms to solve drill problems when more, or less counts are needed to make the maneuvers easier to execute. Doubling note values adds drama. Simplifying complex rhythms saves a lot of stress and rehearsal time.

Examples

Presented by **Roland Barrett** from the *University of Oklahoma* at the *2008 College Marching Band Symposium* at the *University of Washington*.

These examples are from his arrangement of ***American Salute*** to illustrate important arranging considerations for any marching band arrangement.

Example 1 - Within a like section of melodic instruments, if a melodic line approaches the instrument's upper range limit, double it an octave lower, as shown in the second trumpet part. The upper notes are more secure when approached from below (from notes which are more safely within the playable range of the instrument).

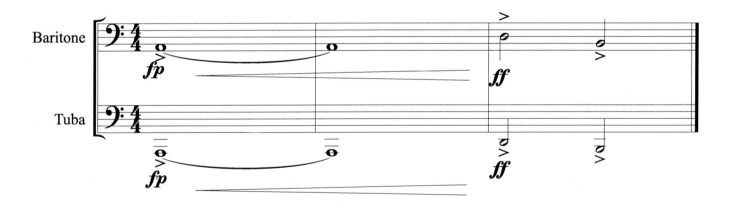

Example 2 - If the tuba part dips below low *B♭*, double it an octave higher.

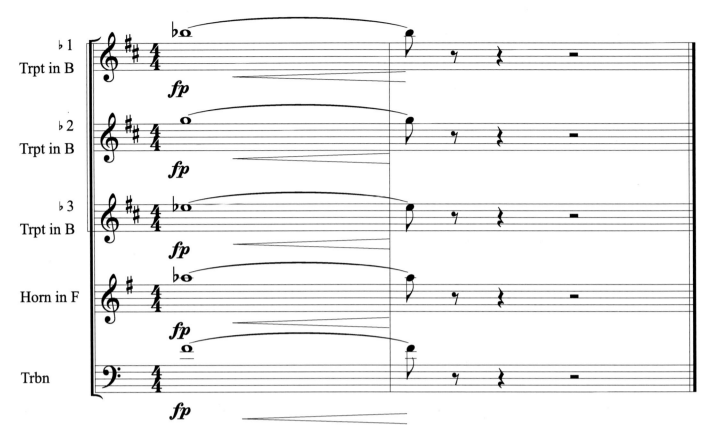

Example 3 - When sheer power is required on any given triad, make sure that the *1ˢᵗ* trumpet, the *1ˢᵗ* horn, and the *1ˢᵗ* trombone are assigned to different pitches of the chord. These players are probably the strongest in the band so assigning them to different chord degrees helps ensure a more solid sound. In a concert *Dᵇ Major* triad, the horn has the tonic, the *1ˢᵗ* trombone has the *3ʳᵈ*, and the *1ˢᵗ* trumpet has the *5ᵗʰ*.

Example 4 - *Linking/Connective Material.* Although the arrangement should have a great deal of variety, it's easy to end up with a very "segmented" sound. Passages such as the one shown below help avoid too much abruptness at those "change of lead" measures.

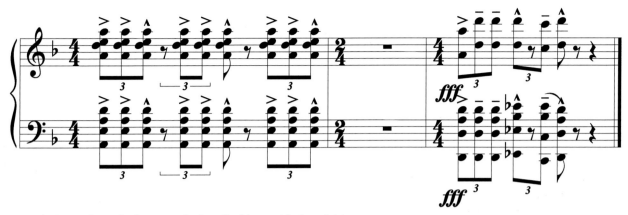

Example 5 - A short rest before final impact helps yield more power

Example 6 - Alternating short phrases often appears like a good idea at the time, but is actually fairly difficult for a band to execute cleanly. The following passage, while musically interesting, can present a constant challenge.

Example 7 - As an alternative for younger bands, a dovetailed, or interlocking approach might assist in ensuring a stronger performance. In the following reduction, one additional note has been added to each of the "dueling" statements.

Common Music Problems

Problem 1

Serious pitch problems occur in extreme temperatures, as several conflicting forces are working against each other. Wind instruments have proven tendencies to be flat in cold weather and sharp in hot weather. Keyboard and membrane instruments do the opposite. As strange as it sounds, piccolos sound flat when the temperature is hot and sharp when it is cold. This is due to the instrument's smaller size; therefore, their pitch will be affected to a lesser degree than that of the larger instruments.

Solution

Ideally, it is best for students to adjust their tuning apparatus the least amount possible. This means the center of pitch must be allowed to move up and down with the temperature to avoid excessive adjustments on the wind instruments.

Tune a B^b clarinet to a tuning device indoors at normal temperatures (around *75 degrees*). Leave the clarinet physically adjusted when moving to the performance location. Allow the clarinet's pitch to rise or fall with the climate of the performance location. Tune one person from each section to that clarinet reference pitch in the conditions in which the performance will occur. Then tune the section to that person. This allows for more precise tuning of like instruments, to the pitch center.

Using tuning devices in extreme temperatures will not allow the pitch center to deviate. This will cause excessive adjustments of the instruments resulting in serious pitch problems for each instrument. For colder temperatures, once the tuning process has been completed, keep the internal air temperature constant by blowing air through the instrument until the performance begins.

Pit-type instruments should be protected from weather related damage with coverings (such as shipping quilts). This also helps large pitch conflicts with the wind instruments during extreme temperature swings.

Keeping instruments up to temperature requires preparing for a performance. Bands typically complete a thorough warm up, which includes a carefully executed tuning sequence. With a normal body temperature of 98.6, it can be estimated that even in cold temperatures the wind instruments are brought up to a temperature much warmer than the outside temperature. During the transit from the warm up to the performance, the instruments could drop in temperature as much as 30 degrees. To maintain intonation, it is very effective to continuously exhale through the instruments to keep them up to temperature.

Problem 2

Most mellophones usually sound flat in a marching band.

Solution

Pitch is a problem for all instruments in a marching ensemble, but the mellophones have a tendency to sound flat even in ensembles with good overall pitch. This is a result of tuning mellophones to a B-flat concert. This pitch is problematic as it is not in the usual *tessitura* they play in during performances. A better pitch center will be maintained by tuning an *F concert arpeggio* (their upper *C-E-G*). This puts the horns in a higher register for tuning, and will be closer to their normal playing range. In addition, playing a mellophone in tune involves more than adjusting slides. No matter how they are tuned, there will be other pitch problems in other registers. However, it is the upper register that is the most exposed.

Problem 3

The full harmonic balance of sound is not achieved.

Solution

Ever try memorizing a third trumpet part? Melody, bass lines, or counter-melodies are much easier to learn. It is a common tendency for inner parts to gravitate toward the melody or other dominant lines when playing by memory. Sometimes the problem is the result of assigning less experienced players to inner parts. Reassign more evenly across the section and ensemble to distribute the talent levels to cover all parts. For example, eliminate the third trumpet part and transpose it for some of the alto sax players, or eliminate the third trombone part and transpose it for the tenor saxophones. The possibilities are unlimited when transposing various parts to other instruments in order to strengthen inner voicing and improve harmonic balances.

Problem 4

When arrangements have high *tessituras*, the pitch and tone qualities are poor, especially at louder volume levels.

Solution

Before purchasing a new arrangement, check the range and make sure it is within the comfort level of the winds. When hiring an arranger, be sure to provide him or her with the ranges of the players. One possibility is to input the arrangement into a music software notation program and lower the key for the whole ensemble. Another possibility is to re-score/re-voice the portions of the arrangement where the ranges are too high. This must be done with portions of the music in which improvement may never occur. There is no reason to allow strained portions of the music to go on without change.

Problem 5

Impractical placement of instruments during a drill causes a variety of phasing problems.

Solution

The most obvious solution is for the drill writer not to design drills using placement that induces phasing problems. However, if it is too late and the drill has already been taught, then the solutions are more challenging, but possible. To minimize this problem, some players will need to adjust the pulse in order to remain "in sync" with other instruments. All musicians must learn two concepts of pulse: following the pulse of the conductor regardless of what they are hearing from other instruments, or following what they are hearing from other instruments and ignoring the conductor's pulse. The choice is dependent upon the placement of the instruments.

How to adjust for phasing problems

When the marching percussion is backfield (or to the side), they will phase with the percussion in the pit, or the brasses up front (or to the opposite side). In this case, the pit players or the brasses in front (or side) must ignore the conductor and learn how to "listen back (or to the side)" and "sync-up" with what they are hearing from the backfield (or side) percussion. The percussion backfield (or side) must ignore what they hear and follow the conductor.

When the marching percussion players are close to the conductor and the brasses are farther away, the percussion must not follow the conductor, but must "sync-up" with what they hear from the brasses backfield (or to the side). The brasses must ignore what they are hearing from the percussion and follow the conductor.

In all cases, common sense prevails. Sometimes the drills can be modified to resolve phasing problems.

Problem 6

Phrase endings are "clipped-off" during expressive passages.

Solution

During warm-ups, play scales, chorales, or chords to teach "tapered" releases, making sure to stretch note values. Expressive passages should be played in the same style as a concert ensemble, shaping lines with dynamics, stretching phase endings, tapering releases, and using rubato to enhance the lyrical qualities of the ensemble.

Problem 7

Articulations are not uniform or in the proper style of the music.

Solution

Practice vocalizing phrases using appropriate vowels and consonants. This will improve uniformity and help save players' "chops" as well. Use the section on *Teaching Articulations,* earlier in this chapter, to learn how to vocalize articulations to achieve uniformity amongst the wind players.

Problem 8

The winds do not sustain long tones or finish long phrases with substance.

Solution

Wind players must learn proper breathing habits, particularly in a marching ensemble where movement is combined with music. Use the exercises described in the *Marching While Playing an Instrument* section found in *Chapter IV.* These exercises will help to develop breathing, sustaining, releasing, and attacking notes uniformly as an ensemble.

Problem 9

Attacks in the winds are "mushy" and sloppy.

Solution

This is usually caused when the attack is out of ratio with the breath. Here is an exercise that helps to develop clean attacks in the winds: Play a B^b *scale*, holding each note four counts. Attack each note using only the breath (no tongue at all). This will sound very sloppy and first, but with practice, it will become more precise. Start each note on *count 1*, release on *count 3* and take a huge breath on *count 4*. Once the ensemble is able to attack each note precisely using only the breath, start using the tongue on the same exercise. The improvement in achieving clean attacks will be obvious.

Copyright Laws

by **Mark Greenburg**

Contrary to popular belief, Copyright law and compliance is very easy to understand. Copyright Law centers around the principle of protecting creative works from being duplicated without the consent of the rights holder. It is not a "sales" right, or a "profit" right, it is a "copy" right. When band directors ask if they need to obtain licenses for making recordings for DVDs, CDs, Video Streaming, and etc., explain that they are simply giving the recordings away and not making any money from the recordings. It simply does not matter because the important issue is that of duplication of copyrighted work. If one asks themselves the question—"Am I duplicating copyrighted work?." The answer to the question is "yes." Then one will need the permission of the owner of the copyrighted work, which will be the rights holder, who will most likely be the publisher.

Copyright for Sheet Music

For Marching Band Directors, the most common concerns about copyright begin with straight forward duplication issues involving the sheet music.

MOST COMMON QUESTIONS AS REGARDS TO SHEET MUSIC:

1. **The band director has purchased a stock chart**, but if the band director hands it out to the kids in the band, they will destroy it. Can the band director just keep it in their files and hand out photocopies to the kids? The answer to this question is "no", not without the consent of the copyright owner. It is a duplication of copyrighted work.

2. **The band director has purchased two stock charts**, and would like to cut them up and make a medley out of the two charts, and then paste the sections together, photocopy these sections and hand them out to the band members so they can learn their parts. Is this permitted? The answer to this question is "no", not without the consent of the copyright owner. It is a duplication of copyrighted work.

3. **The band director has purchased a stock chart**, but does not like the drum section. Can the band director has make their own drum parts and hand them out to the student?

In general, drum parts, and drum parts only, are not unique enough to enjoy the protection of copyright. Therefore, if the band director is making their own drum parts and telling the band members to use the drum parts that the band director or the arranger has created, and to simply ignore the drum parts as they are written, this would be acceptable. If, however, the band director or arranger is retyping the arrangement into notation software and adding their own drum parts into the arrangement, then the band director or the arranger are back to being on the position where they are duplicating music under the protection of copyright, and it is forbidden to do this without permission of rights holder.

4. **The band director has purchased a stock chart for concert band**, but needs to add in their own instrumentation to better fit their marching band's instrumentation. Is this permitted? The answer to this question is "no", not without the consent of the copyright owner. It is a duplication of copyrighted work (i.e. the band director would be making their own sheet music, which is of course, a duplication).

It should be easy to see the common thread in numbers 1-4. Let's turn to the making and commissioning of custom arrangements. It is best to just address the question as to when one needs a custom arrangement license.

WHEN YOU NEED A CUSTOM ARRANGEMENT LICENSE:

A. **Whenever music is altered from it's original form**, it becomes a derivative work. So for example, the song Yesterday, written by *Paul McCartney* and *John Lennon*, was written for guitar and vocals. Therefore, if one wants to make an arrangement of this work for a marching band, one must add in the various instruments and create the parts for those various instruments. Therefore, a custom arrangement license is needed and the permission of the publisher or rights holder is required to make this derivative work. The publishers frequently charge for this license and the amount of money for each license generally varies from **$150.00** to about **$400.00** per song.

B. **If the music is used in a medley:** A medley is defined as a collection of songs or other musical items performed as a continuous piece. Therefore, if one is combining two or more songs in a continuous work, even if the works are not being re-arranged and are just being combined with a musical transition tying the two works together, one must obtain the permission of the publisher or the rights holder.

C. **This is more applicable for show choirs.** Re-voicing a choral arrangement: If one purchases a choral arrangement that was published as an *SSA* arrangement, and wants to re-voice it as a *TTBB* arrangement, that requires a custom arrangement license and the permission of the publisher or rights holder.

D. **Using a small selection of the music:** Rights Holders are frequently asked whether or not the permission of the rights holders or publisher is required if one is using "less than 20 seconds", or "less than eight bars" of music when the music is being used in a continual performance (i.e. where the music does not stop, a medley). The answer is that if one is using any portion of a song that is recognizable, then the permission of the publisher or rights holders is required. So, if one borrowed the first 12 notes from the opening of "Layla", written by *Eric Clapton*, and inserted into a medley, then one would need a custom arrangement license for using those twelve notes. In short, there is no time limit.

E. **Changing lyrics:** Lyric changes of any form require the permission of the rights holder and publisher, therefore a custom arrangement license must be obtained.

F. **Using pieces of stock arrangements** that are combined (i.e. cut out and pasted selections of stock sheet music or re-transcribed) constitutes the need for a custom arrangement license for all of the compositions used. Remember, it is never permissible to duplicate copyrighted material without the permission of the rights' holders.

G. **If you copy the arrangements into** *Finale*, *Sibelius*, *Noteflight* or any other notation program, and you intend to hand this out to the students, then you will need a custom arrangement license. This example would fall under the duplication of copyrighted material and needs the consent of the rights holders.

Copyright for Audio Recordings

Once you move past sheet music based copyright issues, you will be faced with the issues that surround the duplication of audio recordings and audio-visual recordings through the creation of DVDs, CDs, downloads, and streaming.

When making an audio recording and duplicating the audio recording, one must obtain a mechanical license. In general, a mechanical license is statutory, which means that the rights holder must issue the license if a recording of the composition has been created and made available to the general public.

Harry Fox Agency's Royalty Rates Example

9.10 Cents per copy for songs 5 minutes or less or 1.75 Cents per minute or fraction thereof, per copy for songs over 5 minutes.

For example:
5:01 to 6:00 = $.105 (6 x $.0175 = $.105)
6:01 to 7:00 = $.1225 (7 x $.0175 = $.1225)
7:01 to 8:00 = $.14 (8 x $.0175 = $.14)

The statutory mechanical royalty rate for ring-tones is 24¢ per copy.

The rates for interactive streams and limited downloads are determined by a number of factors. These include service offering type, licensee type, service revenue, recorded content expense, and applicable performance royalty expense. Calculate these costs on their website.

Licenses issued after *March 1, 2009* are subject to interest for late payments of 1.5% a month, or 18% a year.

These rates will remain in effect until the next schedule of mechanical licensing rates is determined.

Please note that statutory mechanical license rates do not apply to musical compositions that were created as part of a dramatic presentation. So, making a cover CD of *The Beatles'* songs requires obtaining statutory mechanical licenses, making a cover of music from *Oklahoma* would require getting permission from the rights holders directly, and the statutory rate will not apply and permission can be withheld for any reason.

Copyright for Video Recordings
(DVDs, downloads, and streaming)

Whenever music is set to a moving image, one must acquire a synchronization license from the publisher or rights holder of the music being synchronized to the moving image. Therefore, if one wants to make a video of their show choir performances or their marching band performances and is seeking to distribute or duplicate the video, whether as a DVD, download, or stream (on demand) whether for free or for remuneration, then a synchronization license is required by the publisher or rights holder.

A master use license is a license that is required whenever a master recording is used. For example, if a color guard team performed to a recording of a *Coldplay* song, and made a video of the performance that they wanted to distribute. Another example is, if a performing ensemble used a sample of some other ensemble or band's recording in their performance, and intended to make a video or audio recording of the performance for duplication or dissemination.

Performance Rights & Grand Rights

Performing rights are the right to perform music in public. It is part of copyright law and demands payment to the music's composer/lyricist and publisher (with the royalties generally split 50/50 between the two). Public performance means that a musician or group who is not the copyright holder is performing a piece of music live, as opposed to the playback of a pre-recorded song. Performances are considered "public" if they take place in a public place and the audience is outside of a normal circle of friends, and including concerts, nightclubs, restaurants etc. Public performance also includes broadcast and cable television radio, and any other transmitted performance of a live song.

Permission to publicly perform a song must be obtained from the copyright holder or a collective rights organization. In general, public secondary high schools are exempt from paying performance rights for non-dramatic musical performances even if there is an admission fee sold for the performance if the admission charged at the event is repatriated directly to the school.

All performances of music that were written for dramatic works may have a grand right attached to them, and there are no performance rights exemptions for music that requires a grand right. In other words, one cannot have a concert in which one plays the music from *The Sound Of Music* without checking with the rights holders of the play and determining whether or not a grand rights license will be required.

Grand rights are required when music is used with any type of layering involving costuming, choreography, or the use of props. It is a stretch at this point in time (Summer 2016) to believe that grand rights will be required for marching bands, however it is with certainty that grand rights will be required for show choir and some color guard performances.

Where to Obtain Licensing

Tresóna Multimedia, LLC is the world's largest grantor of arrangement licensing, synchronization licensing, grand rights licensing, and dramatic rights licensing for the world of marching arts ensembles and show choir ensembles. *Tresóna* represents publishers directly and the Licensing Exchange is a highly automated, easy to use, internet-based platform that requires that one only knows the name of the song for which licensing is being requested and either the composer or the person who recorded the song. There is no research involved, just the simple act of typing. There is never a charge for applying for a license, and *Tresóna* represents almost every major publisher for the issuance of licenses.

Tresóna only licenses 100% of every music composition. So if a director obtained half of the license from a publisher directly and informed *Tresóna* that they only needed the 50% of the rights exclusively licensed by *Tresóna*, they would not be able to issue the license because their technology is designed to make sure that every publisher is paid, so what would happen is that *Tresóna* would end up issuing a 100% license, which would mean that the band director would be paying for 150% of the song. There are a multitude of reasons for this, but one of the primary reasons is that it has often been the case that the practice of issuing partial licenses left many other rights holders in the position of not being paid. Therefore, when the system was designed, with the needs of both publishers and licensees in mind, it was designed in this manner.

Tresóna is a one-stop shop for licensing and can obtain licensing for your synchronization, mechanical, grand rights and dramatic rights licensing, and they have a very well developed legal department that services their clients and publishers. Licensees are always able to ask questions of *Tresóna's* legal department, free of charge.

Tresóna is a fee based company that charges a per license fee for every license issued. If *Tresóna* does not deliver a license and collect money for the license on behalf of the publisher, *Tresóna* does not get paid. There should never be a charge for applying for a license from any publisher, and the act of applying for a license should be as simple as providing the name of the song and the performer. There is no research needed on the part of the licensee when applying for a license.

A Note to Custom Arrangers

When creating a custom arrangement of a copyrighted work for an ensemble, an arranger has no right to make the arrangement, deliver it to the ensemble and pass the obligation of obtaining the license to the ensemble. In this instance, the arranger would be infringing the copyright. The music is the property of the rights holder, and the arranger would have no right to take the property of the rights holder and duplicate it and disseminate it without first obtaining permission.

Musical rights are musical rights, and *Tresóna* protects arrangers and publishers by making sure that arrangers sign work-for-hire agreements for every song that *Tresóna* licenses for custom arrangements. And although that license specifies that the resulting arrangement belongs to the publisher, and not the arranger, it is also the case that the arrangement may only be used by the ensemble to which it was licensed. This protects the arranger from having his music used without his permission as a custom arrangement license is required each time arrangement is requested by a new ensemble. The arranger will be required to sign a work for hire agreement each time his music used as a custom arrangement. This helps insure that arrangers are treated fairly and that their work does not proliferate without them knowing how it is to be used and if it must be modified for another ensemble, it gives the arranger the ability to charge a fair price for their work.

It is also the case that copyright protection adheres to the arrangements of public domain music and that arrangers are entitled to sync licensing income if their arrangement of a public domain composition is used in an audio video recording and mechanical licensing income if their arrangement of a public domain composition is used in an audio recording.

www.tresonamusic.com

III.

MARCHING

This chapter contains essential information related to the visual elements of marching ensembles. Improper teaching of the fundamentals result in precision and style problems. There are no shortcuts to building a strong base of basics in marching. The following methods produce significant results. In addition, effective techniques should be designed so there is a continuous process of maturation to more advanced levels of skill. Furthermore, efficient fundamentals produce motivation and momentum for participants to develop impressive work ethic.

TOPICS

- Drill Terminology
- Style & Precision
- Commands
- Standing Basics
- Moving Fundamentals
- Posture
- Various Marching Styles
- Transitions
- Marching While Playing

Drill Terminology

Marching Ensembles are a specialized medium that requires a unique language to convey thoughts in a pragmatic and consistent manner. Unfortunately, there is no standard vocabulary established for the communication of instructions and ideas. The following suggested terms could be used to improve the consistency of communication in rehearsals. Knowledge of these terms can contribute to a steady transfer of ideas during rehearsals.

adjacent forms—groups combined in horizontal planes

axis—The point from which a form rotates

choreography—any movement or visual effect other than drill

closed spacing—individuals or forms spaced 22.5" apart (used only in front positions)

control—maintaining good tone quality at all dynamic levels

conversion—an organized drill connecting two predetermined forms

cover—command used to check vertical alignment

diagonal— two or more individuals placed in an angle

diagonal space—space between individuals or forms in an angle

distance—space between individuals or forms placed one behind another

dress or guide—command used to check horizontal alignment

drifting—gradually shifting left or right from the intended direction during movement

even positions—individuals or forms placed on the grids (even number positions using two- or four-step grid)

fanning—the opening up of intervals during movement

file—two or more individuals placed one behind another

front—two or more individuals placed beside each other

freeze—a command used to encourage no movement at the end of a drill

grid system—a mathematical subdivision of measurements on paper

horizontal form—forms appearing mostly horizontal on paper, or to the audience

intermeshed—two different forms passing through, or placed in between each other

interval—space between individuals or forms placed beside each other

leaning—hips not in line and square with the shoulders

odd positions—individuals or forms placed between the grids (odd number positions using two- or four-step grid)

offset position—forms not positioned between the planes of the zero points

open spacing—individuals or forms spaced 90" apart

phasing—lack of rhythmic precision between sections within an ensemble

pivot—person nearest the axis (fixed pivot is on the axis; moving pivot is off the axis)

precision—uniformity of movement and/or sound

rank—grouping of two or more individuals into a unit, usually within a block formation

regular spacing—individuals or forms spaced 45" apart

sagging—the closing of intervals during movement

sequence—the same movement executed at different times

smooth—a movement executed in ratio to the tempo

snap—a movement executed as quickly as possible, regardless of the tempo

squad—grouping of two or more individuals into a unit (usually four individuals)

stacked forms—grouping of forms combined in vertical planes

stage—the total visual picture of a static form

style—the overall characteristic look and/or sound of an ensemble

timing—the movement which occurs between the starting and ending positions

vertical form—forms appearing mostly vertical on paper, or to the audience

zero points—reference marks placed on the field creating a 180" visual grid system

Style & Precision

Every marching ensemble aspires to achieve a high standard of excellence in both music and marching. Style is defined as the total look and sound of an ensemble. It is important that each participant be able to perform all fundamentals with ease and consistency to attain precision. Participants must understand what is correct and how to accomplish it. In addition, they must be willing to work hard at refining their individual performance skills.

Before you start teaching marching fundamentals

Meet with all participants to describe why learning the basics is important. Ensemble members must have an understanding of the goals and how their achievement will ultimately provide the basis for a great ensemble.

To improve communication while teaching marching fundamentals, the following terms should be clearly explained, listed here in the order in which they should be introduced.

In addition to defining these terms, it is beneficial to use visual demonstrations illustrating the importance of these fundamentals.

anticipation—beginning movement and / or sound before the proper time

dragging—executing movement and / or music increasingly slower than the established tempo

execution—movement and / or music in action

hesitation—beginning movement and / or sound after the proper time

inner pulse—subdividing the pulse mentally to achieve ensemble precision

point 'a'—the clearly defined starting position of any movement

point "b"—the clearly defined ending position of any movement

precision—the uniformity of sound and / or movement

rushing—executing movement and / or music increasingly faster than the established tempo

smooth movement—moving from point "a" to point "b" evenly, in ratio to the tempo

snappy movement—moving from point 'a' to point 'b' as quickly as possible, regardless of the tempo

style—the overall characteristic sound and / or appearance of an ensemble

subdivision—dividing beats into smaller increments to clearly define the timing of movement and / or sound

tempo—the speed of the rhythmic pulse of music and / or movement

timing—defined movement between points 'a' to point 'b'

Commands & Standing Basics

Parade Signals

'FORWARD MARCH' is given by blowing one long whistle beginning on **count 1**, releasing on **count 2** and resting on **counts 3** and **4**, followed by four short whistles in the desired tempo on **counts 5, 6, 7,** and **8**. On the *'and'* of the fourth short whistle (**count 8**), everyone moves the left leg in position for the first step then steps off on the next count. For the fast chair step, the left leg moves up in position for the first step ON the **8th count**.

To switch from marching forward to *'MARK TIME'*, give the same signal as the forward march at the end of a phrase of the cadence or music. The ensemble begins marking time on the fourth whistle for chair step and on the *'and'* of the fourth whistle for glide step. To resume moving forward from mark time, simply signal a forward march.

To *'HALT'*, first signal a mark time. Next, a very long whistle is blown signaling the drums to play a halt cadence at the completion of the current cadence. If there is no halt cadence, the drum major can give a regular halt signal (vocal or with whistle) once the current percussion cadence has ended.

To indicate a *'ROLL OFF'*, give a very long whistle combined with a visual signal near the end of the cadence (circling a hand or baton over the head is a common visual signal). The ensemble begins playing on the first odd count following the last count of the cadence in which the signal was given. The signal should be given facing the ensemble. When the ensemble formation is long, consider using a relay system with someone on the side of the ensemble or in the middle of the parade formation or by having the ensemble members verbally relay the message backwards through the formation.

Verbal Commands

All verbal commands should be given in a strict tempo of **120 beats** per minute. Speeding up the tempo of the commands causes the ensemble to "compress" movements making it difficult to achieve clean and precise execution. The voice should be clear, crisp, deep, and projected with solid air support. Avoid tension in the neck to prevent damaging the vocal cords. Verbal commands for stationary maneuvers should be administered while facing the ensemble and standing at attention with perfect posture, with a minimum of five yards spacing from the front of the group. Commands should never be given casually, but rather with confidence, clarity, and power. This will encourage the ensemble to respond with energy and precision.

The command of preparation identifies who should execute the maneuver and to prepare the group. Use terms such as *'band—squad—file—drums'* and etc. The command begins on **count 1** and is released on **count 2**.

The command of execution consists of one or two short commands, usually given on the **3rd** and/or **4th** counts and identifies the maneuver. Use such terms as *'right hace'—'horns up'—'parade rest'* and etc.

The pulse of the entire command establishes the tempo in which the maneuver should be executed. Maintaining a steady tempo when giving commands facilitates better execution of the maneuver.

Verbal commands for marching maneuvers are similar, with the exception that the command of preparation identifies the maneuver. The command of execution occurs one count in advance of the maneuver's execution. For example, on turns that are executed on the right foot, the command of execution should be given on the left foot.

When giving commands while marching, make sure that verbal commands are directed toward the group, either by facing them and marching backward, or by turning the upper body and head to direct the sound toward the ensemble.

Verbal Commands For Moving Fundamentals

The command of execution for moving commands can be given on any count, as long as it falls on the count that precedes the maneuver. For right foot pivots, the command of execution would be given on the odd counts. Turning on *count 8* is best, especially when the music consists of four or eight-count phrases.

FOR   WARD   MARCH

This command is used to initiate marching forward, either from the position of attention or while marking time. The command of execution should be given two counts before stepping off. The first step forward is normally on the left foot, on an odd count, with the command of execution on the preceding odd count.

TO   THE   REAR   MARCH

This command reverses the forward movement *180 degrees*. Normally, the command is given on the left foot, turning to the left on the right foot.

RIGHT   FLANK   MARCH

(or "Left" or "Right/Left Oblique")

This command changes the forward movement *90 or 45 degrees* to the right or left, and should always be given one count before the turn occurs. When making the turns on the right foot, the command of execution should be on the left foot and vice versa. A *flank* or an *oblique* is a snappy turn which can occur on the 'ON' or the 'AND' of the count in which the turn occurs.

FOUR COUNT TURN TO THE   RIGHT   MARCH

(or "Left" or "To The Rear")

This command changes the forward movement *90 degrees* to the right or left, or in reverse at *180 degrees*. The command of execution is given one count before the maneuver begins. This turn is a slow turn, executed by gradually rotating in four counts, while marking time in place. For the rear, the turn should be executed to the left, unless specified otherwise. For turning right or left, turn in the shortest direction unless instructed otherwise.

Verbal Commands For Stationary Fundamentals

BAND   PA   RADE   REST

(or "At Ease" - for a longer period of time)

The purpose of this command is for resting a short period of time, such as in a parade when the forward movement is briefly stalled or during a pause in rehearsal. There should be no moving or talking while at parade rest, as it is simply a more relaxed position of attention. For a longer period of time, 'AT EASE' would be more appropriate since it is permissible to relax and talk as long as the right foot remains in place. Only the command of 'ATTENTION' can follow when the ensemble is in the position of at ease. While at parade rest, only the commands of 'ATTENTION' or 'AT EASE' can be given.

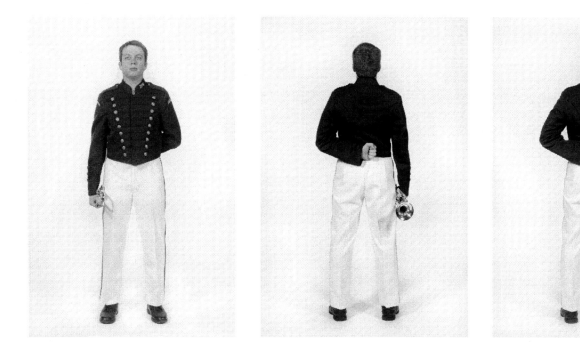

Parade rest style 1

Parade rest style 2

Parade rest style 3

Parade rest style 4

Drum Major Corps Style

On *count 1*, both arms move about *10"* to the side of the legs. Arms and hands are straight with fingers together and palms back. On *count 2*, cross the arms in front of the body, left arm over right arm with hands in a fist position, while sliding the left foot on the ground *15"* to the left (shoulder width).

Count 1   *Count 2*

Drum Major Mace & Signal Baton Style

On *count 1*, bring the tip of the mace to the right of the right toe (almost touching). On *count 2*, push the head of the mace to the right *45 degrees* while sliding the left foot on the ground, *15"* to the left (shoulder width). At the same time, snap the left hand to the small of the back, in a fist position.

Count 1   *Count 2*

Drum Major Traditional Baton Style

On *count 1*, swing the right arm straight out to the right, parallel to the ground. The baton should remain in the crook of the arm. On *count 2*, drop the tip of the baton behind the body and grab it with the left hand with both arms extended straight down with the baton parallel to the ground, while sliding the left foot on the ground, *15"* to the left (shoulder width).

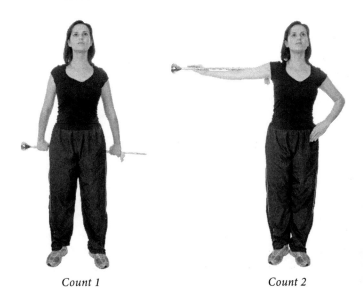

Count 1   *Count 2*

BAND   TEN   HUT

Snap to the position of attention in one count. An optional verbalization can be used, such as 'GO.'

BAND   DRESS RIGHT DRESS

(or "Dress Left" or "Dress Center")

The purpose of this command is to check horizontal alignment. On **count 1**, snap the head in the direction of the command. Check the alignment. Do not lean forward or backward, but rather move the entire body to adjust alignment. Line up the center of the bodies. Note that the end person in a line in the direction of the command, or the center person, does not move on the command, keeping the head forward.

BAND   REA   DY   FRONT

This command reverses "dress right, center, or left" back to the position of attention. Only the head should move.

BAND   HALT

The purpose of this command is to cease marching forward, or marking time, and assume the position of attention.

The command 'HALT' can be given on any odd count. Take one more step on the next count and yell 'STEP AND.' The left leg should be extended back, toe pointed on the ground (in place for mark time). Close (left foot) to attention on the next count and yell, 'CLOSE.' For chair step, the left leg should be in chair position during 'AND.' Vocalizations are optional.

BAND   MARK TIME MARK

The purpose of this command is to march in place. On the 'AND' of count 4, raise the left leg and begin to mark time in place. Be careful not to drift out of position. The fast chair step is begun *ON* the **4**th count.

(or "Right Face" or "Half Left / Half Right")

BAND   LEFT   FACE

The purpose of these commands is to change the direction the body is facing while in a stationary position.

Left Face or Half Left: On **count 1**, execute a **90/45 degree** left turn by pivoting on the right toe and left heel. On **count 2**, snap the right foot back to attention by sliding the foot on the ground.

Right Face or Half Right: On **count 1**, execute a **90/45 degree** right turn by pivoting on the left toe and right heel. On count 2, snap the left foot back to attention by sliding the foot on the ground.

BAND   A BOUT FACE

The purpose of this command is to reverse the direction the body is facing while in a stationary position.

On 'AND' extend the left leg straight forward, toe pointed, directly in front of right foot and close to the ground.

On **count 1**, the left toe makes contact with the ground. The left leg is straight, toe pointed and the weight still on the right foot.

On **count 2**, pivot on both toes, to the right **180 degrees**, keeping the weight on the right foot and the left leg straight with toe pointed.

On **count 3** slide the left foot on the ground, back to attention with the heels together and the toes at a **45-degree** angle. Do not allow the body to rise up or to anticipate the action with the shoulders.

'AS YOU WERE'

The purpose of this command is to cancel a previous command and resume activity in progress.

Posture & Styles

Good Posture Habits in Rehearsal

It is very important that students carry their instruments, preferably in the playing position, when learning or practicing marching fundamentals. This enables the students to develop the strength and endurance needed in their upper torso and arm muscles before learning how to march and play at the same time. If the basics are learned without instruments, the body positions will be different, causing incorrect posture habits and making playing with marching more difficult.

Once proper posture and marching style are firmly established, the students can begin to play simple scale and long tone exercises while marching. Practicing these types of exercises is important before incorporating the two elements. If this stage of development is omitted, the first attempt at playing while marching will be disappointing.

> **UNTIL THE ENSEMBLE CAN MARCH WELL WITHOUT PLAYING, AND PLAY WELL WITHOUT MARCHING, THEY ARE NOT READY TO COMBINE THE TWO.**

Position of Attention and Instruments Down

When standing at attention, the heels should be together with the toes at a 45-degree angle, or in one of the positions illustrated later. The body should be stretched upward with the head held high. Do not make the body stiff or raise the shoulders up. For good posture while marching or standing, try to maintain this "stretched upward" feeling, as if the body is suspended from above, and the feet are barely able to reach the ground.

There should be no moving or talking. The eyes should be forward with the head held high. Body posture is best checked by rising up on the toes while stretching the body as high as possible. Commence by giving the command 'UP,' at which time everyone stretches his or her body up. While up on the toes, maintain good balance so that the weight is properly distributed. The command 'DOWN' indicates to let the weight slowly down until the heels barely touch the ground. This procedure results in consistent body angles, weight distribution and good posture. Think of being stretched upward, like a rubber band. The posture while playing and/or marching is the same, but with the instrument in the playing position.

Instruments in the Down Position

There are many ways to hold the instruments, depending on stylistic preferences. A common approach is to hold the instrument with both hands in front of the body, parallel to and ten inches away from the body. The most common arm position is with the elbows positioned at a 90-degree angle; however, some prefer a 180-degree angle, parallel with the ground. A third option is to tuck the elbows in tight to the body. Section leaders should demonstrate the proper hand and instrument (or equipment) positions and should set the exact height for each instrument (or piece of equipment).

Members of many sections can position their mouthpieces at eye-level (these include mellophones, trombones, trumpets, flutes, piccolos, clarinets, and saxophones). Baritone players should hold the horn on the right side of body with the hands in playing position. Sousaphone players should keep the right hand on the valves and the left hand on the tubing on the left side of the horn. Saxophonists should keep the left arm parallel to the ground. For percussion, the most common procedure is to simply alter the normal grip used for the playing position.

For snares, mallets, and tenors, turn the sticks toward the center, gripping the sticks with both hands together and over the center of the drumhead. The bass drummers should move their hands in playing position up near the top two sides of the heads, near the rims. The cymbals should be held in playing position, tucked into both sides of the body, at shoulder height. All instruments should be held in the same manner within each section. It is the section leaders responsibility to check the height, angles, and hand positions for perfect uniformity.

Various Positions of the Arms While at Attention

Various Positions of the Feet While at Attention

Feet open at first position

Feet closed at third position

Feet at 45 degree angle

Feet together

At-ease: formal   Close quarters marching

'*At ease*' is a resting position of attention. The body is relaxed while maintaining good posture. In formal situations, any talking or moving of the feet is not appropriate. For informal situations, talking and moving the left foot is permitted.

Keep the right foot in position so when the command *attention* is given, the left foot can close to the original position of the body.

Stand by is a defined resting position used during rehearsals, usually when instructions are being given. It allows the participants to relax while staying focused to instructions being given.

Close quarters marching is an instrument carrying position employed for marching in tight places.

Drum Major Corps Style

The arms should be extended down at both sides, relaxed and slightly bent at the elbow. The hands should be in a fist with the thumbs over the top of the first finger and in line with the seam, or middle of the leg.

Drum Major Signal Baton & Traditional Style

The hands should be on the hips with the first four fingers in front and the thumb behind the hips. The fingers should be together and in a straight line with the wrist. The elbows should be straight out to the side. There should be a slight arch in the back so that the shoulders are back slightly. The baton should be resting along the top of the right arm with the first finger slightly over the top of the shaft and the ball of the baton extended about three inches beyond the fingertips.

Drum Major Mace Style

The mace should be held with the right hand and extended straight down the right side of the body. The first finger should be pointed straight down the shaft toward the ball with the mace extended about eight inches beyond the right hand. The palm should be turned in toward the leg. The left arm should hang straight down the left side of the body with a slight bend at the elbow. The hand should be in a fist position, turned toward the leg, with the thumb on top of the first finger.

Horn parallel

Horn elevated

Horn "to the box"

There is little difference between the down position and the playing position with the exception of the angles of the horn and head. With most instruments, the elbows remain at either a 90-degree angle or parallel with the ground.

The desired horn angles can vary based upon the height of the bleachers, acoustical considerations, visual effects, or stylistic preferences.

Marching Steps

There are many styles of marching steps, each with individual characteristics and purpose. Uniformity of marching steps can be accomplished only by utilizing effective teaching techniques. The following marching fundamentals describe movement forward, backwards, sideways, in place, and switching (transitions) from one step to another.

TERMS TO BE USED FOR THE FOLLOWING MARCHING STYLES:	
Relevé—raising up onto the toes or ball of the foot *Tendu*—the leg is fully extended, foot pointed with the toe lightly touching the floor, all weight is on the other foot *Coupé*—the foot is placed next to the ankle in a toe down position, the knee is usually turned out	*Plié*—lowering the center of body by bending the knees *Demi-plié*—half plié; the knees are bent half as much as a regular plié

The Bracket

The Bracket is an exercise which quickly and easily solves many posture problems all at once. It can be used to teach perfect posture at attention and while marching. This procedure should take place at the beginning stages, before using any instruments.

Steps to Define the Bracket

1. Put the arms in the *bracket* position, right arm on the top, parallel to the ground.

2. Next raise the arms to the angle that of the desired horn angle

3. Then stretch the head up until the chin is at the height of the arms. Do not roll the head back, but stretch up from the neck.

4. Raise entire body up as much as possible on the tips of the toes. Hold this position maintaining balance. This distributes the weight to the center of gravity resulting uniformity of body angles in the group.

5. Slowly lower the weight, keeping the head high, until the heels barely touch the ground. Strive for about **60%** of the weight on the balls of the foot and **40%** of the weight on the heels. Doing so creates a perfect posture at attention.

6. Use this same body position when teaching standing and marching fundamentals. It will develop strength in the upper torso and be a faster method to achieve uniformity in the group. Use this position whenever drilling without instruments rather than letting the arms hang down at the sides.

Achieve uniformity by teaching the proper technique.

THE SYSTEM: IV. MARCHING / POSTURE & STYLES

The Glide Step

The Glide Step is a stylized version of walking and is the most practical for playing and marching simultaneously. While shifting the weight forward, roll from the heel to the toe, creating a smooth "gliding" action. Stylistic variations of this step are possible, depending on the defined foot and knee action. The standard size step is generally a *22.5"* step (eight steps per five yards, or "eight to five") for corps-style groups, although a *30" step* (six steps per five yards, or "six to five") is common for military-style groups.

To understand the basics of the *glide step*, think of taking a normal walking step with toes turned forward and with the inner edges of the feet parallel and close together. This concept can be easily taught by utilizing a visualization known as "ski-line." Imagine a person skiing down a hill. In order to proceed, the skier must keep the skis perfectly parallel. If the toes turn in, crossing the skis in front, or if the toes turn out, crossing the skis behind, the skier will likely fall down. While marching, the feet must remain in a similar position. Care must be taken especially when stepping off out of a foot position with open toes.

When stepping forward, keep the toe turned up and roll from the heel to the toes while shifting the weight. This slight difference from walking gives the glide step its characteristic appearance. The "gliding" action is caused by smoothly shifting the weight through rolling from the heel to the toe. This action can be practiced by rocking back and forth; from the back to the front foot while keeping the body level. Keep the body erect, as if balancing books on the head. The articulation point should be the back edge of the heel (not the ball of the heel). Smoothly roll from the heel to the toe in a straight line to shift the weight forward.

A feeling of stretching upward must be maintained to achieve a gliding action. The shoulders should be square with the hips. There should be no movement from the waist up; do not bounce or swing the shoulders from side to side, and do not lean forward or allow the shoulders to move ahead of the hips.

The following teaching technique is geared toward achieving a relaxed, straight-leg style. A more exaggerated style can be gained by increasing the action of the knee. Generally, either technique should be taught with as little discussion of the knee as possible, although instructors must be completely familiar with how the technique they desire will occur.

A slight knee bend happens in the straight-leg version, but it is best to encourage students to keep their knees as straight as possible without locking them—while concentrating more on accurate heel attacks, weight distribution, and proper posture. The bend in the knee of the exaggerated style is more easily taught by concentrating on the increased action of the foot in the roll-through (in addition to the above). It is challenging to be aware of the angle of one's knee (to say nothing of trying to control it). Therefore, it is much simpler to focus on the angles and attack points of the foot.

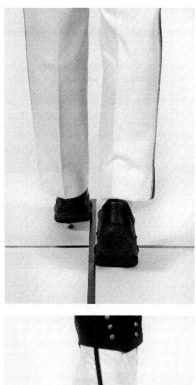

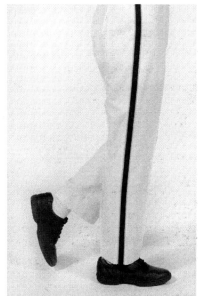

Each step can be broken down into four incremental parts to develop perfect timing and uniformity of movement, weight distribution, and body posture. These parts are labeled as such: 'ONE' (or the number of the step being executed), 'EE'—'AND'—and 'UH', just as beats are subdivided into four parts in common music notation counting systems. Keep all movements smooth and flowing from one part to the next. The weight of the body must be constantly gliding forward from foot to foot. Begin the teaching process by breaking down the glide step, defining key positions and movement of the body using the following procedure.

1. Start with the feet together. Make sure the body is stretched upward and the horn angle is defined. Give a four-count prep to establish the tempo and prepare the movement. On the 'AND' of **count 4,** or ON count four, the left heel raises slightly off the ground and the body begins moving forward. Push off the right foot to get the body moving forward. On 'UH' of count four, the left foot and the body continue to move forward. The front heel should pass by the back toe on 'UH.'

2. On 'ONE', the body should arrive in the position of a perfectly symmetrical upside down 'Y', with the weight distributed evenly between the left heel and the back toe. *This is the key position of the glide step.* Hold this position and define the exact position of the body and the distribution of the weight. The left toe (the height may vary depending on desired style) and the right heel should be up off the ground. The legs should be straight but not stiff to avoid *squatting.* The body should be stretched up forming an upside down 'V' from the hip to the ankles. The shoulders should always remain in line with the hips to avoid *leaning,* and the upper body should be erect.

3. On 'EE' the body continues moving forward, rolling from the left heel, shifting the weight to the front foot. The left leg is straight and the right leg is bent with the heel off the ground, toe pointed touching the ground. The shoulders should be in line with the hips.

4. On 'AND' the body continues moving forward until the right ankle is in line with the left ankle. The heel is up slightly with the foot barely off the ground. The right leg should be slightly bent, the left leg is straight.

5. On 'UH' the body continues moving forward. The back edge of the right heel should pass by the front edge of the left toe on 'UH.'

Glide Step

Upside down 'Y' position

6. On count *'TWO'* the body arrives to the upside down *'V'* position with the right foot forward. This body position should be the same as count *'ONE'*—with the exception of the right foot forward.

Once these positions have been defined, it is best to combine parts of the movement, as it is impossible to stop the forward motion without losing one's balance. It is also more productive to practice this exercise with the instruments in playing position to help achieve proper balance and develop strength and endurance in the upper body.

7. Practice combining *'AND—UH—ONE'* in one motion. Be sure to push off the back foot in order to arrive on the front heel exactly on *'ONE.'* A common problem is arriving on count *'ONE'* late because the movement of the first step must be initiated from a static position. Be thorough about checking the upside down *'V'* position of the lower body for uniformity. This position is the key for developing stylistic consistency. It will take a significant amount of time until everyone is able to hit this position precisely without losing their balance. This can also be practiced in the beginning stages without instruments and locking arms to help maintain balance.

8. Once this has been perfected, do the same exercise and add the *'EE'* position by shifting the weight to the front foot. Hold this position and make sure the shoulders are in line with the hips, the left leg is straight, and the back leg is slightly bent with the heel off the ground. *'AND-UH-ONE-EE.'*

9. Next, practice the exercise adding the next *'AND.'* Hold this position making sure the ankles are in line with each other. The right foot is slightly off the ground with the toe pointed. The left leg should be straight. *'AND-UH-ONE-EE-AND.'*

10. Finally, practice this step to *'TWO.'* Check the posture in the upside down *'V.'* *'TWO.'* *'AND-UH-ONE-EE-AND-UH-TWO.'*

22.5" Glide Step
A standard glide step used for marching eight steps in five yards.

30" Glide Step
A longer glide step is used for marching six steps in five yards. Shorter people can have a tendency to bounce while executing this step. Pushing forward with the back foot can eliminate the bouncing.

31.8" Stride Step
This larger step used to maintain eight steps to five yards while marching at *45-degree* angles.

Glide Step Demonstration

START

'AND'

'UH-ONE'

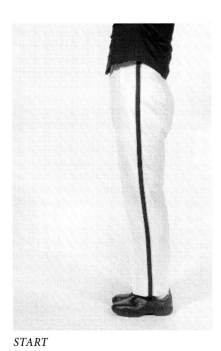

'EE'

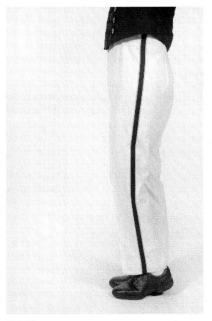

'AND'

'UH-TWO'

THE SYSTEM: III. MARCHING / POSTURE & STYLES

The Ankle-Knee Step

The Ankle-Knee Step is executed by bringing the foot up along the inside of the opposite leg on the *'AND'* of each count. Depending on the tempo, the height of this step can vary from raising the arch of the foot to the calf muscle for a lower step, to bringing the arch to the knee for a higher step. This step can be altered at the *'UP'* position by either pointing the toe down the inside of the leg or letting the foot hang naturally. This step is ideal for *marcato* style music at moderate to slower tempos.

The Drill Procedure Breaks Each Step Down Into 4 Parts to Achieve Uniformity of Style

1. *'TOE'*: Lift the left heel until just the tip of the toe touches the ground. Make sure the knee is pointing straight forward and the weight is on the right foot.

2. *'UP'*: Slide the left foot in a straight line, up the inside of the right leg, until the arch is lined up with the inside of the right knee. Keep the toe pointed downwards along the inside of the right leg (some prefer to let the foot hang naturally). The weight is on the right foot.

3. *'TOE'*: Step forward with the left foot 22.5 inches by sliding the foot down the inside of the leg in a *"scooping"* motion until the tip of the toe touches the ground with the weight remaining on the back foot. A variation of this step would be to use a bicycling foot action. Think of stepping over a wire. For marking time, the foot moves straight back down to the original toe position. The weight is on the back foot (right foot for *mark time*).

4. *'DOWN'*: Shift the weight evenly to both feet as the front foot flattens and the body moves forward. The toe is pointed on the back foot. For *mark time*, keep the weight evenly distributed to both feet. There should be a constant feeling of being suspended upward so that the feet lightly touch the ground, which assists in maintaining good balance. All movement should flow smoothly, avoiding stiffness and jerky movement.

Ankle-Knee Step Demonstration

START

'TOE'

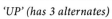

'UP' (has 3 alternates)

'TOE' (MT-step forward for FM)

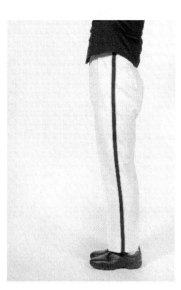

'DOWN'

'UP'—alt—Ankle-calf—relaxed foot   *'UP'—alt—Ankle-calf—pointed toe*   *'UP'—alt—Ankle-knee—relaxed foot*

Two Count Locomotion Drill

This drill progresses closer to the actual step and is accomplished by connecting *'TOE UP'* and *'TOE DOWN.'* To begin, there are four preparatory counts or whistles given. On the *'AND'* of the 4th count, bring the left foot to the *ankle-knee* position.

On count *'ONE'* step forward *22.5* inches with the toe touching the ground first. The weight is on the back foot but begins to move forward after the left toe hits the ground. On the *'AND'* of count *'ONE'*, raise the right foot to the *ankle-knee* position. The weight is then shifted to the left foot.

On count *'TWO'* and the *'AND'* that follows, repeat the previous motions with the roles of the feet reversed. This drill should emphasize the *'UP'* position of the foot, showing that the weight is not shifted until after the front foot hits the ground. This drill should be gradually accelerated until the subdivision is eliminated and the step becomes smoother.

When stepping forward, the foot should slide down the inside of the leg and "*scoop*" into position. Keep this motion smooth and flowing. Be careful not to slam the foot on the ground, jarring the body.

The power of the foot action is on the *'UP'* position while the gentle action of the foot is on the down position during each step. A variation of this step would be to step forward in an arching pattern, as if stepping over a wire. This same procedure can be used for *mark time*.

THE SYSTEM: III. MARCHING / POSTURE & STYLES

START

'TOE'

'UP' (has 3 alternates)

'TOE' (MT-step forward for FM)

'DOWN'

The Chair Step

The Chair Step emphasizes more leg action and uses a pointed toe and bent knee. The height of the upper leg, the lower leg angle, and the foot position can vary, depending on the desired style and the tempo. The advantage of using this step is that it is easier to maintain body control and execute proper timing at a very fast or slow tempo. The same teaching procedures described for the **ankle-knee** *step* are used, except that the 'UP' position is in the "chair-like" position. Lock the knee and ankle joint and pivot at the hip when raising the leg to the 'UP' position.

When raising the leg, roll off the heel and allow the toe to leave the ground last. Conversely, the toe should touch the ground first when stepping down, and the foot should roll from the toe to the heel. The foot acts like a shock absorber to prevent jarring the body while marching. For fast **tempi**, the upper leg is raised with a snappy movement, and only halfway from the 'DOWN' position to the aforementioned 'UP' position. Placing the upper portions of both legs at a **45 degree** angle when viewed from the side.

THE CHAIR STEP EMPHASIZES MORE LEG ACTION AND USES A POINTED TOE AND BENT KNEE.

'UP' - alternate- leg extended   *'UP' - alternate - High Chair*   *'UP' - alternate - Low Chair*

The Double Time Quick Step

The Double Time Quick Step is basically a smaller-sized chair step, with the foot lifted about one inch off the ground. The toe is pointed and the leg is brought out in front of the body while the shoulders are held slightly back.

Execute two steps per count. Begin by lifting the left leg on **count 4**. On **count 1**, initiate the double time step, executing two steps per count. The halt is executed by closing the left foot to attention on the count following either the halt command of execution, or the last count of a cadence. This is a flashy step used for fast action movement. Note that it is impossible to play while doing this step.

The Jazz Walk

The *Jazz Walk* is suitable for slow, smooth, lyrical pieces such as ballads. It draws heavily from dance and can be highly effective when properly utilized. This step works best for intermediate step sizes.

To begin, the feet must be in first position and this turnout must be maintained throughout the movement. The impact occurs as the big toe is placed on the ground on the beat. Then the foot smoothly rolls down through the ball and finally to the heel. As the pulse moves to the *'AND'* of the count, the foot gradually arrives at the **coupé** position next to the stationary foot, with the knee in a *45-degree* turned-out position. The inside of the big toe remains in contact with the ground during each step,

lightly grazing the ground as the foot is moved forward. After the *'AND'* of the count, the foot returns gradually to first position for the completion of the step. To close at the end of a move, the trailing foot may either travel through the **coupé** position and then close, or go directly to the first position.

The **coupé** is not utilized during the initial step-off from a stationary position, although if desired it could be used in transition from a glide step. Move to **count 2** reversing the feet in the *'AND'* position.

The Jazz Walk Demonstration

START

'ONE'

'AND'

'TWO'

The Jazz Run

The Jazz Run should be used whenever the ensemble is marching in a glide step and individuals or sections need to take a *45″ step (4–5)* or larger. Very tall individuals can execute a glide step in this size, but it is generally better if a larger group employs this step if one or two people need to use it. This step helps prevent the look of bouncing or leaping to achieve the largest step sizes, and once a marcher is proficient, it permits playing while using this step size. Jazz running cannot be done effectively at slow tempos; in those cases, marching double time might be a better option. *Corps-style* auxiliary groups frequently employ *Jazz Run* to cover large distances quickly.

Some of the basics of this step are similar to the *Jazz Walk*, especially the turnout of the feet and the movement through the *coupé* position on the *'AND'* count. The impact of the toe on the beat is extremely important; the failure to anticipate this, can lead to injury, and will in all cases cause the marcher to bounce and leap. In addition to these similarities, an understanding of the *plié* position must be added.

The *plié* is a dance movement involving lowering the center of the body. It is not necessary to do a full (grand) *plié*, only a half (demi) *plié*. Begin in first position, although if necessary second position can initially be used. The center of body must be lowered straight downwards, with the knees over the toes. The posterior must be tucked underneath as if lowering onto a stool, not pushed backward as if trying to find a chair behind you. The upper body position remains static. Move slowly into and out of this position from the position of attention, until the motion and position are fully understood.

Once the *plié* position can be accomplished, it is possible to learn the *Jazz Run*. Although awkward, it is best to learn the initial step-off position slowly. Starting from a station

Incorrect plié position

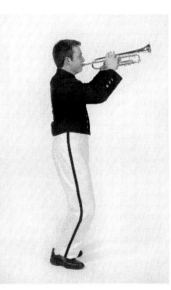

Correct plié position

Plié position—front view

ary position, move to a very slight *plié* position on the *'AND'* count prior to the step-off into the *Jazz Run*. This applies as well when it is preceded by a transition from a *glide step*.

On the first beat, push forward with the rear leg, utilizing the power muscles in the leg. The tendency will be to leap upward, but it is not necessary to bound like a gazelle. The left toe should be turned out and impact the ground about *45″* from the starting point. The body should now be in a position similar to a *plié*, with the center of body lowered and the front knee bent and slightly turned out, while the rear knee is straight due to the pushing motion. The upper body should remain erect as in the position of attention. This initial step-off motion should be practiced until comfortable.

Once the step-off feels secure, it is possible to begin taking several *Jazz Run* steps. Initially, it may be best not to try to stop abruptly. Instead, take four to eight steps and then transition into a smaller step size. As in the *Jazz Walk*, the trailing foot passes through the *coupé* position on the *'AND'* count with the knee turned out. This allows the *plié* position to be maintained throughout the move. Again, be careful that all impacts are in the toes and not the heels, and that there is no bounding motion. There must be constant motion; no pauses or stutters can be allowed.

Once the step itself feels comfortable, the halt or transition is relatively easy to learn. During the *'AND'* count before either the halt or the new move, the body must begin to lift out of the *plié* position. In a halt, the lead knee and foot must be used as shock absorbers to stop the momentum of the performer. When transitioning to a smaller step size, the downbeat of the next count must be in the proper direction and of the proper size and style.

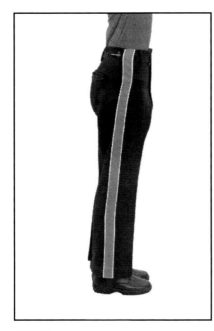

START

'ONE'

'AND'

'TWO'

72

Lateral Marching

Lateral Marching is used by wind players when marching in one direction while pointing their sound in a different location. For directing the sound *45 degrees* to the right or left, have the students first rotate from the hips at a *45-degree* angle keeping the upper body, head, and instrument set. For directing the sound *90 degrees* toward the right or left, have the students rotate from the hips *45 degrees*, then rotate the upper body another *45 degrees*, leaving the hips at the initial *45-degree* angle. This motion should feel like the rib cage is lifted up and out from the hips, and should be maintained throughout the slide. The horn height angles can vary.

Practice marching in these positions up and down the yard-lines to learn how to prevent drifting. The *ski-line position* of the feet, a *45-degree* hip position, and a *90-degree* upper body position must all be maintained simultaneously. Concentrate on keeping the trailing hip and shoulder pulled back, as the tendency is to try and pull them around the same direction as the feet.

Direction of travel

45-degree angle

90-degree angle

Side Stepping ('Crab Crawl')

Side Stepping allows one to move from side to side while keeping the upper body facing forward. Percussion players use this step frequently, to allow their drums and/or sound to stay directed toward the audience. It can also be used as a visual effect for the horn line. The basic step is accomplished by crossing one foot in front of the other, remaining in *relevé* throughout.

To initiate movement to the left from a stationary position, the weight is placed on the right foot on the count previous to the movement. On count *'ONE'* step left with the left foot, skimming along the '*ski-line.*' On count *'TWO'*—the right foot skims lightly along the ground over an imaginary line that runs directly between the starting and ending positions. On count *'THREE'*—the left foot begins moving parallel to the path of the right foot. To halt, plant the right foot and bring the left foot behind and in, to close.

To initiate movement to the right from a stationary position put the weight on the ball of the right foot on the previous count to the movement. On count *'ONE'*—the left foot crosses in front of the right, again skimming the imaginary ski-line. On count *'TWO'*—the right foot begins moving parallel to the path of the left foot. To halt, the right foot must be brought forward to the front foot's line of movement, as the last step is taken. The left foot is brought straight in to close next to the right foot.

Start position moving right

Prep count moving left

Count 1 moving left

Count 2 moving left

Start position moving right

Prep count moving right

Count 1 moving right

Count 2 moving right

All steps taken during any given drill move must be of symmetrical size. Both toes should remain pointed directly forward (similar to the ski-line in forward and backward marching). Be careful that the foot does not roll from side to side, as this can lead to ankle injuries. The point of impact should always be on the ball of the foot. Keep the upper body square and maintain a slight natural flex in the knees to retain a gliding action. To help maintain the hips' square forward alignment, imagine a pair of headlights on the hips and imagine that the headlights must always be pointed forward.

Most transitions into and out of the crab crawl are related to how the step is initiated in the intended direction from a stationary position. For instance, when going from forward marching into a left crab crawl, the foot positions on the last two counts of the move already place the feet on their individual lines of travel for the side step.

Other transitions require the use of a *'dead step'*—such as going from forward marching into right crab crawl. On this transition, the foot positions must be reversed from the final two counts of the forward move. One method of accomplishing this is, on count *'ONE'* of the right crab crawl move, the left foot re-articulates in place. The right foot moves right and back on count *'TWO'*— and the left foot begins the crossing motion on count *'THREE.'* Because there is no motion on count *'ONE'*— all of the preceding steps must be bigger than if a step had been taken on count *'ONE.'*

During the final count of a forward move that transitions to a side step, make sure that the performer rolls up into the *relevé* position on both feet. These transitions should be well defined for each ensemble, and can be effectively taught using a box drill.

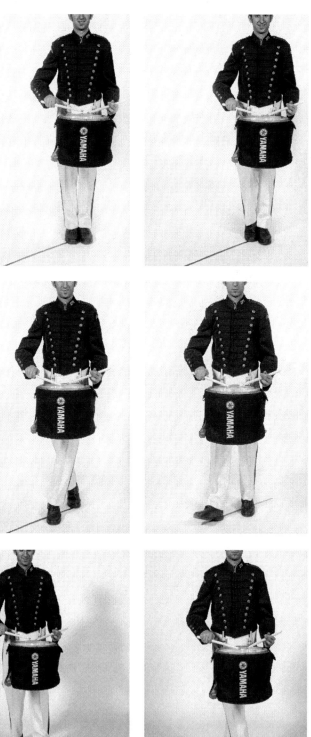

THE SYSTEM: III. MARCHING / POSTURE & STYLES

Backwards Marching

As with the glide step, there are two variations of the basic backward marching step. The description below is for a straight leg style, but can also be modified by utilizing a roll-through from the toe to the heel to allow the knee to bend. Again, the knee should not be locked, and a slight bend is allowed on the *'AND'* counts.

To achieve fluidity, it is best to remain in the *relevé* position at all times with the weight centered on the balls of both feet. Demonstrate the *'triangle'* concept to define how the weight is distributed on the front portion of the feet for normal size steps. The heels should remain at the same height throughout the movement. There are two methods to arriving in the *relevé* position. The first is to pop up to *relevé* on the *'AND'* count prior to the beginning of the backwards move, and then push away for the first step on count *'ONE.'*

The second method is to push away for the first step on count "one" while simultaneously moving to the *relevé* position, like backing up on a ramp.

No matter what style of backward technique is utilized, the toe of the foot in motion should lightly skim along the ground. The beat should be on the ball of the foot to minimize bouncing. As in the forward glide step, the ankles should cross on the *'AND'* count, and the feet remain in the "ski-line" position. The shoulders should remain in line with the hips, while the upper body is lifted upwards and away from the lower body.

For small step sizes, such as those smaller than the 22.5" (eight to five) step, the knee should be nearly locked for the duration of each step and the body raised up on the tip of the toes. For larger step sizes there is a very slight knee bend and the weight is lowered close to a flat foot position.

Do not squat or slump the upper body in an attempt to take a large step size. Continue to lift up and out from the hips and utilize the muscles of the lower leg to push away, not up, from the ground. For the largest step sizes, push away from the ground and become almost airborne to keep the legs straight. The feasibility of this must be evaluated on an individual basis, for the drill move and height of the student.

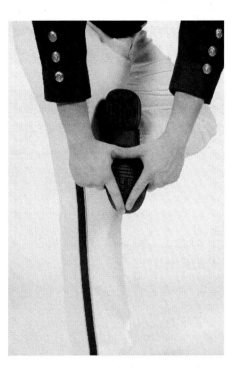

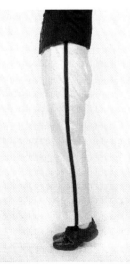

Lift to precede back step

Regular size step back

Small size step back

Large step back

Mark Time

There are several purposes for *mark time*. The first, is to maintain a tempo while holding in a stationary position. This can also be used to reinforce the timing of the feet while rehearsing music. The second, is to maintain motion while in a stationary position in the drill.

Ankle-Knee Mark Time
Variations in the UP positions

Ankle knee—pointed toe   *Ankle calf—pointed toe*   *Ankle knee—relaxed foot*   *Ankle calf—relaxed foot*

Chair Step Mark Time
Variations in the UP Positions

   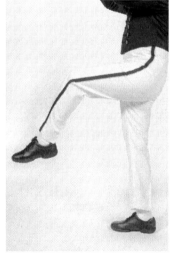

Low chair   *Pure chair*   *Half chair*   *High chair—leg extended*

Low Mark Time

THREE BASIC VARIATIONS OF LOW MARK TIME:

1. *Flat Foot Mark Time*
The foot is raised up about 1" off the ground and kept flat in the *'UP'* position. Bring the foot up until the arch is in line with the ankle. Avoid bouncing and squatting, and keep the body stretched upward.

2. *Heel Mark Time*
The heel is raised, and the toes remain in contact with the ground. Think of "peeling" the foot off the ground. How high the heel comes off the ground can vary, depending on style and tempo. Keep the body stretched up.

3. *Toe Mark Time*
The toe is curled up slightly, and the heels are kept on the ground. How high the toe is raised can vary, depending on style and tempo. Keep the body stretched upward.

ALL THREE TYPES OF MARK TIME STEPS CAN BE EXECUTED WITH EITHER SMOOTH OR SNAPPY MOVEMENTS.

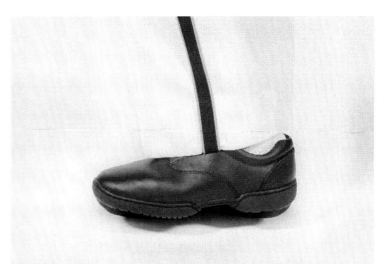

1. *Flat foot mark time*

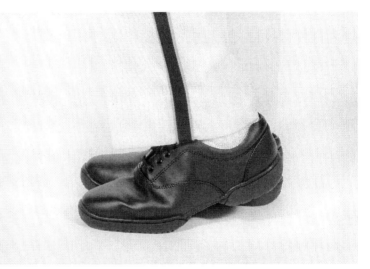

2. *Heel mark time*

3. *Toe mark time*

Transitions

No matter what style of movement is done, it is always necessary to transition during drill. Sometimes the transition is within the same style, and at other times the transition changes to a different style.

CHANGING DIRECTION OF MOVEMENT.

When shifting between a forward or backward *glide step*, there are three central transitions—*the pivot, the roll-through,* and *the jab* or *tendu*. The ensemble can use one type consistently throughout a drill, or they can mix and match types depending on the mood or portrayal of the music. For example, the jab and pivot are especially effective in sharp, angular music, while the roll-through might be better suited for a lyrical ballad.

The pivot is commonly used by marching ensembles and has its origins in the military style. It is achieved by rotating on the ball of the trailing foot from the previous direction of travel to the new direction of travel. The pivot is most often done on the 'AND' prior to the new move, but can also be done on 'ONE' of the new move, creating a delayed effect. The pivot can be added to either the jab or roll-through transitions.

The basic utilization of the roll-through technique is realized when the final count of a move is identical to any of the steps before it. On the final count, the foot is still in ski-line, and articulates on the back of the heel, then rolls all the way through as if no change will occur. On the initiation of the next move, the trailing foot will not pivot, but instead will remain stationary. This technique produces a much more stylized motion than the pivot.

The *jab* or *tendu* transition is indicated by the articulation of the point in the toe. *Jab* transitions can be used for changes in any direction. The toe of the foot articulates on the ground on the final count, and is then used to transfer momentum to the new direction. Make sure that the upper body goes immediately from the old direction to the new without curving through an arc. The foot should remain in ski-line during the articulation.

The *tendu* can be used on both forward-to-backward transitions or backward-to-forward transitions, and is most effective when both the forward and backward step sizes are nearly identical. These transitions are sometimes called '*stop and go*' transitions. No weight is put on the foot during the *tendu,* and the effect generated is that of a static count.

On the next to last count of the move, the momentum is stopped, and all weight is centered on the planted foot. On the last count of the move, the non-planted foot is placed in the *tendu* position with the toe only lightly touching the ground; again, no weight is put on this foot. Finally, count 'ONE' of the new move is motionless, and on count 'TWO'—the *tendu* foot takes a step in the new direction. Use a verbal, such as '*PLANT*'— '*POINT*'—'*ONE*'—'*AND*' (or '*CROSS*') '*TWO*'—when learning this move.

With both the roll-through and jab techniques, additions known as '*foot placements*' or '*prep angles*' can be used. This method allows the placement of the foot at an angle, typically occurring on the last count of a move. The angle of the foot placement should be about halfway between the previous direction of travel, and the new direction.

Alternatively, the foot placement angles may all be defined at a prescribed angle, for example, 45 degrees in relation to the front sideline and yard-lines. These angles should be clearly defined for each ensemble when utilized, and can be effectively taught in a box drill.

Shifting from Forward-To-Backward and Backward-To-Forward Movement

Roll-through Forward—Go Back

Tendu—Touch and Go Back

Tendu—Touch and Go Forward

Shifting from Forward to the Right

Another type of transition is the conclusion of *ankle-knee* or *chair steps*. When transitioning out of these styles, the *'UP'* position on the *'AND'* count should not be employed on the *'AND'* count prior to the new style. This is analogous to the idea that the *'UP'* motion starts on the *'AND'* count before the ankle-knee or chair-style move. On the final count of the move, the verbal *'LOCK'* should be used to remind performers to lock into the new style and not raise their feet into the *'UP'* position on the next *'AND'* count.

Turn the toe on the right foot 45 degrees to the right, on the ball of the right foot, then pivot to the right on the ball of the right foot.

Shifting from Forward to the Left

Turn the toe on the right foot **45 degrees** to the right on the ball of the left foot, then pivot to the left on the ball of the left foot.

Reversing the Direction of the Movement

Spin Turn

The decision on which type of turn to use is usually determined by the direction the instrument is held.

Military Turn: Turn on the opposite foot of the direction of the turn.

Cross-Over Turns: Turn on the same foot of the direction of the turn.

Counted Turn: Use when changing to any direction with any amount of counts. Turn slowly while marking time in place.

Delayed Turns: Stop on a determined count then making a snappy turn on the next count.

Spin Turns: Execute this flashy turn by turning in the opposite direction of the new path.

Moving Fundamentals

Forward March—A long whistle is blown on ***count 1***, with a release on ***count 2***; ***counts 3***, and ***4***, are silent. Four short whistles at the desired tempo then follow on ***counts 5, 6, 7, and 8***. When marching with a glide step, bring the left leg to the appropriate position on the 'AND' of the eighth count (or any even count). When marching with a chair-type step, the left leg is placed in the appropriate position 'ON' the eighth count. On ***count 1***, following the command, step forward with the left foot in tempo with the signal. A verbal command "forward march" can be given in place of a whistle signal.

Halt—A halt is signaled by the command 'BAND' on counts 1 and 2. This is followed by the command 'HALT' given on any count as long as it occurs on the left foot (an odd count). Everyone then responds with 'STEP AND CLOSE', (optional) while taking one more step forward with the right foot, and closing on the next count with the left foot in attention (all this is done in place when halting during a mark time). A whistle signal, using the same counts, could be used in place of a verbal command.

Right Flank, Left Flank, and To-The-Rear—*(right foot pivot)* When using a right foot pivot system, all turns are made on the right foot by executing a snappy turn on ***counts 2, 4, 6, or 8***. When using the slow chair step, turn on the 'ANDS' of the even counts. When using fast chair step, turn 'ON' the counts. Check the left foot after turning, to ensure that it is in the correct 'UP' position of the step currently in use. For a '*to the rear*,' turn to the left. Be sure to take a full-sized step in the new direction after the turn. To achieve smoother and more graceful turns, the pivot foot can be turned ***45 degrees*** in the direction of the turn. This makes the motion of the pivot smaller.

Right Flank, Left Flank, and to the Rear—*(left foot pivot)* These turns are executed in the same manner as those above, pivoting on the left foot on the odd counts.

Right or Left Obliques—These turns are executed in the same manner as flanks, except that the turns are ***45 degrees*** from the original direction of movement. Following such a turn, switch to a ***31.8"*** step, in order to maintain eight equal steps per five yard increments.

Four Count Flanks, and To-The-Rear—*(slow turns)* These turns are executed by marking time in place and gradually turning to the desired direction in four counts. Turn to the left on '*to the rear*.' While turning, make sure that the speed of the movement is in ratio with the distance. For example: On a four-count to the rear, the turn should rotate ***90 degrees*** in two counts and ***180 degrees*** in four counts. These turns can be executed using any amount of counts, and any type of mark time foot action.

Marching While Playing

Learning how to march while playing an instrument is a critical and challenging process for beginners. The procedure begins by teaching the music and marching separately. Once the marching fundamentals have been taught, it is important to develop exercises that introduce the process of marching while playing. Many ensembles skip this process and begin teaching the drills, resulting in poor execution when the drill and music are combined. Once the music is prepared, and the ensemble is able to march while playing, the drill can be taught. Practicing the drills with recordings makes it easier to understand the relationships between the music and the drill. The last step of this process is combining the music and drills.

The following exercises are designed to help students learn how to march and play before combining the music and drill. By using simple musical exercises that are memorized easily, the students can concentrate on the coordination of breathing, articulation, sustaining long tones, and phrasing; combined with various fundamental marching routines.

These exercises help the ensemble learn to project sound with clean attacks and releases by instilling the practice of breathing uniformly. The overall sound of the winds eventually becomes fuller as the group develops confidence in marching while playing. Each exercise can be rehearsed with or without percussion and auxiliary groups. When the percussionists participate, they should play simple repeated patterns with a solid pulse, that fits rhythmically with the musical exercises. When the auxiliary groups participate, they can add fundamental routines with their equipment, that also are compatible with the phrases of the music exercises. The three exercises below are straightforward and can easily be memorized. They must be rehearsed first, without marching until they can be played with confidence.

Students should play each pattern one time, on each note of any scale, ascending and descending. Play the pattern twice on the top note of the scale, creating an exercise of **128 counts** (**64 counts** ascending and **64 counts** descending). The ensemble should breathe uniformly in tempo on **count 8** of each pattern, filling their lungs completely during each breath. All articulations must be solid, using the tip of the tongue. For each long tone, the air should move for the full duration of the note. Stylistically, the longer notes will have more weight and volume; the shorter notes will have less weight and volume.

Once these exercises have been taught without marching, they can be combined with various marching routines. Keep the routines very simple at first, and restricted to **8-count** patterns to coincide with the phrasing of the exercises.

To begin, practice each exercise while marking time, adjust to moving the feet in sync with the music. Transition to exercises marching forward on yard lines, taking eight steps per five yards, as this corresponds to the breath that occurs each time they hit a yard line.

This eight-count exercise helps to develop solid attacks and clean releases. The quarter notes should be played long with a heavy attack, and the *eighth notes* played short, with a crisp attack. Play the last note with a solid attack, drop the volume quickly, and then make a fast crescendo with a clipped release on the *count 7*. On *count 8*, take a full breath. As mentioned above, marching eight steps per five yards allows breathing when stepping on the line.

This exercise emphasizes sustaining long tones, and the concept of phrasing. Make a solid attack on *count 1*, and soften to a *piano* dynamic level on *count 2*. Play a gradual *crescendo* with a clipped release on *count 7*, and a breath on *count 8*.

This exercise teaches clean articulations and the concept of weighting notes on primary and secondary *accents*. On the first measure, play the quarter notes heavy and long, and the *eighth notes* light and detached. On the second measure, play the *eighth notes* heavy and short, and the *sixteenth notes* light and short. Breathe on *count 8*.

This eight-count percussion vamp can be memorized and played with the ensemble on all of the previous exercises.

Once the students become comfortable with these shorter exercises, more challenging drill sequences can be created, to incorporate turns or alternating forward march and mark time with turns.

Here is an excellent example of a routine for 128 counts, which can be used to review the basics of marching while playing:

1. Forward march eight, and right flank four times (box), forward march eight, and left flank four times, forward march eight, and to the rear four times, forward march eight, and mark time eight twice.

2. Create various simple drill patterns to help the students relate musical phrasing with marching patterns.

3. Once success is achieved with this process, practice marching the full length of the field while playing the school song ,or a musical selection the students have thoroughly memorized. This helps the players develop endurance, confidence, and a more advanced level of marching while playing.

Common Marching Problems

Squatting

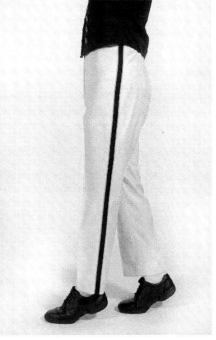

Proper small size glide-step backward

Proper small size glide step forward

Problem 1

When marching with larger step sizes, some individuals tend to bounce or sway the upper body.

Solution

Bouncing when marching forward is a typical problem, particularly when taking larger steps. To eliminate the bounce, keep the upper body stretched upward and keep the body moving forward on the 'AND' of each step. Keep the back straight and head up to avoid slouching. Practice marching forward at six and four steps per five yards, to develop uniformity and comfort with this larger step size. Avoid "squatting" by keeping the legs straight.

Problem 2

Typically, many marching groups "shuffle" their feet when taking very small glide steps, and tend to "slump" their upper bodies. This is common on "adjust"-type drills when everyone is taking various sized steps during a drill transition.

Solution

Keep heads and sternums high. To remedy this, line up everyone in vertical forms on the yard line with instruments in playing positions. Have the students practice tapping the back edge of their heels on the ground a few times on their own to regain the "feel" for where the articulation is. Practice marching 16 steps per five yards, keeping the full body weight entirely on the heels with the toes curled up. This will look very awkward and stiff, but it forces everyone to make contact with the ground, on the heels at the beginning of each step. After repeating this several times, allow marchers to roll from the heel to the toe, with each step. Define how high the toe should be curled.

In general, the smaller the step, the less pronounced the curl of the toe. Remind students to keep the upper body stretched upward at all times. A common side effect of posture work, is better foot technique, and uniformity of the foot action. Correcting poor posture can produce immediate improvement in the feet.

Problem 3

Marching backwards with very large or very small size steps is not uniform, looks awkward, and is sometimes out of rhythm. Marchers also tend to lean the upper body forward with the shoulders in front of the hips. "Squatting" is another common problem with large or small size steps.

Solution

To correct *squatting*, practice small backwards step sizes to immediately improve style. To make large steps easier and more uniform, teach students where their "power muscles" are. Begin with both feet flat on the ground, then launch up onto the toes. Be aware of the muscles used to accomplish this. Use these muscles to propel the center of the body backwards. Be careful not to rise upward first. One final consideration is the motion of the foot for backward steps. If no roll down is desired, make sure that the foot is almost "locked" into position, as it slides against the ground and pushes off into the next step. Too much play in the foot will usually cause instability.

Shoulders ahead of hips

Physical correction

Proper alignment

Problem 4

When marching forward, many students moved the upper body and bounce.

Solution

Without instruments, have students pretend to hold an imaginary bowl of water in front of their face with the tips of their fingers. Pretend the bowl is filled with water to the brim. Practice forward marching without spilling any water. This exercise helps develop the concept of smooth and graceful movement, while maintaining upper body control.

Problem 5

Individuals do not arrive simultaneously at the end of each drill segment.

Solution

When teaching or cleaning drill, have everyone freeze on the last count of each drill segment. The leading foot on that count should be in the assigned position of that form. Next, close the other foot, and correct any alignment problems until the students understand their positions in that form. Retrace that drill to the previous form. This saves time and teaches the drill backwards and forwards. Run the drill again, instructing students to correct their paths, and step size, until they can reach their exact targets on the same count. Once this is accomplished, they are ready to practice the same drill using the "overlap" concept. This is by doing the same maneuvers, but taking one more count into the next drill.

Possibilities might include a turn into the next form, halt, or mark time. Helping to eliminate false turns, stops, or step offs, as everyone is learning to make these changes at the *end of drill one,* instead of at *the beginning of drill two.*

Problem 6

When standing in a stationary position, many performers tense up their shoulders, or allow their upper body to slouch.

Solution
This exercise can be done with instruments in playing position, or in the down position (while standing at attention or parade rest). Have everyone rise up on the tips of their toes as high as possible. Hold this position while maintaining good balance.

Tell them to imagine themselves as rubber bands being stretched upward as tightly as possible. This forces the student to center their weight in the same place.

Once they have gained control of this position, tell them to slowly lower their weight from the shoulders down. Just until their heels barely touch the ground, while pretending to leave their heads in the 'UP' position. The body angles should be uniform. Tell them to develop the feeling that they are constantly being stretched upward, whether marching, or in a still position.

Another concept to facilitate proper upper body positions, is to instruct the marchers to imagine that each one is a puppet suspended from above, by a string attached to the top of the head. The string is so tight that the feet are barely able to touch the ground. This should give them a constant feeling of being pulled upward from the head, demanding the feet to be pushed down to make contact with the ground.

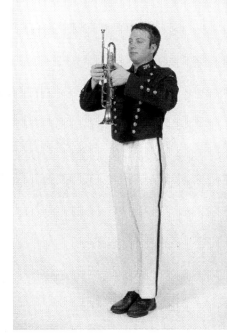

Slouching shoulders

Tense shoulders

Relaxed shoulders

Problem 7

Good posture requires the upper body be stretched upwards and erect. This includes the head angle. Bad head angles affect posture and horn angles.

Solution
The bracket check is an easy way to quickly resolve bad head angles.

Bad head angle

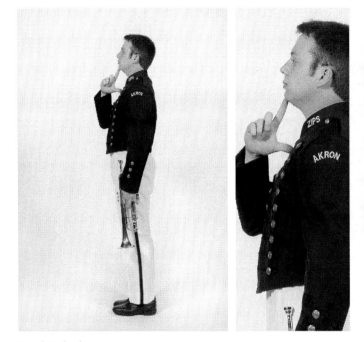

Bracket check

Problem 8

Spacing and alignment are inconsistent.

Solution

This problem is multi-faceted and ongoing at all levels of achievement. During the teaching of fundamentals, each individual must learn about maintaining equidistant spacing in all forms, covering down in files, and keeping curves and arcs smooth. Learning to use one's peripheral vision takes time, and must be exercised from the early stages of aligning formations. When making adjustments to correct flaws in various drills, the most common dispute is whether an individual should go to the wrong position in order to be in the form, or go to the correct position and be out of the form.

The rule of thumb for this situation, is to adjust to the form for performances, but go to the correct positions during rehearsals, hoping to correct the accuracy of the drill set for the future. If inaccurate forms do not get corrected in rehearsal, they will deteriorate until they become unrecognizable from their original design.

Problem 9

Horn angles tend to droop, especially at the end of the show.

Solution

This tendency is usually the result of ensembles that practice drill without instruments. Marching without instruments completely changes the balance of the body when marching. In addition, upper body strength must be built over a long period of time in order to develop the endurance to perform with good posture for the entire show.

The only time instruments should not be carried during drill, is while learning new maneuvers/commands, while holding drill charts. Most drill cleaning and review of fundamentals should be done with instruments in playing positions. Vary horn angles by pointing the bells toward a defined object, such as the press box or the podium.

Problem 10

Neck extension is another typical problem.

Solution

Think of keeping the ears centered with the shoulders.

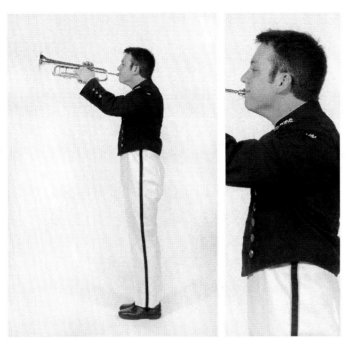

Improper neck extension

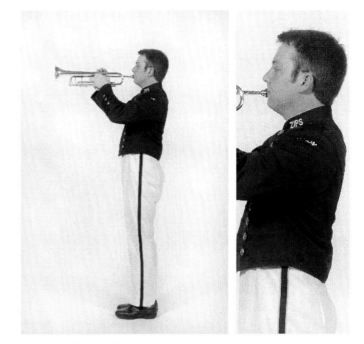

Proper neck extension

Problem 11

Turning the toes outward or inward while doing the glide step is a common problem. Spreading the feet is also a common occurrence.

Solution

Practice marching parallel to yard lines. The yard lines provide a visual aid and a "ski line" concept to keep the inseams of the feet parallel, and in line with each other.

Problem 12

When preparing to move, if performers stand with all of their weight toward the back of their feet, some students will have difficulty with the weight shift necessary to achieve the correct step size on count one. This can also cause problems with pulse on count one.

Solution

Establish the concept of "the platform" of the foot. Ask students to perceive the front half of their foot as the "platform". Prior to a step-off, have the students shift their weight to the platform. They should only feel the shift, but not lift the heel. This will be an internal shifting of weight as preparation, not a visual shift. In the same way that all moving changes of direction take place on the platform of the foot; count one from a standing position will be improved, if this technique is used with consistency.

91

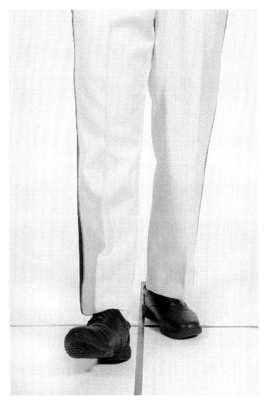

Toeing out

Spreading

Ski line correction—Forward

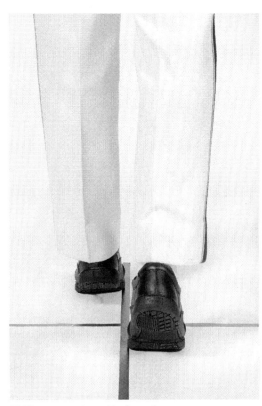

Ski line correction—Backward

IV. REHEARSALS

Band Camp

Successful marching ensembles result from a mastery of the fundamentals of musicianship and marching. They also require an understanding of a total system of administration, goals, philosophies, policies, and purpose. Accomplishing these goals is time consuming, and planning procedures is challenging. Band camp provides an ideal opportunity to prepare for an outstanding marching season.

People seek leadership roles for a wide range of reasons, from personal recognition to a passionate desire to help others. Potential leadership tendencies are present in everyone and can be developed to various levels.

> *SUCCESSFUL MARCHING ENSEMBLES RESULT FROM A MASTERY OF THE FUNDAMENTALS OF MUSICIANSHIP AND MARCHING.*

- Enjoying recreation, & entertainment
- Scheduling master classes, & educational clinic sessions
- Organizing recitals, or a talent show
- Scheduling a final performance to demonstrate accomplishments
- Taking pictures, and/or videos for press releases

EXAMPLES OF ACTIVITIES AT BAND CAMP:

- Issuing instruments, music, uniforms, equipment, & supplies
- Making friends, meeting new people, & planning social events
- Training leaders, & define their responsibilities
- Distributing season schedules, handbooks, & fundraising materials
- Discussing rules, regulations, goals, philosophies, & purpose
- Defining rehearsal procedures, warm-ups, tuning processes, & work ethic
- Refining music fundamentals
- Memorizing music
- Teaching, & refining marching fundamentals
- Conducting effective sectional rehearsals
- Reviewing traditions, cheers, cadences, school songs, & membership requirements
- Observing videos, & listening to recordings of model ensembles
- Reading, & memorizing drill charts
- Hosting special guest clinicians, or specialized instructors
- Meeting band parents, coaches, & school administrators

Band Camp Locations

A local band campsite would provide the least expensive option. Camp sessions could be held at school or another nearby facility. Meals could be provided by the school cafeteria, parents, or be catered by local food establishments. The advantage is reduced expenses. The disadvantage is potential distractions, and attendance problems. Regardless, a local band camp, is better than no camp at all.

Ideally, having band camp at a remote location offers an ideal scenario for avoiding distractions, and attendance problems. It also provides an excellent opportunity to develop stronger bonds amongst students, to attain a higher level of concentration during instruction, and to allow for flexibility in adjusting schedules. The disadvantage is a higher cost.

Overall Structure of Scheduling

FIRST DAY

The first day sets the mood for camp and the entire season. Before instruction begins, a highly organized registration procedure should be planned. This process could include issuing instruments, music, equipment, materials, schedules, handbooks, uniforms, etc. It could be accomplished with the assistance of the parents, or perhaps by student leaders, giving them an opportunity to visit with old friends, and meet new students. The entire event should be a positive experience to ease tension with new students, and to create enthusiasm for the season.

Once students complete registration, they should report to their section leaders to review, or learn a few basic fundamentals. This could include defining posture for the position of attention and parade rest. Also the hand positions for holding instruments, or equipment, in the down and playing positions. This will save a great deal of time for the first marching fundamental rehearsal.

The second activity could be sectional and auxiliary group rehearsals. This provides the section leaders with the opportunity to make introductions, welcome new students, and begin introducing warm-ups, and tuning procedures. Instruments and equipment should be checked for proper maintenance and condition. This is a great time to review hand positions, horn angles, and body posture while at attention and parade rest. The sectional time, could also be spent preparing music that will be rehearsed in the full band rehearsal, something simple or familiar, like the school song. Concentrate on good tone, pitch, posture, breathing, rhythm, and articulations. The ultimate goal for sectionals is to assure that the first full ensemble music rehearsal, will be successful in creating excitement for the season. Make sure everyone is carefully tuned, so intonation in this rehearsal will be impeccable.

> **THE ULTIMATE GOAL FOR SECTIONALS, IS TO ASSURE THAT THE FIRST FULL ENSEMBLE REHEARSAL WILL BE SUCCESSFUL IN CREATING EXCITEMENT FOR THE SEASON.**

Conclude the first day with a full music ensemble rehearsal, (inside) while auxiliary groups continue their specialized training.

Rehearse the music that was prepared in sectionals. The director should do everything possible to prepare the ensemble for a successful and positive rehearsal. Make sure the band room is clean and organized with the rehearsal goals written on the board. Talk little, and play much. End the rehearsal with something exciting to energize the ensemble.

SECOND DAY

Like the first music rehearsal, the first marching rehearsal should be geared to assure a high degree of success. Begin early in the morning with stretching exercises, and marching fundamentals when the weather is cooler (during summer months). Make them fun, but productive. Wild and crazy music helps get the students alert. To save time, the exercises should be done in the same teaching formation that will be used for learning standing fundamentals; the creation of this formation should be charted with student leader assistance. Discipline breaks down when time is wasted, when there is confusion, or when students do not understand what to do. Before rehearsals, have drinking water sources available, fields lined, sound systems tested, podiums in place etc. The students will be positive, if they see everything is organized and prepared when they arrive.

The rest of the morning should focus on marching fundamentals. On the first day it is important to go slowly, and to clearly define each fundamental. Work to achieve detail, snap, precision, and uniformity, to such a degree that every student is experiencing success. Staff members should stand by to assist individuals having trouble. The goal is to instill confidence and spirit, and to create momentum for the entire camp. It is not important to cover a lot of material, but rather to perfect a few basic movements so the students experience the positive feelings of success. Always end each rehearsal with something that is uplifting, and exciting.

After lunch, when the weather is typically warmer, concentrate on music; starting with sectionals, so that the entire afternoon is dedicated to music. Make sure the goals and procedures are clearly defined for every rehearsal. In sectionals, the section leaders should continue to establish productive warm-up, and tuning procedures. Also, rehearse only music that will be played in the full ensemble later. Auxiliary groups should spend the entire afternoon working on their specialized material. After sectionals there should be a short break followed by a full music ensemble. When appropriate, the winds and percussion may be split up to rehearse separately.

After dinner when it is cooler, marching fundamentals can be reviewed, followed by a continuation of teaching basics. This is a good time to begin playing outdoors, in the teaching formation. Start with something simple, such as a warm-up, to become accustomed to playing in this new atmosphere.

THIRD DAY – LAST DAY
Essentially, the mornings will be devoted to teach marching fundamentals and drills. The afternoons should emphasize music fundamentals, leaving the evenings to focus on reviewing and eventually combining drill and music.

LAST DAY
This should be the high point of the week. The culmination of band camp on the last day could include an informal performance for friends and family, demonstrating the accomplishments of the week, and presenting a preview of things to come. Include only demonstrations that are well prepared. End the performance with something impressive.

Effective Rehearsals With Results

Every marching ensemble should strive to attain a distinctive look and sound. All visual elements define style, including uniforms, type of drill, marching fundamentals, the size of the band, and the use of auxiliary groups. The musical style, which is the overall sound, is determined by factors such as the size of the ensemble, instrumentation, scoring techniques, type of music, interpretation, and other musical elements.

Marching and musical styles are primarily determined by the fundamentals and the manner in which they are applied to the performance. The degree of success is determined by how effectively the fundamentals have been learned and applied. Therefore, the teaching process during rehearsal must be organized, thorough, productive, consistent, and effective.

Since all movement, including drill and choreography, is an extension or variation of fundamentals, it is critical that marching rudiments are taught well, so that the band's performances can be executed with precision, confidence, and uniformity. Great marching ensembles emphasize the qualities that cause the drills and music to happen, rather than emphasizing the performance itself. To improve an ensemble's performance level, improve the fundamentals.

Consequently, the rehearsal becomes the most important aspect of the maturation process, as this is when marching and music basics are defined, practiced, and perfected. Efficient rehearsals are the key to developing outstanding marching ensembles. Unfortunately, the quality of many marching groups suffers due to poor rehearsal procedures.

Positive attitudes, good discipline, and enthusiasm result from experiencing success during exciting, productive, and effective rehearsals. When rehearsals are profitable, students motivate themselves as a direct result of enjoying their achievements. They are conscious that progress is taking place. Student pride

and dedication increase in direct proportion to the level of accomplishments achieved in rehearsal. Healthy attitudes are products of success.

"Success breeds success. Failure breeds bad attitudes."

COMMON CAUSES FOR INEFFECTIVE REHEARSALS:

- Wasted time
- Fear & stress
- Boring teaching procedures
- Improper teaching pace
- Terminology not explained
- Unenthusiastic and/or impatient instructor
- Students' poor discipline & concentration
- Teaching techniques not productive
- Long & short-range goals not defined
- Support staff responsibilities not accounted for
- Negative atmosphere
- Unclear instructions
- Lack of encouragement & praise
- Not enough individual help
- Schedules not followed
- Movements' lack of detail
- Underutilization of visual models or demonstrations
- Poor logistics of rehearsal facilities
- Student leaders not properly trained
- All personnel not treated equally

 Practice Formations

MARCHING FUNDAMENTALS OR CHOREOGRAPHY TEACHING FORMATION

The diagram illustrates an ideal formation for teaching marching fundamentals or choreography. It can also be used for stretching exercises and music warm-ups. By placing the instructor on an elevated platform in the center of concentric circles, it is easier for everyone to hear and see. In this formation, communication and discipline are improved because of direct eye contact between instructor and participants. Another advantage is that the instructor can easily monitor how well each individual is progressing. Smaller groups can use one circle, and larger groups can add more circles as needed. Notice that the percussion and auxiliary groups have their own circles, so they can be removed when rehearsing the winds separately.

The circles should be divided into sections and assigned to support staff, making it efficient for assisting students needing individual instruction during rehearsal. Those who require individual help can be taken out of the circle and assisted without disrupting the rehearsal. The circle formation makes it possible for the instructor and assistants to "scan" everyone quickly and identify individual differences and make corrections. When large errors occur, clarification and review are needed for the entire group. When mistakes are minimal, individual help is more appropriate.

This formation is ideal for teaching stationary fundamentals, choreography, marching steps, mark time, halt, and basic body posture. By placing like instruments together, it is easier for section leaders to demonstrate, and examine uniformity of horn angles, hand positions, pole angles, body position, etc.

Marching steps should be taught in this formation, by having the group march in a follow-the-leader drill around the circumference of the circles. Step size, alignment, and spacing need not be emphasized until the group is placed in a formation on yard lines. This makes it easier to concentrate on achieving uniformity of body movement. When marching around the circumference of the circle, wind players should hold their instruments in the playing position at a *45°* angle, in the same direction, to prevent possible collisions during forward movement. The distance between individuals should be a minimum of two steps.

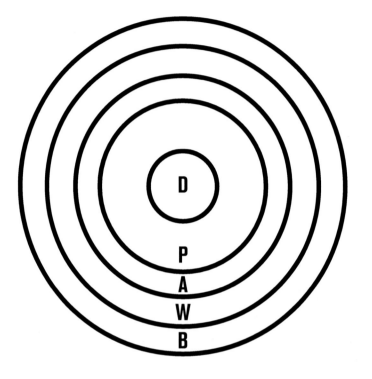

D - DIRECTOR ON PODIUM

P - PERCUSSION

A - AUXILIARY GROUPS

W - WOODWINDS

B - BRASS

Drill Formation on the Yard Lines

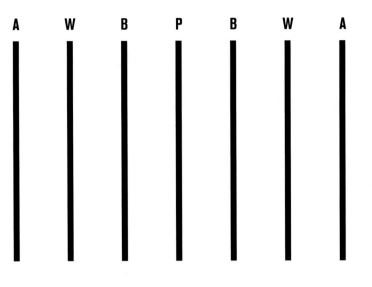

A   W   B   P   B   W   A

P- PERCUSSION should be placed in the center for better acoustics, and so the winds can rehearse separately.

B- BRASS should be placed symmetrically around the percussion for a tighter ensemble sound.

W- WOODWINDS should be placed around the brass symmetrically for a balanced sound.

A- AUXILIARY groups should be placed attractively on both ends of the formation so they can be removed without affecting the winds and percussion formation.

Once all the standing fundamentals and marching steps have been taught and perfected in the circles, a drill formation similar to the one above can be used to complete the process of learning marching basics. By putting the group on the yard lines with good instrumentation, the emphasis can then be directed towards spacing, alignment, turns, step size, and playing while marching. The purpose of this formation is to complete the process of learning the marching fundamentals needed to teach drills. Notice that this formation is ideal for exercises involving playing and marching simultaneously, since it is constructed so that the sound is the same going in any direction.

Music Rehearsal Formation

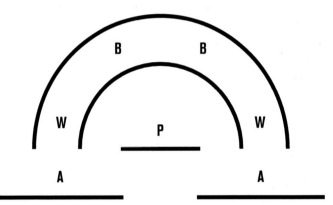

An outdoor concert formation should be utilized for warm-ups, rehearsing, taking attendance or performing music. Setting up with good instrumentation will ensure that the groups can hear each other, and that the ensemble is visually attractive and musically balanced. It must be compact enough for the sound to be tight, to facilitate rehearsal of intricate rhythms. The auxiliary groups should be positioned so they can practice their routines simultaneously, with the music rehearsal. This formation can also be used for musical performances.

TYPICAL RUDIMENTS TAUGHT IN THIS FORMATION:

- Marching with standard 22.5" & 30" steps
- Learning fast & slow turns
- Marching oblique with a 31.8" step
- Marching backwards
- Marching with an adjusted size step
- The 9 concepts of movement
- Playing while marching
- Alignment & spacing
- Marching with a large jazz-run
- Marching with a jazz walk-step
- Practicing various transitions & turns
- Practicing lateral marching with various horn angles

Wellness Considerations For Band Camp

by **Chris Borgard**

Before band camp even starts, band directors should seek out a wellness expert on campus, (assuming none is staffed) that can come in during one of the first mornings of camp and spend at least 30 minutes providing expert advice to the group, to prepare them for the physical challenges associated with camp. This professional could be a licensed physical therapist (PT), certified athletic trainer (ATC), or certified strength and conditioning specialist (CSCS). Their presentation should include education regarding sound nutrition and recovery from day to day, as well as recommendations to prevent dehydration, heat illness, fainting spells, and overuse injury.

Note: Any handouts or postings to the band website can be helpful here. Examples of educational material regarding these topics can be found on the *Marching Band Member Wellness Program* (MBMW) website.[1]

Hydration & Heat

It is important to maintain the hydration levels of all personnel, especially in an activity where the majority of time is spent outdoors in the heat. Both students and instructors should carry water bottles to outdoor rehearsals. Frequent quick water breaks should be given, as often as every 10 to 15 minutes, especially during hot days. Consider carrying extra water during parades, and other hot-weather performances. The timing of water breaks is critical, band directors should not bypass these opportunities.

The placement of water bottles or containers for instrument groups can be equally important, and under some conditions the availability of electrolytes should be included. This can be done with types of sports drink mixtures that also contain simple carbohydrates (and possibly even caffeine), thus ensuring that energy and blood sugar levels are maintained during practice sessions, even in extreme conditions. Some examples of great solutions of optimal sport drink mixtures can be found on *Live Fluid* website.[2]

On days that are excessively hot or humid, the use of ice-water towels kept in large containers can also provide a huge relief to the body's cooling mechanisms. Certain members of the staff should be delegated with this responsibility, to be taken seriously without fail, every time the marching unit takes the field. During summer and early in the season, clothing permitted during practice should be lightweight and moisture wicking with lightly-colored reflective (rather than absorptive) properties, while substantial enough to help prevent sunburn when possible.

[1] Website address: marchingbandwellness.com
[2] Website address: livefluid.com

Stretching Exercises Before Marching

It must be understood that some portions of a marching program routine will often lead to much higher loading forces placed on muscles and joints (*ex: instrument group dancing or run-on periods, etc.*) For this reason, it is necessary that band directors incorporate *<10 minutes* of dynamic movement warm-up exercises prior to each rehearsal, for an optimal stretch. These movements should be of sufficient intensity, to match the physical requirements of each day's activities. Research has shown that a dynamic warm-up is an effective means of increasing muscle temperature, and is ideal if the warm-up can be implemented prior to a static stretching period. For all major muscle groups, have band members hold each static *stretch for >30 seconds* at each position, to eliminate overly tight or shortened muscles, which are more likely to cause injury.

CONSIDERATIONS FOR A HEALTHY STRETCHING PROGRAM:

- Aerobic exercises, such as jumping or running, should not be excessive. Use enough to warm-up the muscles only.

- Avoid exercises that put a strain on joints, such as deep knee bends or push-ups.

- Keep the exercises simple, to accommodate those who might have limited coordination.

- Do not use exercises that are awkward for those who have physical limitations.

- Have someone qualified lead the exercises, assuring the process is appropriate.

- Have someone qualified lead the exercises, assuring the process is organized and appropriate.

- Enhance the exercise activity by adding exciting or crazy music to make it more enjoyable for the students.

- Help students realize the importance of stretching, and how it helps prevent injuries.

DIRECTIONS *(See Figure 004)*

Head: Drop the chin to the chest.

Shoulders: Roll the shoulders up towards the ears, and then forwards and down; bring the hands together as shown.

Upper Back: Push the hands down slightly, resulting in the curving of the upper back.

Lower Back: Release the back muscles, and lean over to the ground.

Knees: Release the knees, allowing the body to collapse as small as possible, release all muscles.

A short pause should occur in this position, allowing the muscles to relax. If using instruments, the hands should be placed on the instrument in such a manner that it can be easily picked up.

The exercise should then be reversed—*Knees, Lower Back, Upper Back, Shoulders, and Head.* The instrument should be held in front of the body with one or both hands until **Shoulders**, at which point it should be in the dominant carrying hand. A final four counts brings the instrument to playing position. At the conclusion of the exercise, the students should feel as if they are stretched upwards.

Insufficient warm-up or stretching is only one example of a factor that can contribute to injury during marching. The status of marching band members' footwear or body composition can both either create or manage injury likelihood. The development of muscles and tendons in key areas of the body can act to manage physical loading forces, while excess body weight in the form of fat can quickly increase these forces to greater than tolerated levels. Footwear that provides ample support and cushioning, can also help lower body joints to absorb these loads.

Figure 004

Warming Up & Tuning The Winds

Warming up and tuning marching band winds is unique because of logistic and temperature variables. The warm-up process should be productive resulting in musical progress and mental preparation.

CHARACTERISTICS OF AN EFFECTIVE WARM-UP PROCEDURE:

- The process should result in improved tone, intonation, range, endurance, and posture.
- The routine needs to have many variables built in to prevent predictability and lack of concentration.
- Using hand signals to control the procedure establishes non-verbal communication, which is ideal for a marching band.
- Insist on good posture and utilize an attractive and acoustically effective formation at all times.
- Help students realize the importance of stretching and how it helps prevent injuries.

Step 1 - Scales

With the horns down, standing at attention, take three huge breaths, and exhale through the mouth. This is signaled by the conductor with three large and slow preparatory motions with the arms, up for inhaling and down for exhaling. On the third deep breath, the horns should be brought to playing positions.

Next play the *concert F scale,* in the lowest possible octave. This encourages wind players to drop the jaw and move a larger volume of air. Tell them not to take a breath until the air is gone. When breathing, take in as much air as possible. Play until the air is depleted on each breath to develop a larger lung capacity. This will not only improve tone and pitch, but will also have a positive effect on sustaining long tones and playing longer phrases.

WHILE PLAYING SCALES, USE THESE HAND SIGNALS TO AVOID STOPPING & USING VERBAL INSTRUCTIONS:

1. Point the first finger up or down to move up or down one scale tone.

2. Point to the ear to indicate when the pitch is not good. The students will listen and adjust.

3. When the pitch does not improve, cut off the ensemble, and cover the mouth with a cupped hand, to signal the players to hum the pitch they were playing. This requires the players to adjust to the pitch they were humming. This also teaches players to learn how to tune to themselves, after identifying and humming the *center pitch.*

4. Incorporate traditional gestures such as *crescendo, decrescendo, legato, marcato, staccato, accent,* and *releases.*

5. Move the air between the notes to keep the scale smooth and seamless. Using one hand motioning in a circular pattern, indicates to the players to move the air faster (not louder). This will improve the fullness of the tone quality.

6. Repeat this process with the concert *B♭ scale.*

Step 2 - Tuning

With marching bands, the winds should tune in the climatic conditions in which they will perform. When the temperatures are very hot or cold, tuning to a fixed pitch device will cause players to adjust their tuning mechanisms to the extreme, that results in serious pitch problems. Take in consideration that the larger the instrument, the larger the adjustment of the tuning mechanism. It is for this reason it is best to allow the pitch center to adjust naturally, moving up in hot weather and down in cold weather. The result is a less drastic adjustment of the tuning mechanism. To accomplish this, have one clarinet player tune their instrument to a tuning device in a room with a normal temperature (*72-77 degrees*). Leave the clarinet mechanically set when moving to the performance environment. Have the section leaders tune to that clarinet and then transfer that pitch to their own sections, tuning on like instruments to one *pitch center*.

When tuning the entire ensemble simultaneously, start with *concert F* from the reference (a player or a tuning device). Have everyone hum that pitch, as they will then tune to themselves once the pitch has been transferred from the reference. Tune from the low to high instruments, in groups with about a five second space.

Group 1: Bass instruments
Group 2: Tenor instruments
Group 3: Alto instruments
Group 4: Trumpets
Group 5: Soprano woodwind instruments

PROCEDURE:

1. Listen to the pitch reference.

2. Hum the pitch.

3. Play that pitch and compare.

4. Adjust the pitch (that is the pitch center).

5. Repeat the same process with B^b concert.

A WARM-UP ADD-ON:

- While playing a *concert F* the conductor can hold up three fingers to indicate that the players should slowly alternate pitches at random on *concert F, A* and *C*.
- Play these pitches very slowly in the mid-range of each instrument, to avoid extreme high or low pitches.
- Bass instruments should check only the B^b concert in octaves. This allows the woodwind instruments to check their *concert A* and all instruments to check the pitch relationships between the tonic, third, and fifth.
- Move the right hand back and forth, parallel to the ground to indicate that all players should return to the unison *concert F* pitch.
- Repeat this process with B^b concert.

Step 3 - Lip Slurs

This valuable warm up only takes about 90 seconds. After the long tones described in the second paragraph, have the wind players perform the following lip slur exercises. Woodwinds play them as arpeggios. Each form is played seven times, descending through the chromatic fingering series.

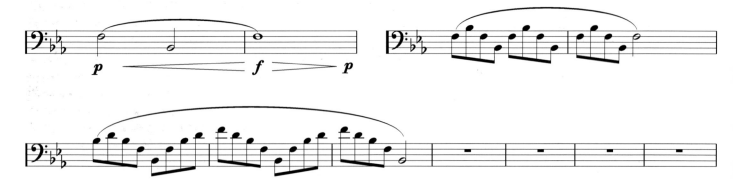

Teaching & Cleaning Drill

The procedures for teaching and refining drill must be logical, productive, efficient, and thorough. The process of combining the drill and music will be more efficient if they are learned independently first.

Obtain or produce a recording of the music as it will be performed. This recording does not need to be the highest quality, provided, the counts and *tempi* are accurate. Copies of the recording should be given to the auxiliary groups, so they can begin creating their choreography, to the percussion so they can begin to write and memorize their parts, and to the drum majors so they can memorize the music and practice conducting. One copy will be used for teaching the drill to the entire group, or various units within the group.

Teach the drill, using this recording, in segments; matching up with the major segments of the musical phrases. Once several segments have been taught, review the drill with the recorded music played through an amplified sound system. This helps to learn the relationship of the music to the drill. Make sure to define horn angles, turns, and body positions during this time. When counting the drill verbally, use the proper tempo changes to match the music as it will be performed.

If you possess the technological skills, create *mp3* audio tracks to match up, with each drill maneuver. Each track should begin with a metronome '*count-off*.' After the count-off, the music should begin precisely on count one of the drill being learned. Each of the tracks should play to the end of the song, so it can be stopped after one set, or they can also be used to combine 2 or more drill sets into larger chunks.

When halting after an assigned segment, the ensemble should freeze in place (depending on the desire of the director) in minus one, halt, or plus one. Several commands are useful at this point, given by either an instructor or the drum major. During this sequence, no additional information should be given from the instructional staff. *CHECK* means move the eyes only, observing the form and being aware of what needs to be fixed to make the form correct. Equipment is not moved. *ADJUST* means fixing the form (guiding), without moving equipment or the head. This helps the ensemble become aware of the corrections they should begin to make on the move. *MARK* is used to allow the ensemble to mark off and set the

form exactly. When *MARK* is called, students should place pencils or other markers on the ground between their feet, and then mark off their position. Observe where the markers were placed and how far off the individuals and the form in general were from their desired locations, and then retrieve the markers. Finally, the individuals should return to the set positions in which they ended the drill segment, make any needed minor adjustments, and observe the form as it should be. Comparisons should be made mentally, to the form that they saw during both *CHECK* and *ADJUST*. At this point, the command *STANDBY*, or similar should be given, signaling the relaxed position of attention. Instructions can then be given by instructors.

Although this seems like a lengthy procedure, *CHECK* and *ADJUST* should take no more than *5-10 seconds* once the ensemble is accustomed to the process. *MARK* should take about *20-30 seconds*, and students should be encouraged to mark their positions off as speedily as possible while still maintaining accuracy. If instructors can refrain from giving instructions during these commands, the students will be able to concentrate and apply corrections easier.

Drill rehearsals should be alternated with music rehearsals, putting emphasis on the perfection and memorization (if possible) of the music. Sectional rehearsals and individual practice can expedite the time for learning the music. Periodically, as music performance improves, more current recordings should be made for drill rehearsals.

Once the drill and the music are at a respectable performance level, it is time to start combining them. Begin by alternating drill with recorded music and playing the performed music. Do this in segments using proper horn positions, turns, stops, and mark times.

A great process for teaching and rehearsing drill segments is the *OVERLAP* method. *OVERLAP* simply means that following the execution of a drill segment, everyone takes one more step (also known as *'PLUS ONE'*) into the next drill, and then freezes on that count. Next, pull the front foot back to the closed, attention position and check alignment and spacing. Be sure to include proper horn angles, turns, or other changes in marching that might occur during the last count. After the drill is learned, the *OVERLAP* method can also be used to begin a drill move from the count prior to the drill segment to be executed. This is also known as *MINUS ONE*.

It is imperative that the feet be placed in the path of the prior drill. The best way to achieve this is to set the entire body as if traveling in the direction of the prior drill move, and then rotating the upper body into the appropriate facing, as in the method for teaching lateral slides.

The advantage provided with MINUS *ONE OVERLAP* is that the direction change, and other considerations usually thought of at the end of a drill move, are now placed at the beginning of the next drill move, where they can be executed with fresh attention, building better muscle memory.

Execution of a drill move is followed by *RETRACE*, meaning the reversal of the drill to the previous position. During *RETRACE*, face the body in the opposite direction of the original drill, and use the same number of counts, amount of path, and step size. Walking back to the previous position wastes valuable rehearsal time. This procedure doubles the amount of run-throughs while simultaneously learning the drills backward and forward.

Once all the segments within a given musical selection have been taught, the **whole** approach would be appropriate. This means running the entire drill (or large segments) with the music. Use this process even if it is rough.

After the ensemble begins to gain confidence in combining drill and music, it is time to refine the total routine. This usually means reviewing the end positions of each segment, and developing consistency in the transitions between each form, with equal distance step size and proper paths.

The most common execution problems in performance, are when individuals do not hit forms accurately on the appropriate counts, or make clean changes to the next move. Reviewing the *OVERLAP* process is the best way to refine those drill problems.

Various Positions of the Body when Passing Over, or Standing on Coordinates.

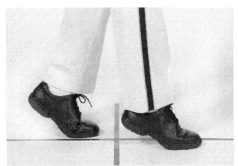

Moving backward centered

Stationary front view

Stationary side view

Moving forward centered over coordinate

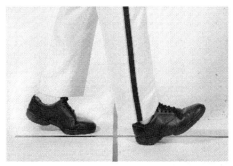

Moving forward centered over coordinate

Dot Books

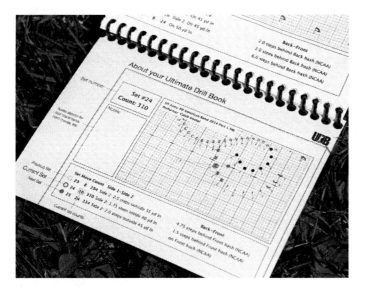

Dot books can be used in place of drill charts once the drill has been learned. This is especially practical for ensembles that spend long periods of time learning and refining a single show. A *dot book* should contain all information necessary for proper execution of the drill. A spiral bound *3" x 5"* index card book that can be "weather-proofed" with duct tape is ideal for this purpose. The dot book must be easily accessible, and carried at all rehearsals.

TIP: *Tye the book around the waist with a shoelace to secure it while marching.*

One page of drill should be written on each card to allow maximum space for additional information and changes to be notated.

WHAT TO INCLUDE:

- Page number
- Count structure
- Dot – relationship to yard-lines, side-lines, hashes, or zero-points
- Interval
- Form picture
- Dress point (if used)
- Subsets
- Horn or body moves
- Music (measure numbers, letters, or copy of the actual music)

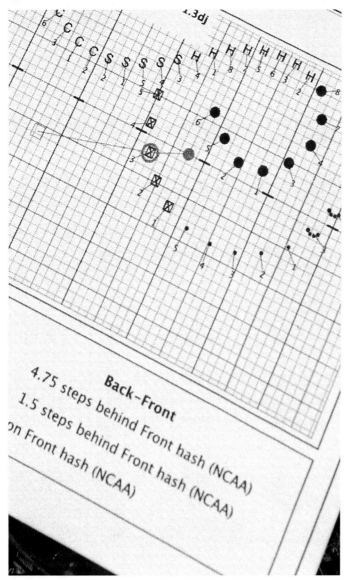

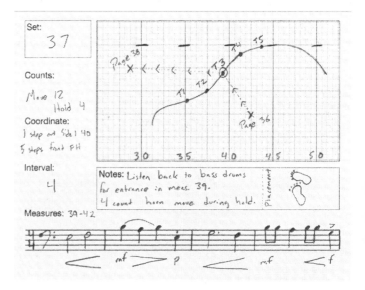

THE SYSTEM: IV. REHEARSALS / TEACHING & CLEANING DRILL

V. PARADES

Music Selection & Formations

Music Selection

Parades are traditionally festive in nature. The make-up of the audience is usually diverse. The spectators are there to be entertained and their taste in music will be varied. Therefore, the selection of the music should be recognizable and popular with the majority of the spectators. Marches, Broadway tunes, and popular music of enduring value are some good choices. Upbeat tempos and spirited melodies will render a good response from the crowd. Individual mistakes, cracked notes, and distorted tones are highly exposed in music with high *tessituras* and complex rhythms, and should be avoided.

Visual Elements

The parade formation of the total ensemble is important for visual appeal and musical balances. The color combinations of the uniforms, flags, props, and banners should all be coordinated. Visual effects with the percussion, drum major showmanship, and auxiliary routines, also add visual impact. Drills and choreography enhances the overall effect for the audience. Motion, color, excitement, energy, variety, and spirit are what excites audiences.

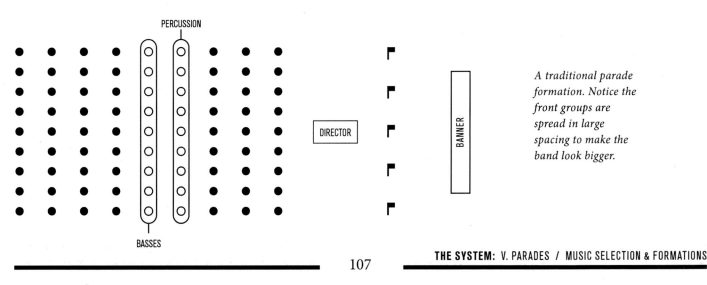

A traditional parade formation. Notice the front groups are spread in large spacing to make the band look bigger.

107

Sound Elements

The parade formation has a profound effect on the balance of the music ensemble. Keep in mind the formation travels from down the street, passes the listener, and then away from the listener. Here are some sample formations which all result in different balance results.

1. With the brass up front and the woodwinds in the back there will be more volume and impact, but less balance.

2. With the woodwinds up front and the brass in the back there will be less volume and impact, but better balance.

3. This is a reversible band which sounds the same going in any direction. The front is in score order and mirrored in reverse score order in the back. The percussion and basses are centered

1. _____

W	W	W	P	B	B	B	B
W	W	W	P	B	B	B	B
W	W	W	P	B	B	B	B
W	W	W	P	B	B	B	B
W	W	W	P	B	B	B	B
W	W	W	P	B	B	B	B
W	W	W	P	B	B	B	B
W	W	W	P	B	B	B	B

W- WOODWINDS   P- PERCUSSION   B- BRASS

2. _____

B	B	B	P	W	W	W	W
B	B	B	P	W	W	W	W
B	B	B	P	W	W	W	W
B	B	B	P	W	W	W	W
B	B	B	P	W	W	W	W
B	B	B	P	W	W	W	W
B	B	B	P	W	W	W	W
B	B	B	P	W	W	W	W

3. _____

W	W	B	B	P	B	B	B	W
W	W	B	B	P	B	B	B	W
W	W	B	B	P	B	B	B	W
W	W	B	B	P	B	B	B	W
W	W	B	B	P	B	B	B	W
W	W	B	B	P	B	B	B	W
W	W	B	B	P	B	B	B	W
W	W	B	B	P	B	B	B	W

Alignment & Spacing

Using a *2 or 1 step interval* in the ranks makes it easier to maintain good horizontal alignment. A *4 step distance* between the ranks keeps the sound from being dampened or "muffled." Traditionally the right guide is responsible for maintaining vertical spacing. It is for that reason marchers should guide right in their ranks, and cover down in their files. If the vertical and horizontal alignment is accurate, it will result in straight diagonals throughout the ensemble.

This block is a formation in which the ranks are staggered. It opens up the sound, and makes is easier to maintain file alignment. Diagonals are still visible. This unique concept actually makes it easier to cover down, since each marcher is aligning themselves between the people in front of them.

This block is set up with *1 step intervals,* and *4 step distance.* It is easier to maintain good rank alignment and execute pinwheel turns with closed intervals. This is ideal for large bands, or for marching on narrow streets. The *4 step distance* keeps the sound from being dampened.

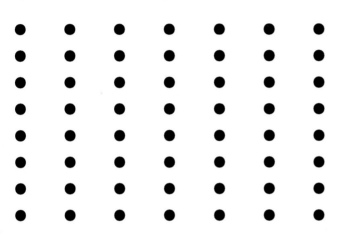

This block left is set up in *2 step intervals,* and *4 step distance.* It makes the band wider, useful for making small bands look bigger.

Parade formations can be in various shapes, such as this wedge. Experiment with creative formations, with combinations of various shapes within the different groups of the ensemble. Even though block formation is most common, experiment with other shapes for the entire ensemble.

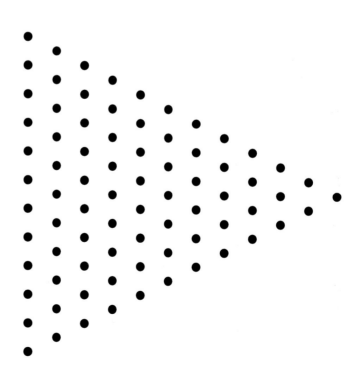

109

Turning Corners

There are three basic types of turns that can be used when maneuvering around corners. The examples below use a **4 step** interval, and a **4 step** distance. The illustrated turn will be to the right.

The Column Turn: This maneuver is executed sequentially in files. First the files move to a staggered position in four count sequences. The file on the right begins the sequence by marking time just past the edge of the corner. Each file switches to mark time sequentially from the right to the left. Once this is completed the file on the left begins to turn the corner, turning to the right sequentially. The remaining files step off every 4 counts, turning to the right in a follow-the-leader pattern.

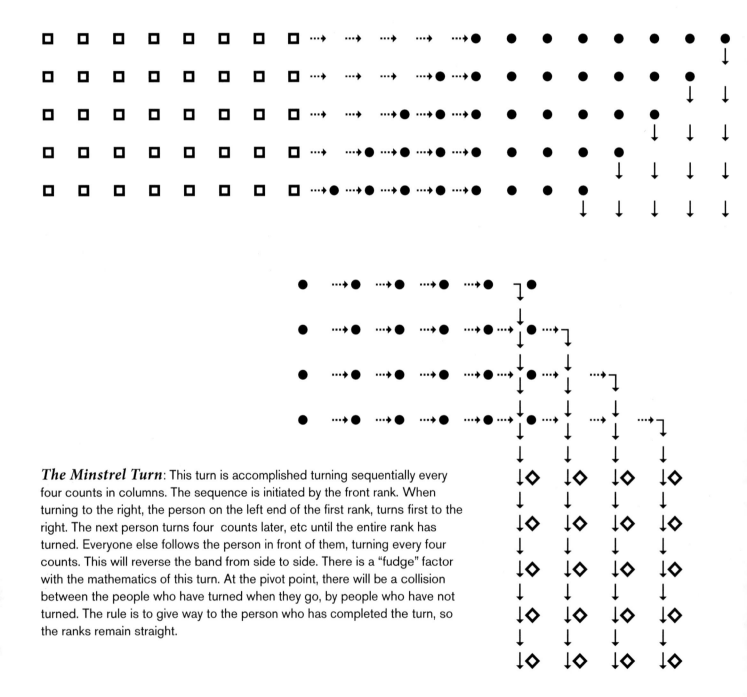

The Minstrel Turn: This turn is accomplished turning sequentially every four counts in columns. The sequence is initiated by the front rank. When turning to the right, the person on the left end of the first rank, turns first to the right. The next person turns four counts later, etc until the entire rank has turned. Everyone else follows the person in front of them, turning every four counts. This will reverse the band from side to side. There is a "fudge" factor with the mathematics of this turn. At the pivot point, there will be a collision between the people who have turned when they go, by people who have not turned. The rule is to give way to the person who has completed the turn, so the ranks remain straight.

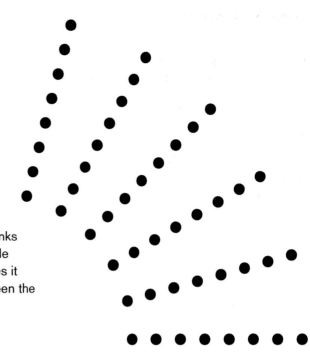

The Pinwheel Turn (gate): This block is a formation in which the ranks are staggered. It opens up the sound and makes is easier to maintain file alignment. Diagonals are still visible. This unique concept actually makes it easier to cover down, since each marcher is aligning themselves between the people in front of them.

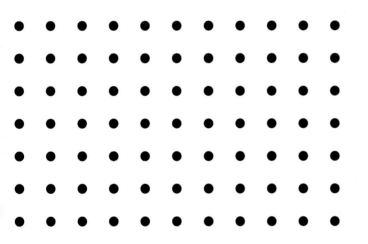

Decreased & Increase Front: The intervals of the band can be increased or decreased when the street width changes. Decreasing the width of the band before turning a corner makes it much easier to maintain good alignment during the turn. The intervals can be changed with an adjusted step, or with sequential turns. The collapsing effect can be made to the left, right, or toward the center. The horizontal alignment should remain straight while executing this maneuver.

Stopping & Starting: Avoid collapsing and expanding the formation when there are delays in the parade. There must be a signal that can be given at any point in the parade to alternate between mark time and forward march. For extremely large groups establish a relay system so the back of the ensemble can hear the signal. When there is a long delay it is wise to halt the group and put them "at ease".

Parade Signals

See Chapter III. Marching / Commands & Standing Basics

VI. MEASUREMENTS & GRID SYSTEMS

Simply defined, a grid is a subdivision of measurements, on paper or marked on the field. These increments are usually indicated on charting paper, with vertical and horizontal lines or dots, superimposed over the regular markings of a football field, which include *yardlines*, *sidelines*, *endzone* lines, and hash marks (*inserts*). These enable the drill writer to place individuals or groups on the field in mathematically accurate positions. When charts (or *dot books*) are duplicated for the band members' use while learning drill, the grid system simplifies the process of determining coordinates, and calculating paths for transitional movement.

Using Reference Marks on the Field

The 22.5", 45" and 90" grid systems are the most common. When teaching a drill, save valuable rehearsal time by placing reference marks or objects directly on the field. Position these reference markings so they represent the grid system in use.

Ideally, there should be a reference marking placed on the field every *180"*, vertically and horizontally, creating a visible grid which covers the entire field. All three of the grid systems illustrated below will work since *22.5"*, *45"*, and *90"* measurements are increments of *180"*. This procedure will enable the students to envision a smaller division of measurements on the field, for determining the accurate location of their positions (coordinates) throughout drill stagings and movement. In addition to saving hours of rehearsal time while learning the drill, refinement and perfection will be more efficient and productive. Also, students will have a better understanding of how their positions relate to the total form.

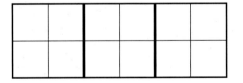

90" GRID SYSTEM

Divides each 5 yard increment into 2 equal parts vertically and horizontally.

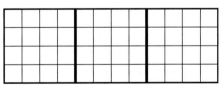

45" GRID SYSTEM

Divides each 5 yard increment into 4 equal parts vertically and horizontally.

22.5" GRID SYSTEM

Divides each 5 yard increment into 8 equal parts vertically and horizontally.

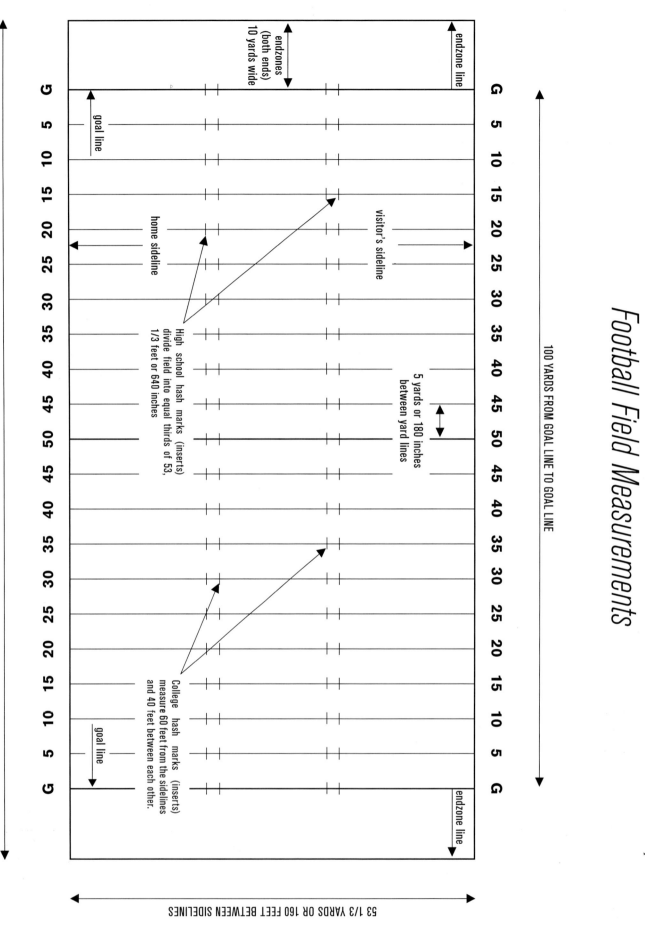

Football Field Measurements

endzone line

endzones
(both ends)
10 yards wide

goal line

visitor's sideline

home sideline

High school hash marks (inserts)
divide field into equal thirds of 53,
1/3 feet or 640 inches

5 yards or 180 inches
between yard lines

College hash marks (inserts)
measure 60 feet from the sidelines
and 40 feet between each other.

goal line

endzone line

100 YARDS FROM GOAL LINE TO GOAL LINE

120 YARDS BETWEEN ENDZONE LINES

53 1/3 YARDS OR 160 FEET BETWEEN SIDELINES

top

Hash Marks Margin-of-Error

Since any grid system that uses multiples of *22.5"* results in a *30"* margin between sidelines, drill designers and those who teach the drill must be aware of its existence and decide how to deal with it. When choosing to ignore the margin of error, adjustments must be made when setting forms or during transitional movement. If the margin of error is not ignored and the grid paper and actual field marks are coordinated with each other, the formations and all movement will be mathematically correct. The hash marks (*inserts*) placements on college and high school are different, though high schools in some states have chosen to use the college hash marks.

High School Hash Marks (*inserts*)

There is a margin of error when using any grid system with multiples of *22.5"* because the height of a football field is *160'*, or *53 ⅓* yards. Most high school hash marks divide the football field into three equal parts measuring *640"*. When superimposing any grid system using increments of *22.5"*, there will be a *10"* margin of error per third of the field because *28x22.5"* steps equals *630"*.

In other words, if one were to take *28–22.5"* steps from the sideline, they would end up *10"* short of the first hash mark. If they continued another *28* steps, they would end up *20"* short of the next hash mark. If they took another *28* steps they would end up *30"* short of the opposite sideline.

Therefore, there is a total margin of error of *30"* between the sidelines when using any grid system built upon multiples of *22.5"*. This will affect how forms are placed on the field.

THE 3 APPROACHES TO RESOLVE THIS 30" MARGIN OF ERROR

1. Ignore the Margin of Error

Most commercially distributed charting paper divides the field into *3* equal increments, ignoring the *30"* margin of error between the sidelines. If this approach is used, realize that when setting forms on the field there will be accuracy problems with spacing and alignment. Also, when placing reference marks on the field, adjustments must be made so that the field grid will coincide with the charting paper.

2. Incorporate the Margin of Error by Building the Grids from the Home Hash Marks

This approach will result in a *20"* gap on the visitor's sideline, a *10"* gap on the home sideline, with the visitor's hash mark *10"* off a grid mark, toward the visitor's sideline. These gaps should be shown both on the paper and on the field. Setting forms will be mathematically accurate.
Notice that the visitor's hash mark is offset *10"* from the nearest grid mark.

3. Superimpose the True Grid Over the Center of the Field Marks

This approach builds the grids from the center of the field, resulting in a *15"* gap at each sideline. The disadvantage is that both hash marks will be *5"* off a grid mark, away from the center of the field. Setting forms will be accurate if the field marks coincide with the charting paper. Regardless of the approach taken, the drill writer and director need to be aware that this mathematical discrepancy does exist and must be considered. When choosing to ignore the error, an adjustment must be made when setting forms or during transitional movement. If the margin of error is not ignored and the grid paper and field marks are coordinated with each other, the formations and all movement will be mathematically correct.

College Hash Marks (*inserts*)

During the winter of 1993, the *NCAA* voted to change the positions of the hash marks (inserts) to accommodate the kicking game for college football. These changes have already taken effect at all colleges and universities in the United States. To date, the states of Massachusetts and Texas have adopted this change for all of their high schools. Some other states are considering this change.

The measurements for college hash marks (inserts) on a football field are *60'* inward from both sidelines. This leaves a *40'* space between the hash marks for a total of *160'* between sidelines. All other college field marks are the same as the high school markings. The margin of error of *30'* for grid systems using multiple measurements of *22.5'* does exist, regardless of the placement of the hash marks.

THE 2 APPROACHES TO RESOLVE THIS 30" MARGIN OF ERROR & CHARTING COLLEGE HASH MARKS

1. Ignore the Margin of Error

Some types of charting paper ignore the *30"* margin of error by aligning the grid system to *84* equally spaced increments between the sidelines, and calling those measurements *22.5"*. Since the college hash marks no longer divide the field into equal thirds, the *30"* margin of error of the field creates a serious problem if ignored.

There are at least two logical methods for setting up the charting paper to ignore the 30 inch margin of error.

First, is to place the hash marks *32"–22.5"* steps in from both sidelines. This means the entire *30"* margin of error would need to be absorbed within the *40'* between the hash marks in the center of the field. This approach leaves *20'–22.5'* adjusted grid marks (or *10"–45"* grid marks) between the hash marks.

Second, is to absorb the *30"* error equally within the *160'* between the sidelines. On paper, this looks the same. The difference is that the margin of error is handled differently. With this approach there is a margin of error of *11.428"* between each sideline and nearest hash mark and a *7.142"* margin of error between the hash marks.

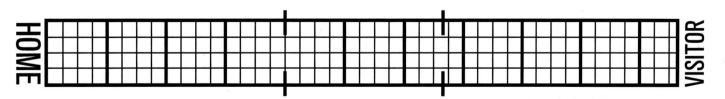

2. Incorporate the True Measurements on the Grid System

For those who want a mathematically correct grid system, the best method would be to begin measuring from the home sideline, and work toward the visitor's sideline. The home hash mark would be on a grid mark, and the visitor's hash mark would be *7.5"* short of a grid mark. That would leave a *30"* gap at the visitor's sideline.

Aligning the grid system with a *30"* gap at the top of the field works very well. If you take *84"–22.5"* steps beginning *30"* onto the field on the visitor's side, the *32nd* step would be *30"* past the visitor's hash mark, the *52nd* step would be on the home hash mark and the *84th* step would be on the home sideline.

Print copies of this *45″* grid paper and use it to practice charting various designs. Experiment with different spacings, shapes and sizes. Consider perspective, proportions and visual appeal. Avoid clutter and sloppiness. For accuracy use tools such as a compass, flexible ruler, french curves, and a ruler.

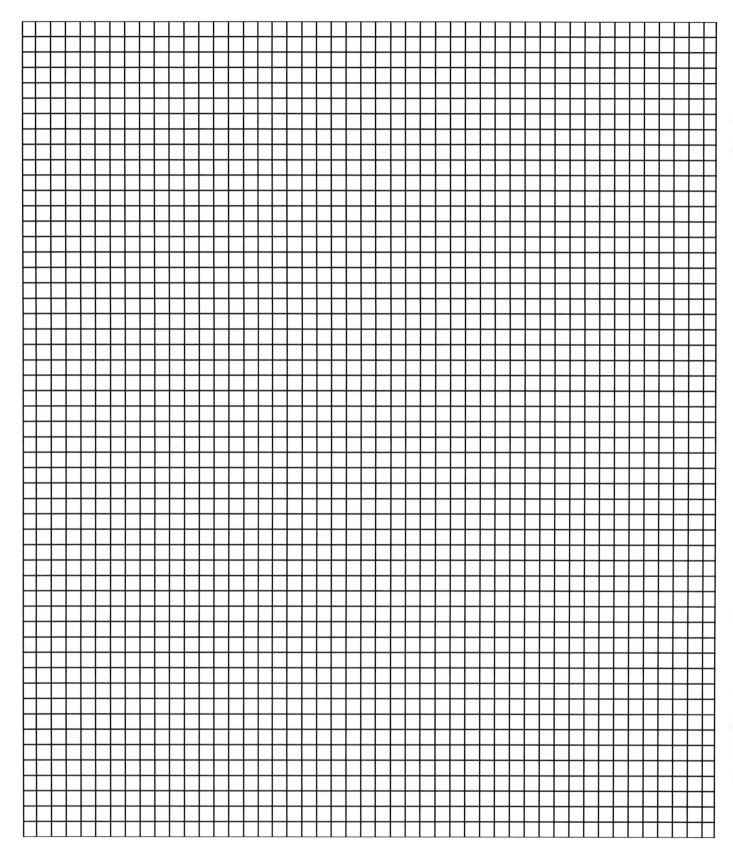

VII. DRILL DESIGN

by **Dr. Corey Spurlin**

Show Development Process

Administrative skills, effective teaching, and good musicianship are extremely important elements for building and maintaining a successful marching program, but if an ensemble is to be successful on the field, directors must also provide students with thoughtful, performable, and effective show and drill design. The most skilled musicians and marchers taught by instructors with the highest level of competency in marching band pedagogy can't overcome poorly conceived show concepts and/or flawed drill design.

Successful show design for marching ensembles hinges on coordination of the two primary elements of marching performance: sound content and visual content. For the purposes of this text, *Sound Content* refers to anything that can be heard during the show, with the actual musical selections serving as the primary sound element. Visual Content refers to anything that can be seen, with drill design serving as the primary visual element. Other visual components include auxiliary choreography, additional body movement executed by instrumentalists, uniforms or costuming, horn movement, poses, theatrics, and special effects.

There are varied approaches to developing marching band shows. The most common practice is to select the sound content first, and then design visual components that accurately depict and portray the musical material. This approach supports the premise that marching bands and corps are first and foremost musical ensembles. Some marching organizations though, have achieved great success by focusing on visual content first and designing a musical package that best represents the visual scheme.

Determine the Unifying Element for the Show

Whether all components are united by a specific theme, as is often the case, or they all portray a particular style or genre, marching shows should have a unifying element that binds all components together. Unifying elements vary, and can stem from musical or visual ideas. Whether a show features music of a specific composer, or a particular artist, period, or movement, or it is united by visual imagery, dramatic context, or narrative. Segments of a show may be starkly contrasting or they may be very similar, depending on the premise for which they are combined in a single production. Designers often start with a particular musical selection or style in mind, and the overall unifying element and other pieces are conceived from that single work. (see section *"Developing A Show Concept"*)

Select the Music

Once the unifying element is in place, designers must carefully select musical material that supports the artistic purpose of the show. Choosing the proper music is the most important task in the planning process. Though it is important that selections relate to the unifying element, they should not be chosen for this characteristic alone. Regarding selection of music, there are three important considerations. First, is musical selections should be appropriate for the medium and for the ability level of the specific ensemble. Second, they should have substance and contrast. Third, they should have aesthetic value to the target audience. When selecting music, consider seeking advice from veteran members of the ensemble, other staff members, arrangers, drill writers, and auxiliary/percussion instructors. This will intensify the excitement of future rehearsals and performances.

Determine the Order of Selections & Analyze the Structure of the Music

Musical selections must be organized such that there is sufficient interest and contrast throughout the show. Certain musical selections will function better as opening segments, middle segments, or closing segments. After the large order is established, it is important to pursue more in-depth analysis of the individual selections to determine which specific segments should be used in the show. Considering the relative brevity of marching shows, it is almost impossible to present complete renderings of musical works, regardless of the style. Thus, it is essential to select segments of the work that will provide the most interest to the target audience and that best support artistic objectives. Since designers ultimately strive to attain compatibility between the musical structure and all visual elements, formal analysis of the music is extremely beneficial in the visual design process. Music analysis aids in determining features, special effects, and drill design that should accompany each phrase of the music.

Determine Additional Sound Elements

After musical material is selected, but before arrangements are initiated or stock music is ordered, designers should determine if any additional sound elements are needed to enhance the show. Additional sound elements might include: percussion beyond the scope of typical battery and front ensemble, sound effects, guest performers, and/or amplification of individuals or sections. Though they are certainly not required to present an entertaining and competitive show, such sound enhancements have become increasingly popular with contemporary marching ensembles.

Initiate Custom Arrangements or Order Stock Music

Once musical material is organized into a logical sequence, the source of the actual arrangements must be determined, and the ordering process initiated. Many marching ensembles, especially those primarily concerned with competition, commission custom arrangements conceived to enhance strengths and hide weaknesses of the ensemble. This option, though more costly and time consuming, offers greater creative flexibility and often yields a product that is unique and that better suits the capabilities of the ensemble. For those that prefer the conveniences of prearranged (stock) music for marching band, there are often several options available, for each desired selection, through the various publishing companies. It is important to explore all options and choose the arrangement that best suits the capabilities of the performers and the mission of the show. Whether opting for custom or stock arrangements, it is important to obtain recordings of the music to aid in the visual design process. Publishing companies often provide promotional recordings, and most arrangers can produce a *MIDI* file that can be converted to *WAV* or *MP3* for use with drill programs or distribution to students and staff.

One of the major advantages of ordering stock music over custom arrangements is that recordings, scores, and parts can be shipped immediately so that the visual design process can begin. Depending on the client list of the arranger and their commitment to the commissioning ensemble, custom material can take months to receive and still may not include percussion parts. For this reason, the source of music is the most critical factor affecting the timetable for completion of the show design.

Design the Overall Visual Scheme

After recordings and/or scores of the music are received, the next step is to construct an overall visual package for the show. This includes drill design ideas, descriptions, and sketches; choreography ideas for auxiliary; color schemes for auxiliary units; additional choreography or dance for winds and percussion; and possible additional props and/or special effects. Visual ideas can be assimilated and analyzed using a *Flow Chart* and/or *Show Planning Sheet*. (*see "Coordinating Sound & Visual Content"*). All visual design elements should be included to insure coherence with the music.

Design and Order Specific Visual Materials

Once the overall design scheme is intact, specific flags and additional props should be designed and ordered. As with music, designers have the option of creating custom flags and props or searching for stock materials that fit the overall design scheme. The same advantages and disadvantages of music acquisition exist with the ordering of visual materials. Custom materials are unique, offer more design flexibility, and better fit the capabilities of the performers, but can be more expensive and take longer to receive. Stock materials are cheaper and can be received quicker, but searching for and ordering stock materials often requires significant artistic compromise. Regardless of the source for acquiring materials, it is important that orders are placed before the drill charting process begins so that the drill designer is aware of all visual elements that must be incorporated into the show.

Design Drill

With musical scores and recordings in hand and planning sheets complete, the drill design process can begin. The process includes creation of specific additional choreography for wind and percussion performers (instrument movement, poses, dance, etc.). Although, for certain arrangements, there are stock drills available that can be adjusted for the specific number of performers, it is common practice for directors to personally chart drill for their ensemble or to commission custom drill from a professional designer. Whether completing the drill design process in house, or hiring another individual, it is essential to the overall success of the marching ensemble that the drill is not only artistic and entertaining, but that it is suitable for the ability level and philosophy of the program. For this reason, a large segment of this chapter is dedicated to charting and/or analyzing marching drill.

Develop Auxiliary Choreography

Once the drill design is complete and auxiliary staging established, choreographers then create specific movement for each count in the music, expanding on broad-based ideas conceived in the "*Design the Overall Visual Scheme*" phase. To get an early start and avoid waiting on completed drill, the drill writer can notify choreographers of predetermined sections where auxiliary units will be stationary.

Design Schedule

With so many facets to the design process, it is important to establish a time-line for the completion of each phase. The following is a proposed strategy that could be altered if stock music and predesigned visual equipment are ordered in place of custom materials.

December–January

Determine the show concept, music, and order of selections. By the end of January, supply the arranger with the show concept and explain expectations.

February–March

Arrange music, final version to be complete by the end of March. Select, design, and order flags and other visual materials.

April–May

Design drill. Supply the drill writer with music and other specifications the first week in April, with final edits to be completed the last week in May.

June

Choreograph for auxiliary units.

Developing A Show Concept

Because there are numerous options for musical content, and at the same time, extensive limitations, the initial stages of show development (establishing the unifying element) can be daunting.

While music has expanded to a seemingly infinite number of genres, there are still few styles that convert easily to the marching band medium. Most works require a gifted arranger to transform them into an entertaining, yet playable piece, for a marching band. Despite the obstacles, concept development can be simplified if approached logically.

Essentially, designers choose from 2 groups of categories from art and music including *orchestral—concert band—jazz—choral—opera/musical—chamber* and *solo instrumental*—to popular music such as, *folk—jazz—gospel—rock* (and its many derivatives) and *country*. Rarely do shows mix musical material from these two categories. Therefore, simply selecting one or the other can eliminate numerous options.

Within these two categories, designers can establish a concept any number of ways, but there are some approaches that have become common practice. Designers often select the music of a particular composer, artist, or performing group. It is also common to select music from a certain genre, time period, or event. It is also possible to select music with a similar programmatic context, either telling a story or relating to a particular word, emotion, or purpose.

Often, music is selected to conform to a nationalistic theme, with each piece originating in a particular country or region. Still other designers select musical material as if programming for a formal concert, intentionally choosing works of contrasting style and heritage with focus on their effectiveness as an opening, middle, or closing segment. This approach forgoes the establishment of a unifying element to seek ultimate contrast between musical selections.

Selection of Sound & Visual Content

Throughout the show development process, there are important considerations that guide decision-making. Both sound and visual content should reflect careful contemplation of the following tenets of effective marching band show design.

Philosophy and Traditions of the Program

Marching show designers must consider the intent of the show, which stems from the director's overall philosophy and vision for the program. Some directors measure success with competition scores, while others are more concerned with audience response at football games. Some directors value the pedagogical effectiveness of their program and the performance and rehearsal experiences provided to their students, over audience enjoyment or competition success. To be successful, the show design must reflect the values of the director and participants. If the mission of the performing ensemble is to illicit maximum audience response at football games, it is likely that students and supporters will consider a costly, carefully-crafted, and highly intricate competition design a failure, especially if it is based on musical material that is unrecognizable to most audience members. Likewise, less creative shows that are easier to execute and include selections recognizable to non-musicians can yield lower scores at competitions, even if performed at a high level.

Quality of the Material

Quality assessment must be applied to all elements of the musical and visual design. Various criteria can be used to determine quality, but all designers/arrangers should insure that materials adhere to standard, accepted conventions. Even the most basic tenets, such as appropriate spacing in drill and stylistically correct articulation in music, are often overlooked. Specifically with music, it is important to evaluate, individually, the melodic, harmonic, rhythmic, textural, and formal elements of the selection, as well as the overall craftsmanship (combination of those elements). To be considered high quality, in addition to being fundamentally sound, musical and visual materials should reflect some ingenuity in their development, they should be genuine in idiom, and they should be consistent in quality throughout. In other words, they creatively generate the desired aesthetic result without including lulls in general effect. Determining quality is one of the major challenges confronting designers. Personal taste is hugely important in assessment, but it is also beneficial to seek recommendations and opinions of experienced colleagues and experts in the field.

Suitability for the Students

Musical and visual materials must match the ability level, size, and instrumentation of the performing ensemble as well as the time and resources available to teach the show. This requires research by the designer, making this consideration difficult for directors constructing their first show for a new program. It is important to remember that even high-quality music and drill still sound and look bad when they are too difficult for the intended ensemble. Likewise, materials that are too easy for the performing ensemble often yield performances that are uninspired and boring. The difficult task is locating or creating show materials that, not only offer an appropriate and surmountable challenge to the intended ensemble, but also lead to exciting and fulfilling performances and enhanced learning.

Suitability for the Target Audience

In addition to being appropriate for the intended performing ensemble, musical and visual materials must also be appropriate for the target audience. Target audiences take various forms, depending on the philosophy of the program. Bands with a sole entertainment function likely consider their target audience to be the football fans for which they perform each weekend. For highly competitive bands and corps, the target audience is the adjudication panel that assesses their performance at each event. It is possible to construct a show that conforms to all principles of successful design, but still lacks effectiveness to the target audience. As designers gain experience, they often enhance their ability to predict how an audience will react to certain music and visual ideas.

Timing, Pace, and Continuity

Because of the relative brevity of marching performances, timing and pace are also important considerations for designers. Timing relates to the amount of real time required for each show segment while pace refers to the frequency of activity within each segment. Pace is affected mostly by tempo. Continuity refers to the organization or order of musical and visual events. Shows require a logical sequence of events so that musical and visual materials flow with an unwavering sense of progress and aesthetic achievement.

All activity should either develop or realize something significant, with musical and visual climaxes strategically placed so that audience members retain a sense of relevant action. It is common for designers to include at least three major "emotional high points" in the show (some more intense than others), with significant space for repose and rebuilding between each. Smaller peaks and valleys are incorporated between major climaxes.

Variety and Contrast

The amount of variety and contrast is perhaps the most important consideration affecting the interest level of the show.

It is important to avoid excessive repetition (musically and visually). One of the basic tenets of good musicianship is recognition of relativity: loud moments only exist when compared to soft. Likewise in drill, angular forms only appear striking when compared to softer, curvilinear forms. When audience members sense little change in the style, frequency, and emotional impact of musical and visual events, they become bored with, and disconnected from, the performers.

Arrangers and composers achieve contrast in music through variation of tempo; changes in style or instrumentation; melodic, rhythmic, or harmonic alteration or embellishment; and/or dynamic shading. Visual contrast can be achieved through changes in field coverage, variety of shapes, and types of movement. Also, different equipment and costuming, and carefully timed visual effects can be effective.

Originality and Creativity

Although imitation is an important part of learning any craft, music arrangers/composers and visual designers must avoid reproducing the same idea exactly. Eventually, the result will become predictable and banal. Designers must not be afraid of experimenting with new ideas and concepts. One of the great advantages of computer-aided drill charting and music notation software is that it allows the designer the opportunity to see and hear new ideas before they are placed in the hands of the ensemble. Often, the best way to develop innovative designs is simply by creating variations of old ideas.

Design Skills For Drill Writers

Drill design is the most critical element in the overall visual package and thus, the focus of the remainder of this chapter. It is the process through which marching band show designers, communicate movement and staging, through a sequence of symbols and related written instructions. Charting systems vary, but if they are functional, logical, and consistent, a common language among staff and students can be established to convey concepts of movement, saving many hours of rehearsal. With experience, students should be able to visualize how the drills will appear and understand how their individual contribution affects the total set. Unlike musical notation, there is no standard language or method for charting drills. The remaining information in this chapter suggests a charting system that will improve the process of creating, teaching, refining, and performing a drill in an efficient and organized manner.

The first step in the drill writing process, after completion of detailed analysis of the musical material, is to develop and sketch an overall visual plan on paper. Sketches should not include labels for individual performers, only desired shapes and field coverage. Thus, sketches take less time than the actual charting process, and designers are not locked into the result. Visual design usually relates better to sound content when designers sketch formations for the musical impact points first, and then work backward to the

beginning and forward to the end. Designers must recognize that it is the actual motion (transition from one set to the next) that will determine the visual impact of the drill, so when sketching a series of formations, consideration should be given to the type and intensity of movement required. Various concepts of movement will be discussed later in the chapter.

Inexperienced drill writers often get overwhelmed and frustrated in the early stages of design. Rarely do designers envision

complete drill sets that they simply transfer to a computer screen. More often, great sets evolve through the addition and subtraction of four basic forms, which are the building blocks of effective drill design.

The following illustrations utilize a 5 yard grid.

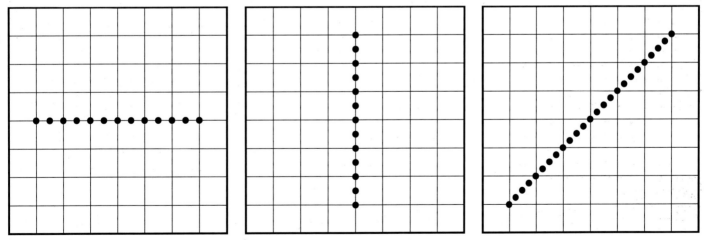

Straight Line Form: Two or more people in a straight line (drawn with a straight edge)

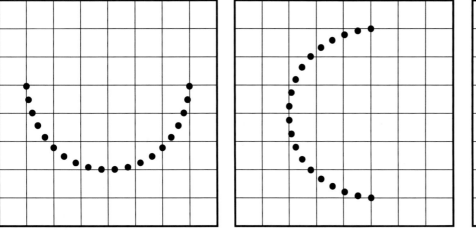
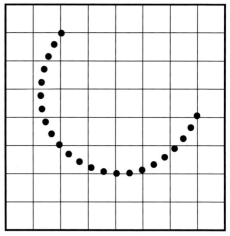

Arc Form: Any portion of a circle; bent lines that are concentric (all points are equidistant from the center)

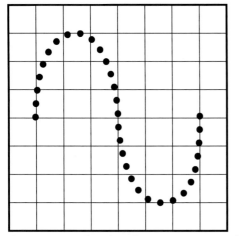
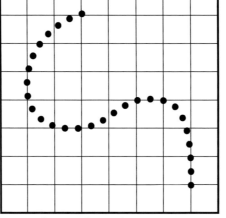
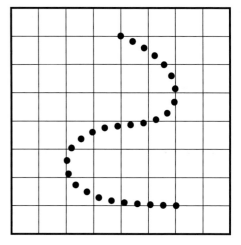

Curve Form: A bent line that is not concentric (drawn with a French curve)

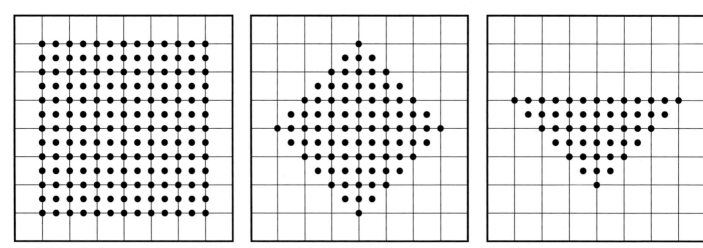

Block Form: Combinations of vertical and horizontal lines (any filled shape)

Basic forms combine to create *elements* (smaller components of a complete picture), and combined elements result in a *drill set* or *page* (the complete picture assigned to a particular count or series of counts in the music). There are numerous possibilities for combining basic forms to create elements. Below is a list of common terms for describing elements, illustrated with various possible form combinations.

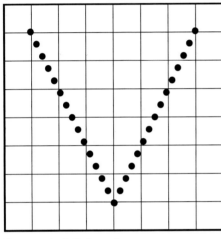

Symmetrical: *Balanced*

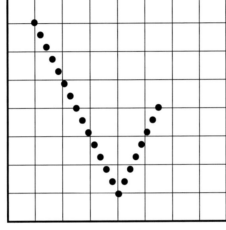

Asymmetrical: *Unbalanced*

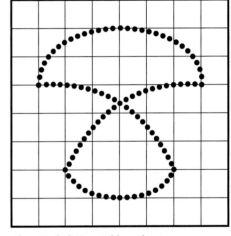

Close Ended: *No visible end point*

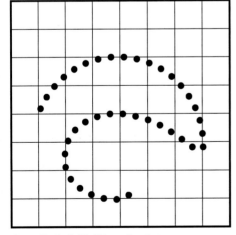

Open Ended: *Visible end points*

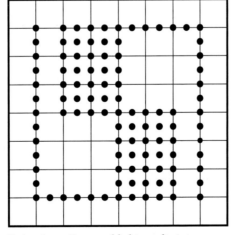

Extensions: *Forms added to endpoints*

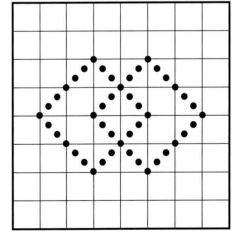

Superimposed: *Shapes on top of shapes*

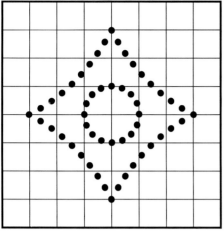

Kaleidoscope: *Same in all directions*

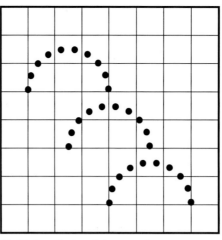

Multiples: *Copies of the same form*

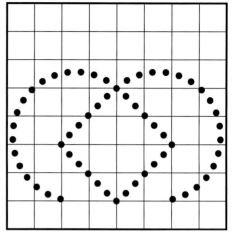

Mirrored: *Multiples with common axis*

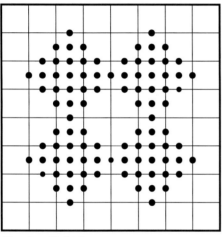

Mosaics: *Multiples creating patterns*

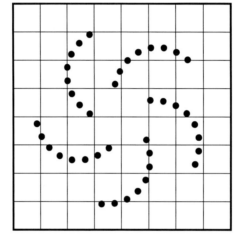

Fanned: *Multiples around axis*

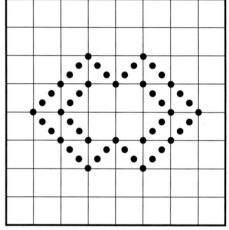

Layered: *Multiples that are parallel*

Sketching Process

When sketching a set for a particular musical segment, whether it is the opening of the piece or an impact point, designers should first consider which basic forms and types of elements best visually represent the music. Once elements are sketched, they can be manipulated in a variety of ways to create a unique and effective complete drill set.

The following approach minimizes anxiety and helps avoid "writer's block" by allowing designers to build complete sets through subtraction and addition of parts from basic shapes and elements. This strategy, though effective with a sketchpad, is most productive when executed on a blackboard or white board. With chalk/marker and eraser, it is much easier to add, modify, delete forms and elements.

The following examples utilizes a 180" grid (8-steps)

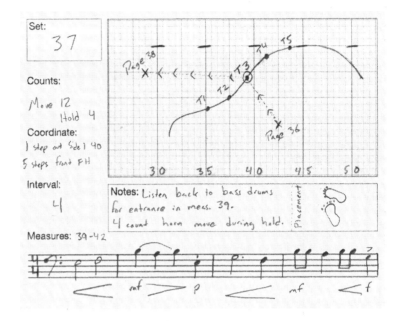

Remove Parts

Designers can generate ideas by first removing a part or parts from an existing shape to create new elements. The following examples illustrate various simple and recognizable drill elements and possible derivations revealed through deletion of segments. After erasing parts of the original form, a new and more interesting element is formed.

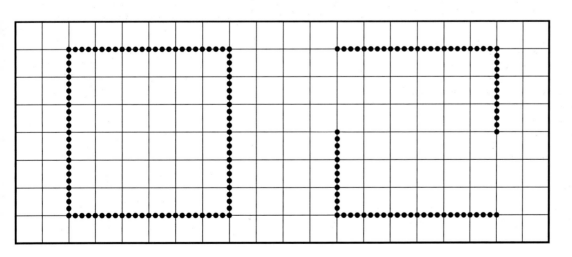

Box becomes open-ended, asymmetrical line combinations

129

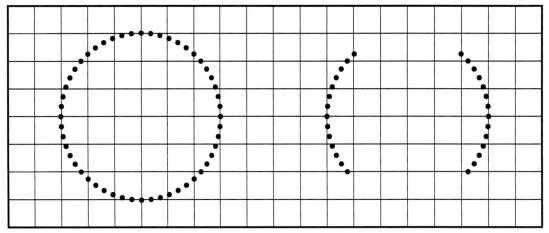

Circle becomes two mirrored arc combinations

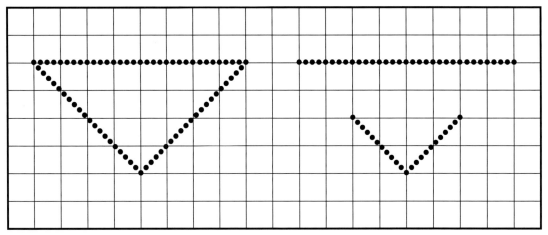

Triangle becomes symmetrical line combination

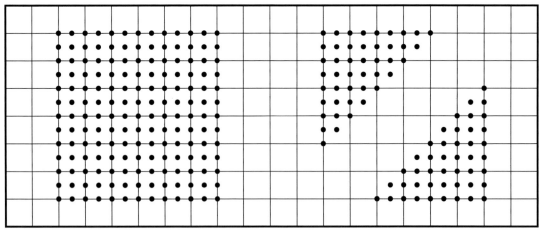

Square block becomes mirrored block combinations

Add Parts

Designers can also generate ideas by adding segments to basic forms and elements. The following examples illustrate various simple and recognizable drill elements and possible derivations revealed through addition of segments. The intent is to strengthen the simple element(s) and add interest with new components.

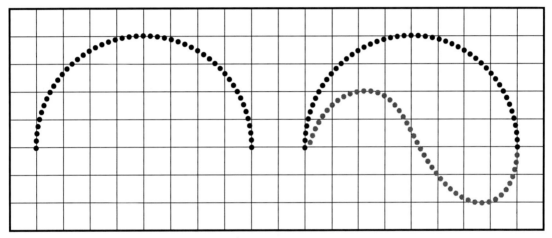

Arc with added curve form (creates asymmetry)

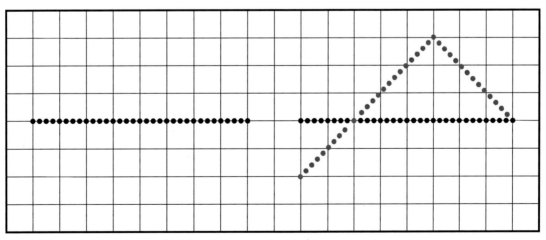

Line with superimposed line combination

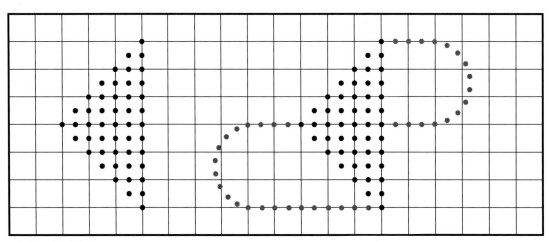

Block with added curve extensions

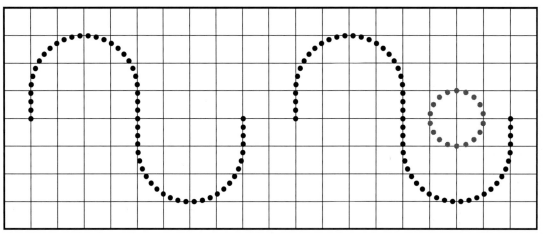

Curve form with added separate form

Complete Sets

Final sketches and complete drill sets are usually the result of the combined processes of addition and subtraction of components. With careful consideration given to potential movement and possible staging of instruments, designers can simply alternate the addition and subtraction of segments until a desirable set is achieved.

Designers must decide whether sets are too intricate and cluttered, or overly simplistic and banal, then make the correct adjustment. The number of *points of interest* often determines the visual appeal of the set. *Points of interest* are noticeable endpoints or intersections of formations within elements. Elements with a greater number of *points of interest* are often easier for performers to set and clean. Those elements that are essentially one large formation (huge arc or long straight line) are the most difficult to clean and should be avoided if possible.

It is important to note though, that well-designed sets have a greater number of *points of interest* in the front third of the field than in the middle and back third. Reasons for this are explained later in the section on perspective. When working towards a complete set, designers must

also decide if a particular section of the music is best portrayed with a set that is completely unified or one that is disconnected. In unified sets (usually closed ended), all formations are connected to create a single large element. Disconnected sets are comprised of various elements (usually open-ended), that support each other but are not joined and thus, maintain their uniqueness.

The following example illustrates the generation of a complete set, which begins with simple shapes, and is transformed using *remove-and-add* technique. Notice the building blocks of the total picture; basic shapes evolve into a variety of elements that comprise the overall set.

The concept of various elements as smaller components of a total set will be especially important later in the *spacing* and *perspective* segment of this chapter. Also notice the addition of *points of interest* as the set evolves.

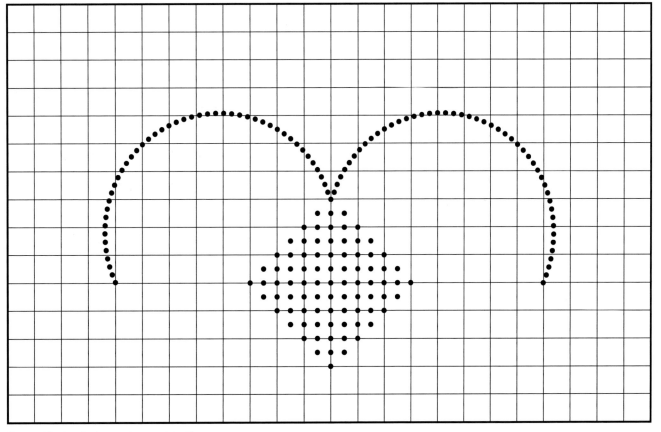

Start with simple shapes (symmetrical)

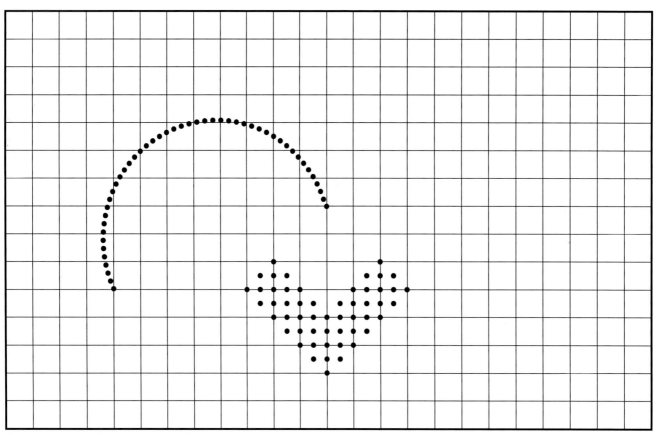

Remove segments (creates asymmetry)

Add segments to strengthen elements

THE SYSTEM: VII. DRILL DESIGN / SKETCHING PROCESS

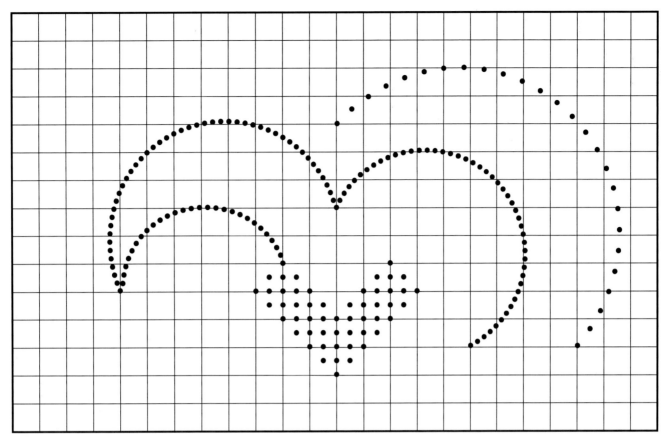

Embellish by adding possible auxiliary staging

Placement of Performers

Once designers progress beyond sketching to the process of charting individual members on a grid, there are a number of other factors to consider. Before beginning, it is important to have a clear understanding of the standard grid system used to chart performers on a football field. As discussed in *Chapter 6*, the standard grid is based on a *22.5″* marching step. Most computer drill programs allow designers the option of seeing and/or printing a line or dot for each horizontal and vertical step (*22.5″* grid system), one for every *2 steps* (*45″* grid system), or one for every *4 steps* (*90″* grid system). Designers should explore these possible grid options and make the necessary adjustments before charting performers.

To create a drill that is easy for performers to interpret and clean, designers should strive to chart members and forms on or through *zero points* as often as possible. The advantages of charting on the grid are further enhanced if a physical grid system of secondary markings is added to the actual practice surface (spraying a small dot for each *zero point*). If *zero points* are marked on the practice surface, students are given numerous reference points to construct forms and locate their positions on the field.

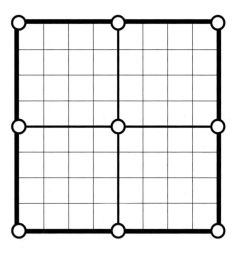

In this example, the dark lines are *180″* apart (*8 steps*). The small circles on the corner of each box are often termed *zero points* and are an important reference marking that can be used to locate exact placement on the grid. The lighter lines are *45″* (*2 steps*) apart.

TERMS TO DESCRIBE PLACEMENT OF PERFORMERS

Even Positions—Individuals or forms placed on the grid lines (*2-step* grid system)

Odd Positions—Individuals or forms placed between the grid lines (*2-step* grid system)

Offset Positions—Individuals or forms not placed between the plane of zero points

File—Two or more people standing one behind another

Front—Two or more people standing beside each other

Diagonal—Two or more people standing in an angle

Closed Spacing—22.5″ (*1-step*) spacing in fronts, 31.8″ in *45-degree* angles

Open Spacing—90″ (*4 steps*) spacing in fronts and files, 127.2″ in *45-degree* angles

Regular Spacing—45″ (*2 steps*) spacing fronts and files, 63.6″ in *45-degree* angles

Distance—Space between people or forms standing in a file

Distance— Space between people or forms standing in a front

The following examples illustrate various forms placed in fronts, files, and diagonals using open, closed, and regular spacing. In general, it is much easier to clean drill when even positioning is used almost exclusively. In the following examples, it is particularly important to note the placement of performers in diagonals. Though the actual space between performers is not an even *2, 3, or 4 steps*, performers are still charted on grid points so that, if one endpoint were to move forward and the other back to form a horizontal line, regular spacing would be intact. The placement techniques implemented in these simple forms are easily applied to more complex elements.

The following illustrations utilizes a 4-step grid (90").

Fronts & Files

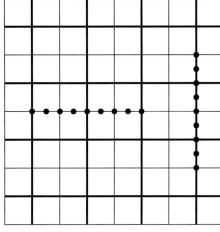

Regular Spacing—Even Positions

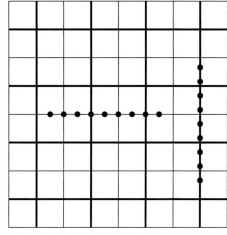

Regular Spacing—Odd Positions

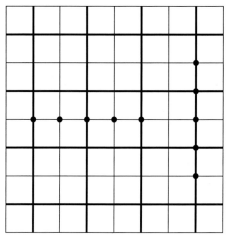

Open Spacing—Even Positions

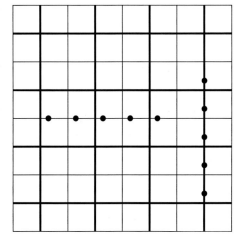

Open Spacing—Odd Positions

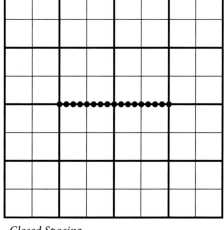

Closed Spacing

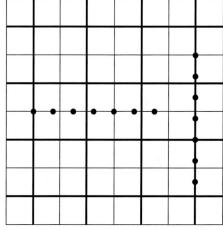

3-Step Spacing

THE SYSTEM: VII. DRILL DESIGN / PLACEMENT OF PERFORMERS

Diagonals

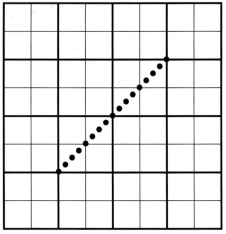

Closed Spacing (45 degrees)

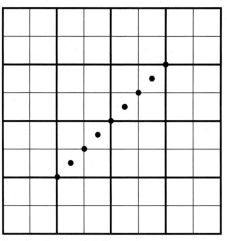

Regular Spacing (45 degrees)

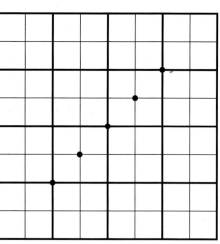

Open Spacing (45 degrees)

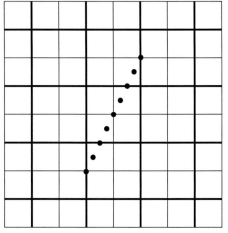

Other Angles

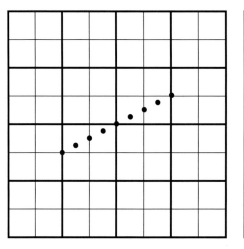

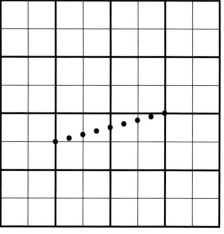

Curves

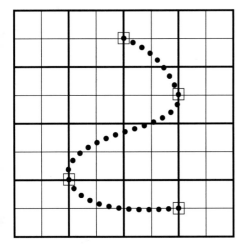

Curve, Regular Spacing

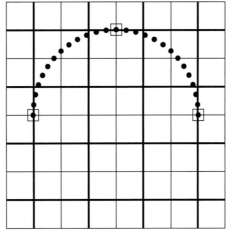

Arc, Regular Spacing

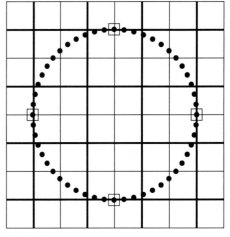

Circle, Regular Spacing

The grid should also be considered when charting curved forms. Though not every performer can be placed on a grid point as with a line or diagonal, designers should strive to chart important dress points on a grid mark. In arcs and curves, the important dress points are those performers that are the endpoints of the form or those that represent the deepest point in the form. In the following examples of arcs and curves, the important dress points are indicated; their position on zero points will make the forms much easier to clean.

Perspective, Spacing & Staging

As designers chart performers, there are certain factors that must remain in the forefront of thought with every set. The following segment explores three important ongoing considerations that will ultimately determine the success and effectiveness of the drill.

PERSPECTIVE

SPACING

STAGING

Perspective

Perspective, as it relates to drill, is the art of charting formations on two-dimensional paper in order to give the correct impression of how they will look when viewed by the audience from a certain three-dimensional vantage point. In other words, it is adjusting for the difference in the way something looks on paper and how it will appear to the audience.

Two factors control the degree of difference:

1. The distance of the formation from the bleachers

2. The height of the viewer in the bleachers

Notice that when the formation is closer to the bleachers and/

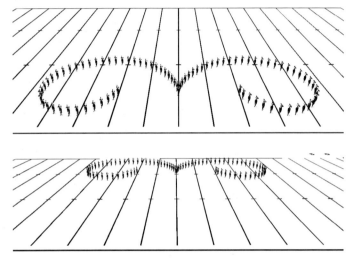

or the viewer is higher, the angle of sight is greater and the formation is more readable. When the bleachers are lower, or the formation is farther away, the angle is less and the formation becomes increasingly more difficult to decipher.

There is one guiding principle when considering perspective.

A FORMATION WIDENS HORIZONTALLY AND ELONGATES VERTICALLY AS IT MOVES CLOSER TO THE VIEWER. CONVERSELY, THE FARTHER A FORM IS FROM THE VIEWER, THE NARROWER AND SHORTER IT APPEARS.

With the square elements below, notice that the spacing in the vertical lines appears smaller than the spacing in the horizontal lines. When viewed by the audience, the square looks more like a horizontal rectangle. Since the top of each element is farther from the audience, the perspective issue is more pronounced than at the bottom. That is why the top of the square appears to be condensed inward, and the intervals in the vertical lines appear to get progressively smaller towards the back of the element.

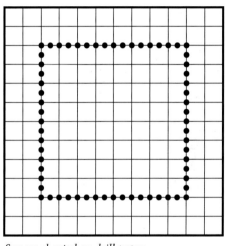

Square charted on drill paper

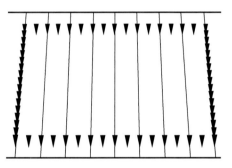

Square as viewed by the audience from higher bleachers close to the field.

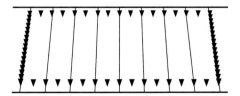

Square as viewed by the audience from lower bleachers further from the field.

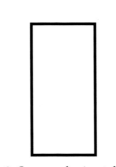

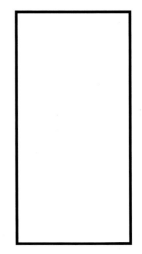

1. Elongate vertically   *2. Compress horizontally*   *3. Do both simultaneously*

Although most drill writers are aware of these principles, many ignore them when designing drills. If perspective is not an ongoing consideration during the charting process, the result can be drill that looks great on paper, but cluttered and unrecognizable to the audience. To ensure the clarity of a form, there are three possible alterations to consider.

These adjustments cannot be made by altering the spacing between individual performers, such as expanding the vertical distance between performers and/or reducing the horizontal spacing. Intervals should remain consistent throughout the element, but to adjust for perspective, more performers are placed in the vertical forms, and fewer in the horizontal.

AVOID SUBTLETIES

When the audience views horizontal forms that are only slightly bent or curved, they will see what appears
to be straight lines that are poorly executed. In the following examples, the adjustments on the right are
necessary for the original form to be perceived correctly from the audience's perspective.

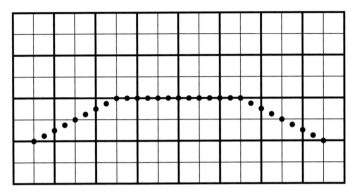

This angle is too slight to create the desired appearance

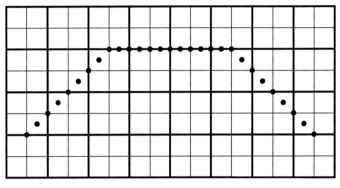

This adjustment improves the definition of the form

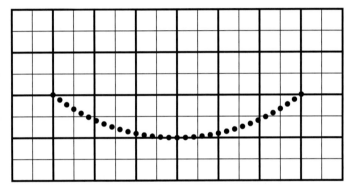

This arc is too shallow and wide

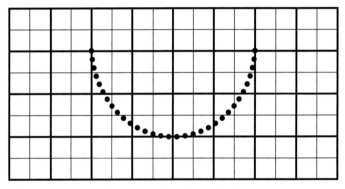

This adjustment adds depth and clarity to the form

It is also important to avoid subtlety in symmetry. Designs that are only slightly
asymmetrical look like symmetrical formations with execution errors. Elements should
be exaggerated enough to be obviously asymmetrical or symmetrical.

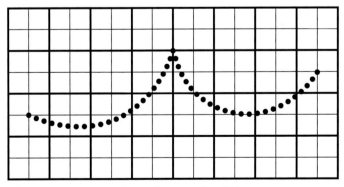

These arcs are very similar in design and could be
misinterpreted as symmetrical forms

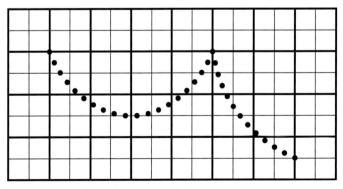

These arcs are obviously asymmetrical

AVOID SCREENING OR MASKING PERFORMERS

When the audience views horizontal forms that are only slightly bent or curved, they will see what appears to be straight lines that are poorly executed. In the following examples, the adjustments on the right are necessary for the original form to be perceived correctly from the audience's perspective.

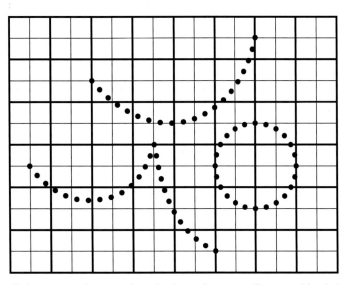

If they are so close together, the front elements will appear blended with the back arc form

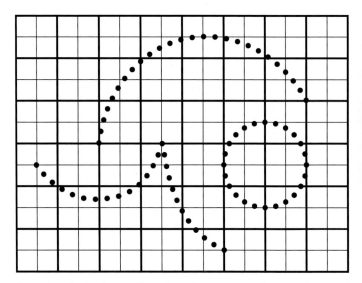

Inverting the back arc allows for adequate space between front and back elements

When stacking elements on the front third of the field, it is important to maintain at least **8 steps** between elements. In the middle and back third of the field, at least **12 steps** should be maintained, though **16–20 steps** will further enhance the clarity of stacked elements on the back third of the field.

In addition to adjusting vertical space, screening and masking can also be avoided by increasing horizontal space between performers. By widening the intervals of the front element, audience members have a clearer view of the performers in the back element, and there are fewer obstacles to block sound.

Again, it is important to remember that intervals should remain consistent within a given element, but can vary between elements, depending on the continuity of the total set. In the following example of a complete set, notice the **8-step distance** between forward forms and elements and the **16-step distance** between back elements. Though there are only **8 steps** between forward elements and the auxiliary element, the **8-step** interval provides enough horizontal space to delineate forms and allow visibility of back elements.

Also, notice the consistency of intervals within elements: **2-step intervals** within line combinations, **4-step spacing** within the block element, and **8-step** intervals within the auxiliary elements.

144

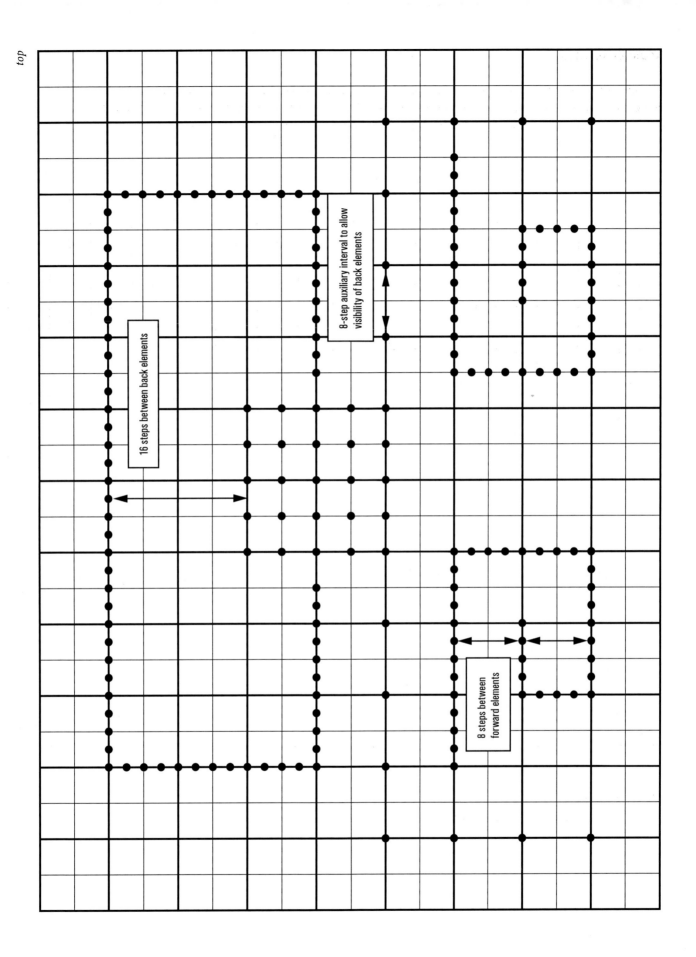

8-step auxiliary interval to allow visibility of back elements

16 steps between back elements

8 steps between forward elements

THE SYSTEM: VII. DRILL DESIGN / PERSPECTIVE, SPACING & STAGING

AVOID CLUTTER

As new formations are added to existing elements, clutter is an increasing concern. Often simple adjustments can greatly enhance the clarity of the element. In the first example below, a straight-line form is added to the arc element, obscuring the focal point. By using an arc form instead, vertical spacing is enhanced, the added form supports other arc forms in the element and the element is clearer, and more appealing to the audience.

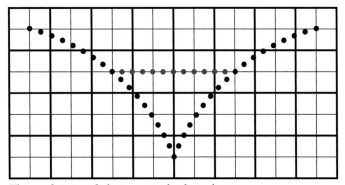

This angle is too slight to create the desired appearance

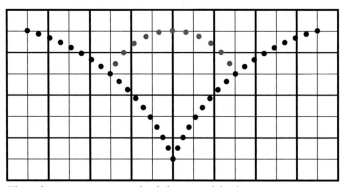

This adjustment improves the definition of the form

PROPORTIONAL ELEMENTS

It is also important to consider the size of individual elements. Because they will appear further compressed from the audience's perspective, especially small elements are not effective. Small forms should be reshaped, resized, or joined to form a larger, well-proportioned element. Larger elements may have segments that are too small. It is important to make sure all components of the element meet the spatial recommendations indicated above. In the first example below, the diamond elements are too small to be accurately perceived by the audience. In addition, the three elements in the set, with only *4 steps* between them, are too close to be viewed as distinct components. They should be joined to create a unified set or further separated to allow sufficient space between.

The second example demonstrates how the four small diamond elements could be reconfigured and joined to create one large element, without losing the angular, striking character of the set. Also in the second example, the three elements are spaced *8 steps* apart so that there are clearly three separate components to the overall set. Though some designers may find the first example to be more visually pleasing on paper, the second will be much more effective on the field.

These elements are too small and too close together

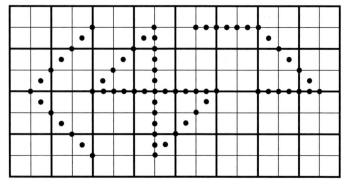

These elements are joined and reconfigured

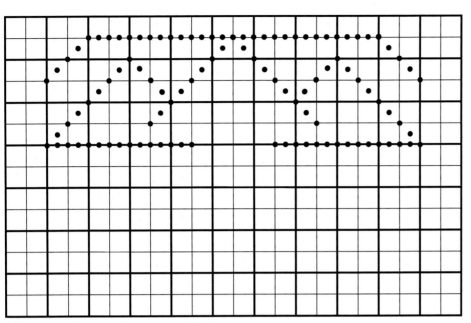

This element is too detailed for backfield charting

As previously mentioned, distance from the field to the audience is one of the critical factors affecting perspective. Backfield drills, especially those that stage the entire ensemble in the back third of the field, are particularly challenging because the line of sight for the audience is at the lowest possible angle. Perspective adjustments must be exaggerated.

The complexity of elements is also a major concern when charting backfield. As previously discussed, elements with multiple *points of interests* are effective in the front third of the field, but because of perspective principles, tend to look cluttered in the middle and back third of the field. It is also more difficult to allow adequate vertical depth when elements have numerous *points of interest*.

For backfield charting, make elements deep and simple.

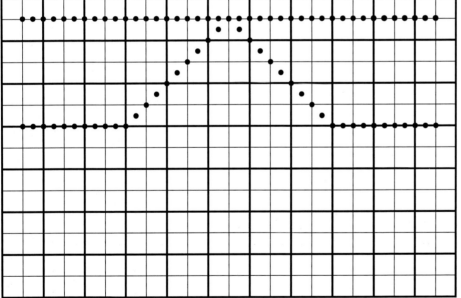

This element is simpler and has appropriate spacing

Spacing

Spacing of specific sections of the band is the second most important ongoing consideration when charting. Aforementioned traditional terms such as open, closed, and regular spacing are relevant, but apply primarily to wind players. In general, execution of a drill is better when even positioning and regular spacing is maintained for wind players. Marching ensembles execute different intervals throughout the course of a show, but most have a default interval at which much of the drill for the winds is written. For large bands, *2-steps* (regular spacing) is most common. Smaller bands, however, appear larger when the default interval is expanded from *2 steps* to *3*. *Three-step* intervals are harder to clean, but the results may be worth the effort.

Depending on the size of the ensemble, formations used, and the desired field coverage, designers should maintain *1, 2, 3,* or *4-step* intervals for all winds. Some specific instruments require a minimum amount of space with certain staging. In files, it is much easier for trombones to maneuver with at least a *3-step* distance. A *2-step* distance requires them to play over the shoulder of the person in front and, if a turn or contrary motion is required, elevate the instrument over the head of the person in front. Sousaphones should not be spaced at a **1-step** interval or distance. For sousaphones, *2-step* intervals are acceptable but *3* and *4-step* intervals are more visually appealing.

Due to the size of the instruments and performance practice, spacing requirements are slightly different for percussion. Because snare drummers are often taught to listen in to the center player, they prefer to be spaced as close as possible, typically at *1½-step* intervals, but *2-step* intervals are also common. Though there are instances where it may be necessary or effective to have snare drummers spaced further apart, it is not typical and should not be common practice. Because of the size of the instrument, tenor and bass drummers require at least *3-step* intervals. Cymbal players can function within *2-step* intervals but it is not recommended. If they are executing visual motions that require them to extend their arms side to side, they need *3* or *4-step* intervals to perform.

The appropriate interval for the various percussion components depends on the spacing of other performers within the same element. If percussionists are charted alongside winds that are *2-steps* apart, it is more visually appealing and consistent to chart the snares at *2-step* intervals and the tenors, basses, and cymbals at *4-step* intervals. Likewise, if percussion are linked with colorguard that are charted at *6-step* intervals, or winds that are charted at *3-step* intervals, it is more effective to chart the snares *1½ steps* apart, and tenors, basses, and cymbals *3-steps* apart.

Auxiliary units for marching ensembles usually fall within one of four categories: flags, rifles/sabers, dancers, or majorettes. Based on the nature of their performance medium and the choreography at any specific point in the drill, each unit has slightly different spatial requirements. When spinning, colorguard members require at least *6-step* intervals, *8 to 12 steps* if oversized flags are used.

Rifles and sabers require at least *6-steps*, but *8-step* intervals are safer and more effective when tossing. Majorettes require at least *4-steps* when twirling, but *6* and *8-step* intervals are more effective when numerous tosses or complicated tricks are incorporated in the choreography. Spacing for dancers is contingent entirely on the choreography. *Four-steps* is common as a default interval, but certain body movement or use of props may require smaller or larger intervals.

Staging

INSTRUMENT & AUXILIARY GROUP PLACEMENT

Since marching bands and drum corps are first and foremost musical ensembles, some of the most important decisions made by drill designers, relate to staging of specific instruments. The placement of the various sections directly influences the production of sound in static, and/or moving formations. Balance, blend, volume, texture, precision, and overall impact can be enhanced or diminished by staging. It also effects the overall visual impact of winds, percussion, and especially auxiliary units.

WIND STAGING

It is common practice in contemporary drill design (especially for a drill that is mostly asymmetrical) to keep all like instruments together in close proximity, as much as possible. Visually, this approach yields a more uniform look than mixing instruments, and provides the designer opportunities to segment and/or create visual effects for sections that present important musical material. With regards to musical execution, players tend to feel more secure when they are around other performers playing the same instrument, thus volume and precision are enhanced. When in close proximity, performers can also react quickly and make adjustments to correct intonation, blend, and precision problems. Designers for larger ensembles, especially if charting symmetrical drill, often split sections so that every instrument is represented on each side of the field. Usually, like instruments still remain together on each side.

Approaches vary with regards to specific staging of the various wind sections on the field. The musical score and the location of the percussion are the two factors with the greatest impact on placement of woodwinds and brasses. Ensembles that are highly competitive typically seek innovative ways to showcase the various sections of the band musically and visually, which leads to both woodwinds and brasses receiving prominent staging in the front part of the field at various points in the show, depending on which color is featured in the score. Conversely, it is typical for entertainment-oriented ensembles to stage brass instruments on the front side of the field, and percussion and woodwinds on the back side of the field. Regardless of the staging philosophy, it is important to consider the acoustical characteristics of the instruments. For timing and execution, it is more critical for brass instruments to be located relatively close together and in close proximity to or in front of the percussion. The volume of the instruments makes it difficult to hear when spread out. Woodwind players can be separated and positioned farther from the percussion; the acoustical quality of their instruments allows them to hear the percussion from a greater distance.

PERCUSSION STAGING

The number of possibilities for staging percussion instruments, hinges on the experience and maturity of both the percussion and brass performers. High-level ensembles with ample rehearsal time to correct timing deficiencies can challenge percussion sections with greater mobility and field coverage.

The ideal playing position for percussion sections is: snare drums in the middle, tenor drums to the right of the snares (from audience perspective), bass drums to the left of the snares, and cymbals behind the snares. The highest bass drum should be staged closest to the snares. Unless absolutely necessary, avoid stacking percussion in multiple fronts (tenors behind snares, basses behind tenors, cymbals behind basses). Because percussionists are accustomed to listening in to the center snare drummer, avoid staging percussionists in "V" shapes.

Less experienced ensembles and/or those with limited rehearsal time will benefit from keeping percussion instruments staged as close as possible to the center of the field and the core of the brass section. Even those designers charting for more mobile percussion units typically stage them in close proximity to brasses during rhythmically challenging segments of the music. Regardless of the level of mobility for the entire line, the percussion section as a group should never be split into multiple units that are more than ten yards apart. As distance increases, it is more difficult for them to hear each other, which results in timing issues and precision problems.

Fear of timing issues or execution problems often inhibits drill designers from properly incorporating percussion members into the overall design scheme. Too often in drill designs, percussionists are staged as a separate entity that contributes little to the overall visual effect of the drill. With forethought and creativity, it is almost always possible to incorporate percussion into other elements in the drill or at least chart them so that they are supporting other formations. If charted correctly, the percussion will enhance rather than distract from the overall aesthetic.

The first of the following examples illustrates possible percussion staging for a curvilinear set with the winds spaced at *3-step* intervals. The second example illustrates percussion staging for an angular set with the winds spaced at *2-step* intervals.

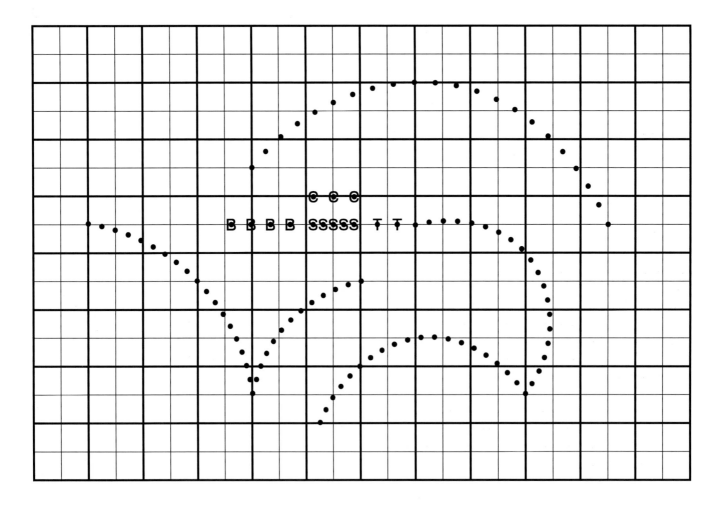

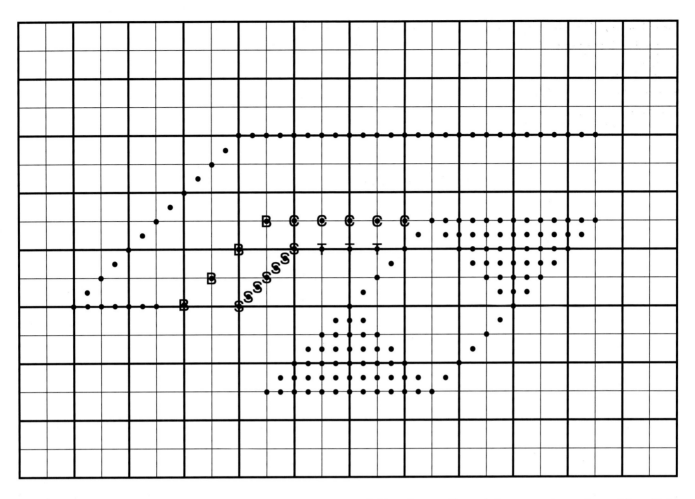

OTHER FACTORS AFFECTING SOUND

In addition to instrument-specific characteristics, there are other general factors that affect staging for wind and percussion instruments. Sound production should be considered not only when placing performers in static sets but also when determining the type of motion from set to set. The sound produced from the brass and bass drums is directional, but the sound from woodwinds, cymbals, and mallets is not. The snare and tenor drums are directional, but, since their sound travels vertically, the audience doesn't hear it as such. For this reason, the percussion and woodwinds do not lose volume when they turn away from the audience. The volume of the brass and bass drums greatly decreases when they turn away, changing the musical balances. Thus, woodwinds can face the line of march without drastically affecting the overall sound quality or quantity. However, it is more prudent for brass and percussion instruments to maneuver in slide position, for the brass to maintain the intensity of sound and percussion, and to sustain eye contact with the conductor.

It is also important to consider the relative *tessitura* of instruments and parts when staging. Higher pitches are easier to hear. For example, just one piccolo can be heard over a full band, regardless of placement. In sections with multiple parts, the first parts are more easily heard than the lower or inner parts. This consideration should not lead designers to place the lowest sounds closest to the audience, but rather, closest to the percussion and behind higher-pitched instruments. Because they often provide rhythmic accompaniment in marching band music, it is important for balance purposes, that low instruments are positioned in close proximity to percussion, and behind the mid and high brass. Because of the acoustics and volume of the instruments, it is difficult for trumpets and mellophones to hear what is in front of them, and they must be able to hear and adjust volume and pitch to the bass and tenor voices.

When staging instruments, it is important to remember that motion also affects musical balance. When a form moves closer to the audience or when performers are compressed in a tighter formation, the volume tends to increase. This concept can be used to emphasize certain sections or soloists, or to enhance particular musical elements.

Because sound travels slowly, ensemble and rhythmic clarity are affected by the size of drill elements. Fast and intricate music requires more compact formations, resulting in increased volume, cleaner definition, and greater impact.

When the music is smoother, slower, and less rhythmically active, it is more effective to chart larger elements with greater field coverage to produce a panoramic sound.

AUXILIARY STAGING

Auxiliary units enhance the music and drill visually through the use of equipment, props, costumes, and choreography. Their contribution to the total effect of the performance is determined by how effectively their choreography characterizes the music, and how well they are staged in relation to other drill elements. Auxiliary units that are most visually effective are those that are part of the overall design of the set, rather than an addendum or distraction to the desired aesthetic. For this reason, it is important to consider auxiliary units when developing a design scheme for the show, and to chart auxiliary units alongside other components of the ensemble. To make this possible, designers must be aware of equipment/costume changes and general plans for choreography before the drill design process begins.

There are a variety of options for incorporating auxiliary units. The following is a list of basic concepts that can be embellished or combined to ensure that visual ensembles contribute to the general effect. An effective visual program would likely contain examples of each concept.

1. Frame: When framing, auxiliary members form a color backdrop or perimeter for the rest of the ensemble. This is the simplest way to chart auxiliary units, and is the most conducive for equipment changes. Already positioned on the perimeter of the set, it is easy for performers to move off of the field to pick up new equipment. Though it can be visually effective at times, adjudicators often consider this approach to be dated and banal, so competitive ensembles should be cautious of overuse.

2. Integrated Frame: With an integrated frame, auxiliary units serve as a color or visual backdrop for other performers, but they are linked to other elements in the set. This approach has the same advantages as a standard frame, but enhances the cohesion of the set.

3. Extension of an Element: Auxiliary units can be staged as an addition to existing elements. If extensions are effective, the visual interest of the original element is enhanced, but the element is not dependent on the extension to be viewed as complete. Because they are easy to create through the "add and remove" sketching process, extensions are one of the simplest ways for inexperienced drill writers to achieve better cohesion between instrumental and visual performers.

4. Fully Integrated: When auxiliary units are fully integrated, their presence is essential for the element to maintain its integrity and fulfill its intention. This is the most challenging approach to auxiliary charting, but adjudicators and audience members often appreciate and reward the enhanced visual impact and design cohesion. When auxiliary units are fully integrated, they are often positioned closer to the center of the field with other performers surrounding them. Thus, it is more difficult to reposition them for quick, and inconspicuous equipment changes.

5. Filler: Auxiliary units can be placed sporadically or in block forms within an element to provide color enhancement. This approach greatly enhances general effect, and is worth the careful forethought that is required, but the technique also includes similar challenges as full integration. Moving the units into position often requires pass-through maneuvers and larger step sizes, and the performers often end up out of position for future equipment changes.

6. Stage: Wind and percussion elements can be used to frame an open area of the field, creating a stage for auxiliary units during feature segments of the show. This technique is typically used when winds and percussionists, or a segment thereof, remain static for an extended period of time, in order to focus audience attention on visual units. The amount of time in the staged set depends on the nature and intention of the show, and the length of the feature segment for auxiliary units.

7. Overlay: With an overlay, a stand-alone complete auxiliary element, is placed on top of an existing element or complete set of winds and percussion. With this technique, the auxiliary and wind/percussion elements could function alone, but are combined to produce an integrated set that is greatly enhanced by depth and cohesion. If charted correctly, the set will appear as though the auxiliary element could be lifted off of the wind/percussion element, and placed on a separate page. An overlay is a type of integration, which produces the same positive results, and similar challenges as other integration techniques.

8. Separate Form: Auxiliary units can be charted as a completely separate form, that is not consistent in shape or style with the rest of the set, or integrated with other elements of the set. This technique can be used to draw attention to the visual unit during a feature segment. Eyes are generally drawn to those elements that are different. This technique is most effective when used sparingly and not as a default approach for staging auxiliary units.

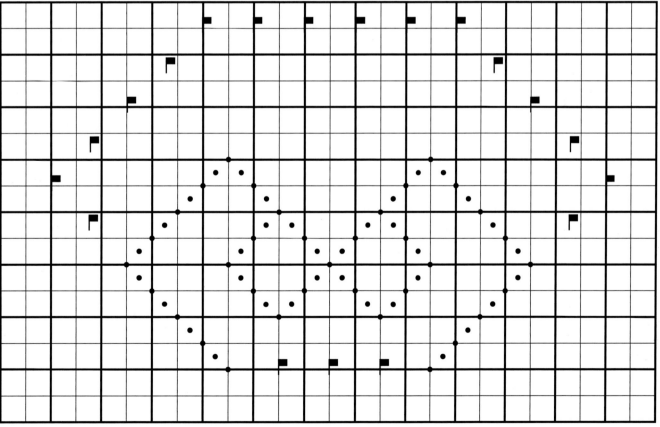

1. Frame

2. Integrated Frame

THE SYSTEM: VII. DRILL DESIGN / PERSPECTIVE, SPACING & STAGING

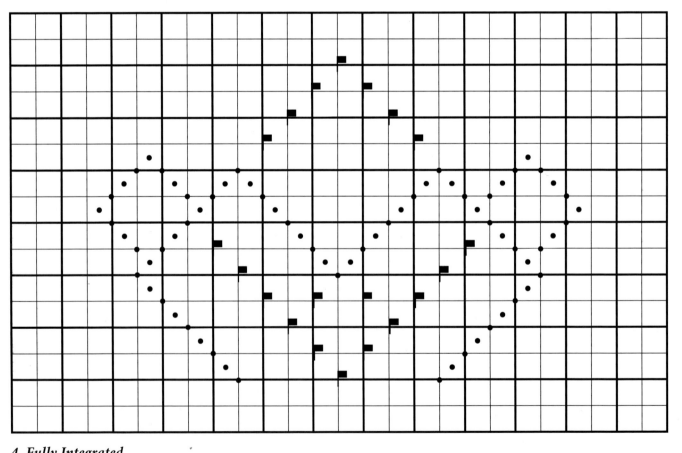

3. Extension of the Element

4. Fully Integrated

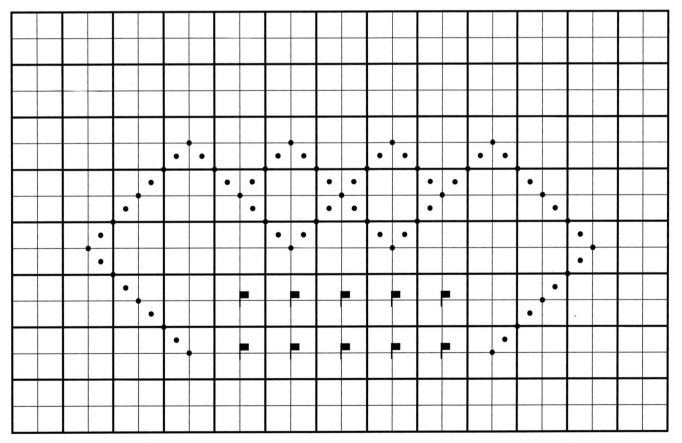

5. Filler

6. Stage

THE SYSTEM: VII. DRILL DESIGN / PERSPECTIVE, SPACING & STAGING

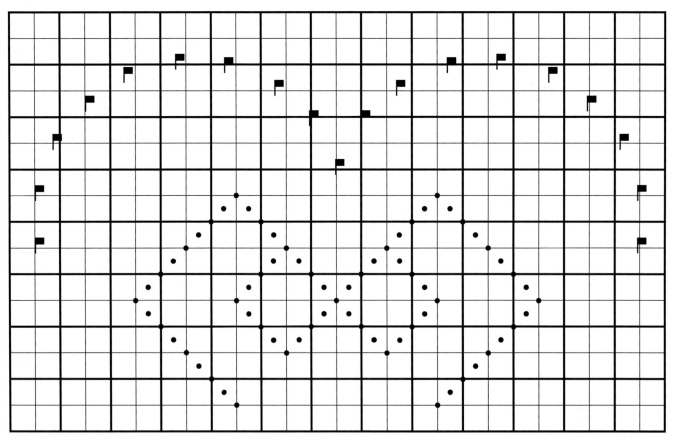

7. Overlay

8. Separate Form

Concepts of Movement

When learning the craft of drill writing, set design principles are generally the first to be presented, however, movement concepts are equally important in the overall process. Too often, designers do not consider movement in the early stages of creative thought. It is important to remember that, in most marching shows, performers are stationary in static pictures a very small percentage of the overall production, relative to the time spent moving. Thus, the overall effectiveness of the drill is primarily based on motion, not pictures.

THERE ARE 9 BASIC CONCEPTS OF MOVEMENT, EACH OF WHICH HAS A NUMBER OF POSSIBLE APPLICATIONS AND VARIATIONS. THESE BASIC CONCEPTS ARE OFTEN COMBINED TO CREATE MOTION WITH GREATER VISUAL INTEREST, IMPACT, AND CONTINUITY.

1. Shift / Unison Movement

2. Morph / Change Shape

3. Expand / Contract

4. Rotation

5. Follow The Leader

6. Curved Paths

7. Sequential Movement

8. Random Movement

9. Combinations

The challenge is to chart movement that represents the music, is visually stimulating, and is within the ability level of the ensemble, but does not inhibit execution of music or choreography. As with the conception of static sets, designers should determine motion for musical climaxes first and then work backward and forward from the impact point.

1. Shift/Unison Movement

Unison movement, the most common movement type for maintaining a form, is the shifting of an element or a complete set to a different position on the field without changing the shape or spacing. With this concept, each performer takes the same size and number of steps simultaneously in the same direction. Though it is the easiest type of drill movement to chart, it can be one of the most difficult for performers to execute. The size and shape of the shifting element, direction of the movement, and step size determine the level of difficulty. Unison movement can also be applied to choreography, in which case all performers execute the same body movement simultaneously.

By shifting two distinct forms (usually straight lines) towards each other, unison movement can be used to combine separate elements into one continuous form. There are two ways to accomplish this objective. Designers can mesh lines so that the two forms truly integrate, and a new order of performers is established. Or, they can simply add one form on the end of another, maintaining the same order of performers for the individual lines. A line mesh that occurs for a single count within a move, with both lines continuing movement in the same direction, is often referred to as a *pass through*. *Pass throughs* are important not only to add interest to the drill but also to aid in moving featured instruments into a more prominent position on the field without separating forward elements.

*The following examples illustrate a simple line
"pass through" and uses a 45 grid system.*

*The first example represents the primary set. During the move, the back line
should be repositioned in front of the forward line.*

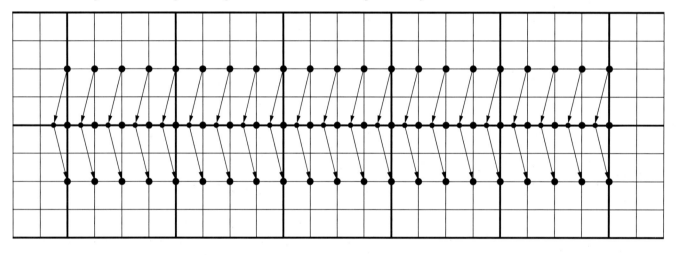

The second example illustrates a "pass through" maneuver that will accomplish the objective.

When looking at drill charts, shifts are usually obvious to performers because the exact dimensions of the formation or element remain intact from one page to the next. However, clarity is enhanced when arrows, pointing in the direction of the move, are attached to key dress points.

In this first example below, unison movement is applied to individual elements, each of which shifts in a different direction.

159

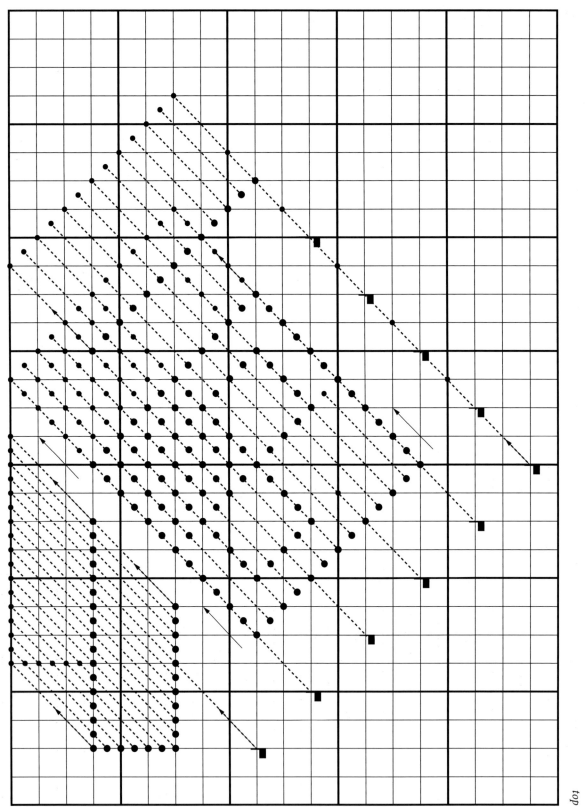

top

2. Morph / Change Shape

Morph is the most common type of movement for changing the shape of an existing form. To morph a form, performers use a maneuver commonly referred to as a float. Using the same specific number of counts, each performer moves in a straight-line path to his/her position in the new form. A consistent step size is used throughout the move, but, contrary to unison movement, the step size required to reach the next set could be different for each performer. With computer technology, changes in shape are easy to chart quickly, especially if little attention is given to the effectiveness and/or complexity of the move.

The ease of computer charting makes it seem as though there are endless possibilities for morphing one shape into another, and designers often become too focused on the appearance of the new form or element and give little attention to the movement required to get there. Designers must recognize that, with any given formation or element,

only certain alterations are visually effective, and achievable by the performers.

It is not necessary to include arrows on charts where morph (or float) is the desired movement from one set to the next. Floats can be communicated to performers simply by using (FL) in the written instructions. Even if secondary sets are not included on the same page, performers can easily flip back and forth between two pages, to see the evolution of the new form.

This first example below, illustrates a morph from angular elements, to curved forms. Notice the straight-line path for each performer. Though the distance from one set to the next varies for each performer, the circles should evolve smoothly over the sequence of counts and lock into place at the same time. This requires each performer to take a different size step.

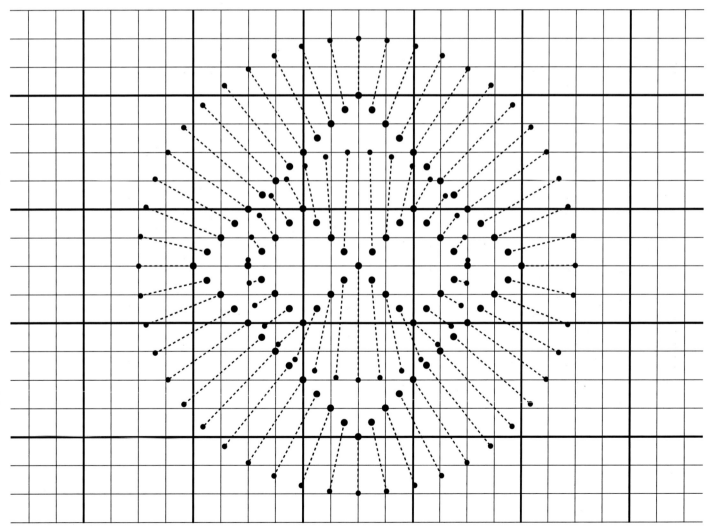

Morph / Change Shape Example 1

2. Morph / Change Shape (cont.)

The second example provides a clearer picture of the desired secondary set.

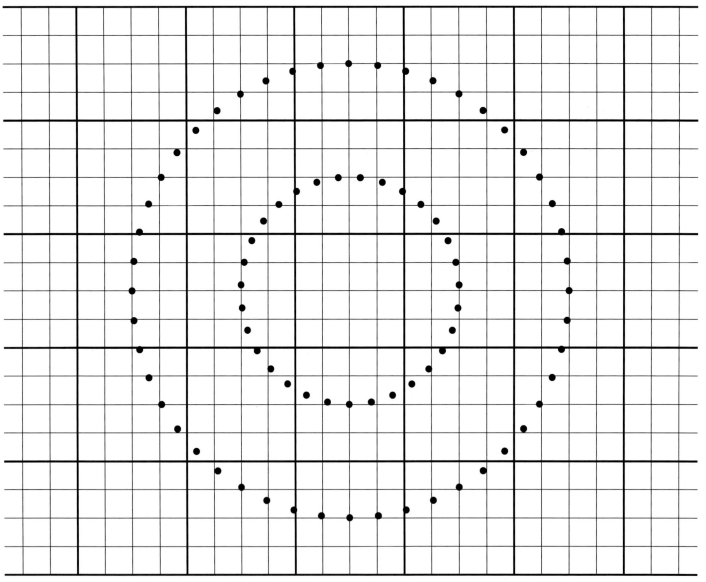

Morph / Change Shape Example 2

3. Expand / Contract

Expansion and contraction alters the size and field coverage of existing forms or elements without changing the basic shape. As with a morph, a float is used to execute expansion and contraction. Each performer begins and ends the move on the same count, travels in a straight-line path from the starting position to the ending position, and uses a consistent step size throughout. Contrary to a morph, but consistent with a shift, the step size is the same for all performers. This is because expansion and contraction is generated from the center of the form and occurs evenly on all sides.

As with a morph, it is not necessary to include arrows on charts, when a simple (not combined with other movement concepts) expansion or contraction is desired. The movement is clear to performers by looking at the secondary set or, if secondary sets are not used, by flipping to the next page. If an expansion or contraction is used in conjunction with a rotation (see combinations), arrows benefit the performers by allowing them to see quickly the direction of the rotation and instructing them that a curved path is required.

The following examples illustrate a simple block expansion. The first example is the primary set and motion, while the second example provides a clearer picture of the secondary set.

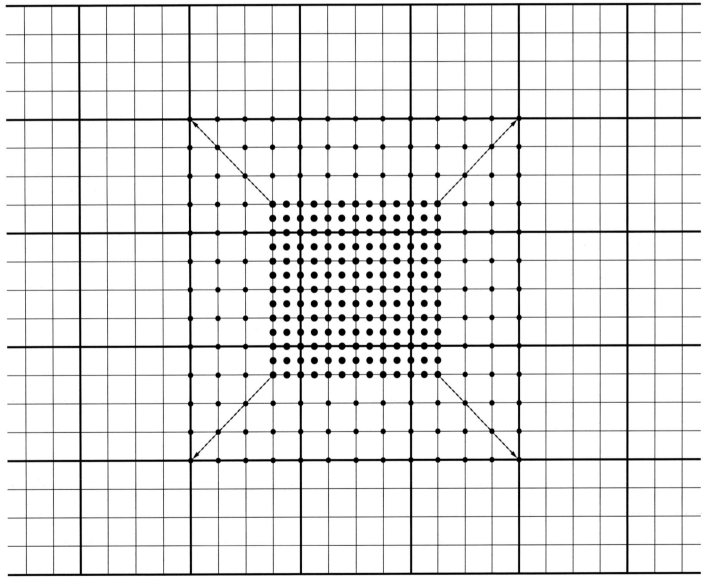

Expand / Contract Example 1

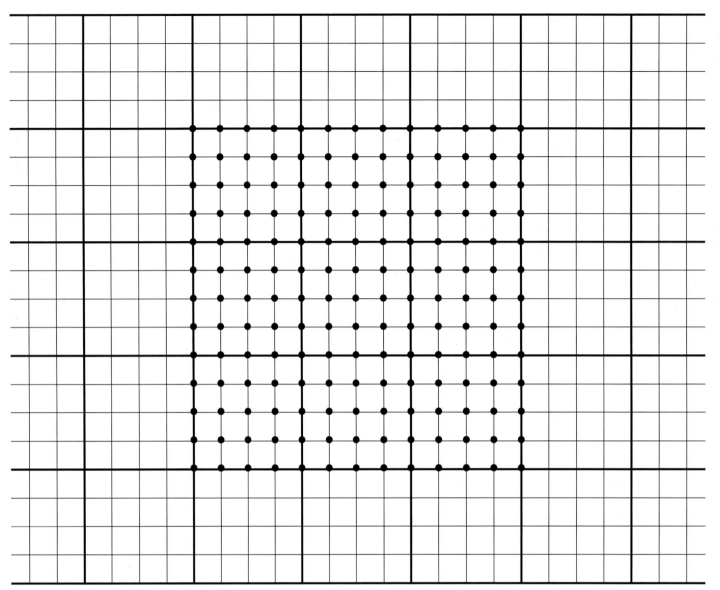

Expand / Contract Example 2

4. Rotation

With rotation movement, the shape and spacing of the form or element is maintained but the position of each performer changes. In some instances, the orientation of the form is adjusted. Each performer follows an arced path around a fixed point, or axis, from the starting position to the ending position. The fixed point can be in the middle of the form, on either end, or a point outside of the form. Each performer takes the same number of steps, but the step size, though even throughout the move, is different for each performer. Those closest to the axis take smaller steps while those further away take larger steps.

The person nearest the axis functions as the pivot. A performer that is charted on the axis point is a fixed pivot and does not move. The larger the form or element and/or the intervals within the form, the more difficult the maneuver is to execute.

To execute a rotation properly, performers need additional information on the chart other than the primary and secondary sets. Performers assume that a straight-line path is used, to move from one set to the next, unless instructed otherwise. Curved arrows stemming from the primary form, and/or specific reference to rotation movement, should be provided in the written instructions. The following examples illustrate counter-clockwise pinwheel line rotations.

The first example illustrates the curved paths necessary to maintain spacing throughout the move.

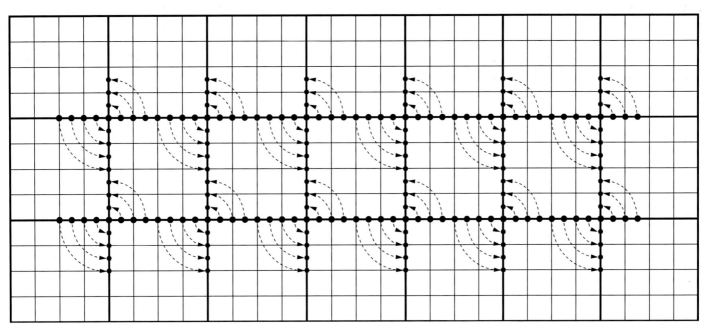

Rotation Example 1

The second example provides a clearer picture of the desired secondary set. In most cases, pinwheel rotations would continue in the same direction, to reform horizontal lines, and possibly continue to reset the original order of performers.

Rotation Example 2

5. Follow-The-Leader

Follow-the-leader maneuvers slightly alter or completely change the shape of a form. They often result in one segment of the form maintaining its shape, while an addendum to the form is created. To execute the move, performers in a particular form, taking the same size and number of steps, follow the exact path of a performer on the end, assigned as the leader. The path taken by the leader, which can be curved or straight, determines the shape of the new formation. The effect is that of the leader pulling other performers through the contour of the new form.

Designers should not chart *follow-the-leader* movement when performers are less than *45"* (2 steps) apart. When charting *follow-the-leader* motion with computer programs, since the designer simply manipulates the leader, it is easy to focus only on the path and destination of the leader, and give little attention to the ending positions of other performers. This can result in a set with limited visual appeal. Especially with angular paths. It is important to ensure that performers end on the grid, and that the resulting angular shapes have true corners.

To properly indicate *follow-the-leader* movement on the chart, designers should establish a system for labeling the leader,

and provide arrows to indicate the path of the leader. If the path changes direction, multiple arrows can be used to indicate the complete path. Curved arrows should be used to illustrate curved paths. It is common to label the leader by circling the appropriate symbol and label. It is also important to indicate *follow-the-leader* movement in the written instructions, typically with the abbreviation **FTL**.

The following examples illustrate curved *follow-the-leader* movement.

In the first example, arrows are included to indicate the path of both the colorguard leader and the instrumental leader. Other arrows are included to label the direction of movement for those following the leader.

The second example depicts the secondary set, or ending positions for the move.

The next 2 illustrations utilize a 90" grid.

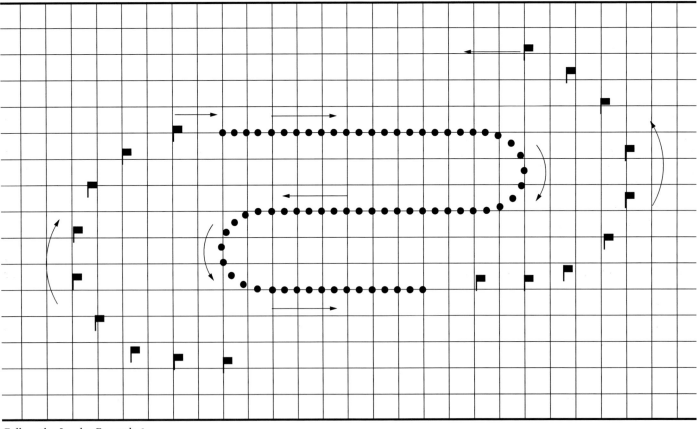

Follow-the-Leader Example 1

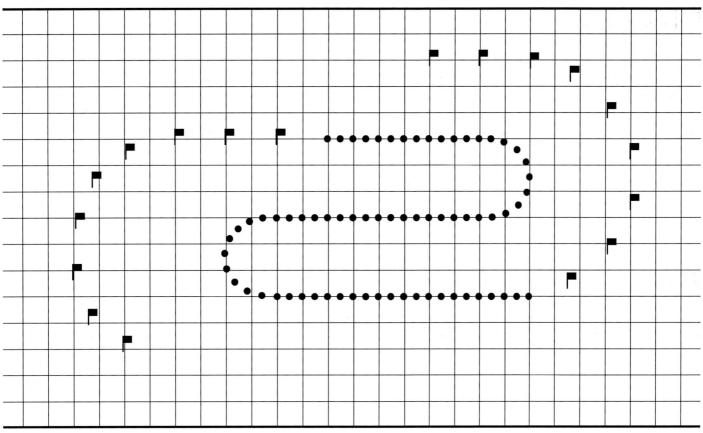

Follow-the-Leader Example 2

6. Curved Paths

Movement with curved paths alters the shape and design of an existing form or element. The maneuver has only one distinguishing characteristic from a morph: performers do not take a straight-line path from the beginning to ending position. The same number of counts is used to execute the move and each performer takes a consistent sized step throughout, with the step size varying between performers according to the distance traveled. As with a morph, the result is that the shape and design of the form changes gradually throughout the move.

When morphing forms, straight-line paths—depending on the disparity between beginning and ending forms—can sometimes cause intervals to condense and expand beyond what is functional for performers. Curved paths, though they extend the step size for performers, help to maintain adequate spacing, and enhance the smooth evolution from beginning to ending forms. Because they are harder for performers to execute, curved paths should only be utilized when necessary to maintain adequate spacing, or when the overall visual effect is worth the added challenge.

In most contemporary drill designs, floats are the most common concept of movement, and unless told otherwise, performers assume that a straight-line path should be used. For this reason, it is important to provide curved arrows and written instructions to indicate when a curved path is desired. Arrows also help performers understand the depth of the path required to achieve the desired effect.

In the following examples, notice that curved paths are necessary for the last six performers on each end of the middle line, and the performers on the far ends of the shorter lines. The curved paths prevent intervals from condensing, as the lines evolve to arcs.

The second example provides a clearer view of the secondary set.

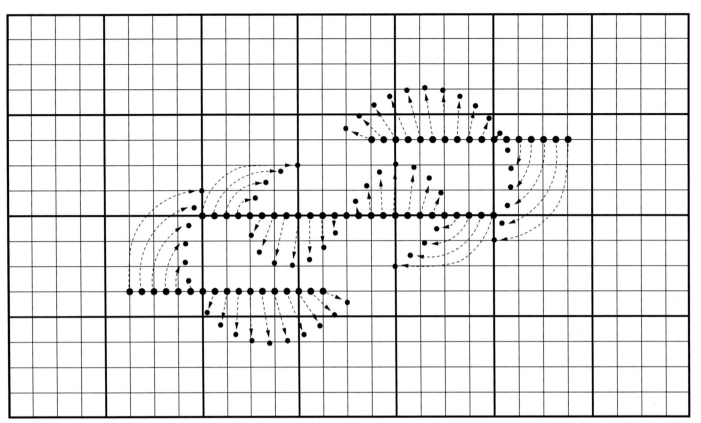

Curved Paths Example 1

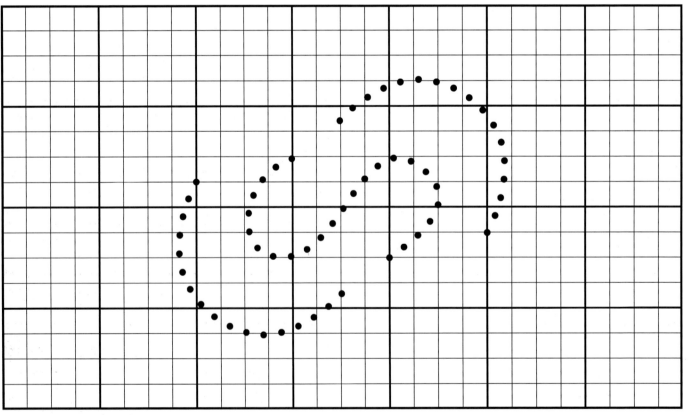

Curved Paths Example 2

7. Sequential Movement

With sequential movement, each performer in a form executes the same drill or choreography, but starts and/or stops on a different count. Because the concept is applied to drill and choreography, it can be used to alter the shape of an element or to enhance a static formation. There are a variety of applications of sequential movement, which can be executed in two counts or over the course of an entire phrase or multiple phrases.

A ripple is a type of sequential movement where only a fraction of a count separates the initiation of movement between two adjacent performers.

To apply sequential movement to larger count structures, performers can start or stop marching (or turning) two or more counts apart, until each member of the drill element completes the move. Sequential movement can also be applied to groups of performers, in which case separate forms or elements start, or stop motion on different counts of the phrase.

Regardless of the approach, sequential movement is more effective when patterns develop without becoming predictable. Though morphs/floats are more common in contemporary drill design, sequential movement is an easy way to add variety to the visual package, without altering design characteristics.

The secondary set/page can remain the same; only the procedure from moving from set to set is changed. In certain situations, sequential movement can also simplify movement for performers, by replacing adjusted step sizes with a standard 22.5" step size.

Sequential movement is indicated on charts in a variety of ways, depending on the desired effect. Sequential choreography is best explained in written instructions, or verbally with modeling. Sequential drill movement that involves performers initiating the move at the same time but stopping on different counts can be described in written instructions, using the abbreviation GTP, which represents *"Go To Position"*. GTP instructs performers to take a 22.5" step from the primary to secondary set, regardless of the total number of counts.

If the performer arrives at the secondary set before the final count, he/she marks time or remains still for the remaining counts in the move. This type of sequential movement (GTP) is opposite of floating, where performers adjust step size to insure that they begin and end a move at the same time. Sequential movement that requires turns in succession can be noted on the chart with a series of broken arrows that indicate the location of the turn for each performer or group of performers in the sequence.

In the following examples on the next page, the secondary set (second example) could be achieved either with a float or with sequential movement. Sequential movement offers interesting contrast for the audience and creates a building effect (secondary set is constructed through a series of similar, predictable maneuvers).

Looking at the first example, if GTP is used, those performers with the shortest path will take two 22.5" steps and mark time or remain still for the remainder of the move. Only those with the greatest distance will maintain forward motion through the entirety of the move.

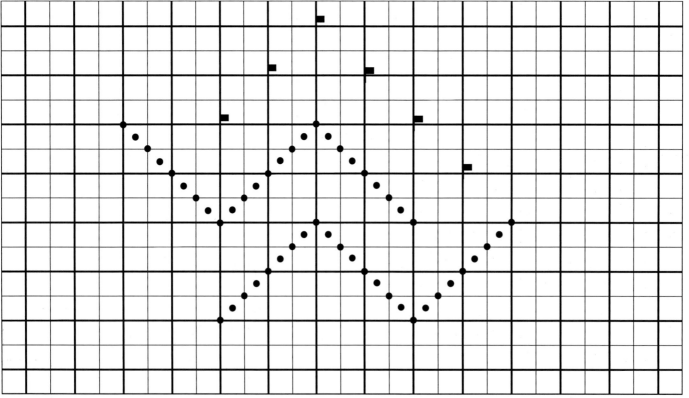

Sequential Paths Example 1

Sequential Paths Example 2

8. Random Movement

Like sequential movement, random movement can be applied to both drill and choreography and thus, can be used to alter or simply embellish the shape of a form. Random movement breaks down and eventually reestablishes unity. This is accomplished by assigning performers, within a single form or element, varying types of movement with fewer restrictions: curved and straight paths, indefinite number of counts, varying step size, and even movement that is in and out of tempo. When applied to drill, this concept is often referred to as a *scatter* and is best used to portray transitional musical material or that which is building towards or relaxing from a climax.

Random movement creates visual tension and is used either to dissolve or resolve a form. Dissolving refers to moving from a defined form to a scattered position while resolving represents the opposite effect. When applied to drill, random movement to and from a scatter set is more effective when each performer uses the same path every time, and when the maximum amount of field coverage is utilized; taking into consideration the step size required to reach the scatter set, and the staging of instruments within the set.

Like sequential movement, there are a variety of approaches for indicating random movement on drill charts. Random choreography, and even some scatter motion, is best explained through verbal instruction and/or modeling. Because of the inherent disorder, movement from scatter formations to unified sets is often the most difficult concept for performers to visualize simply by looking at the drill charts. For this reason, even if the approach is different for the rest of the drill, it is often beneficial to include both the primary and secondary sets on pages that involve scatter formations. Depending on the field coverage and number of performers involved, arrows to indicate paths can be helpful, but there is a risk that the additional markings will only further clutter the chart.

In the following examples, random movement is used to resolve a form. To demonstrate one possibility for piecing different types of motion together, the same design used as the primary set in the previous "follow-the-leader" example is included as the secondary set in this example. *Follow-the-leader* movement is a logical successor to a scatter set; a random movement for the building segment of music and a *follow-the-leader* for the resulting impact segment.

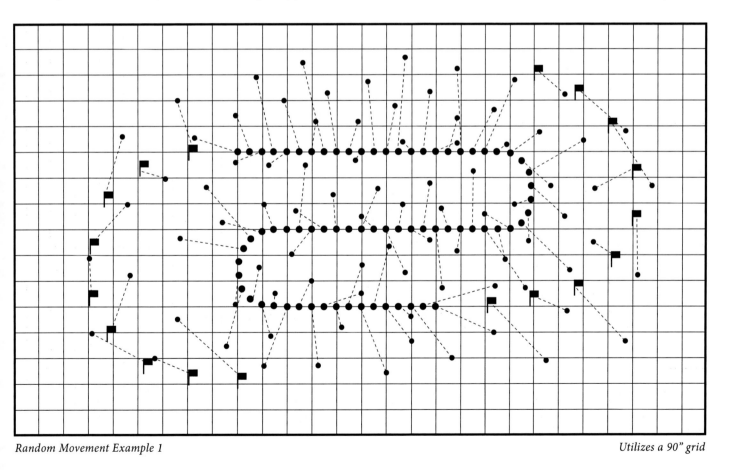

Random Movement Example 1   *Utilizes a 90" grid*

THE SYSTEM: VII. DRILL DESIGN / CONCEPTS OF MOVEMENT

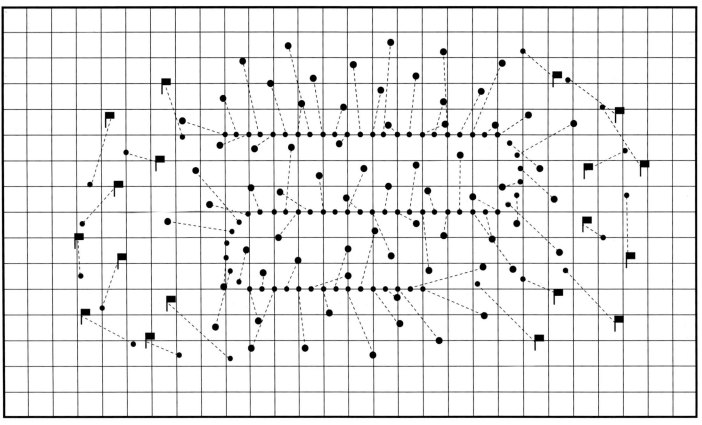

Random Movement Example 2; utilizes a 90" grid

Utilizes a 90" grid

9. Combinations

Motion with the greatest visual appeal is that which combines various movement concepts. To create basic movement combinations, designers can simply chart separate elements that execute different types of movement. For example, performers in the back half of the field execute an expansion, while those in the front complete a *follow-the-leader* maneuver. It is also possible, and often more effective, for designers to combine multiple movement concepts to develop a single drill element. For example, one could chart an expansion that also rotates *(examples 1 and 2)* or a *follow-the-leader* maneuver that pushes another form across the field, combining *shift* and *follow-the-leader (example 3 and 4)*.

The latter is an example of a "this causes that effect," which is a great way to add visual impact, and to draw attention to a particular section. Combinations are most effective when they create contrary motion between various drill components.

10. Body Movement/Choreography

Body movement encompasses any choreographed motion or pose with the body or instrument/equipment that visually depicts the musical content. Body movement can add visual interest to static formations or embellish any of the charted motion discussed above. The possibilities for body movement are seemingly endless, but most options involve some component of dance and/or variation of uniform posture and instrument carriage. Extended choreographed dance segments are common, as are quick, creatively time dance moves. In the competitive marching arts, dance movement with the lower body is often rooted in ballet and can include but is not limited to **Rond de Jambe**, **Plie**, and **Grand Plie**. Lower body poses include but are not limited to: kneeling, leaning, squatting, open seconds, wide seconds, bent leg points, crossed legs, or various combinations thereof. Upper body movement often includes some type of motion with the instrument that is different from the standard, uniform playing position, such as changing the angle or direction of the instrument bell or moving the instrument in a circular motion. Upper body pose options include but are not limited to: bent wall poses, wall poses, pin poses, t-poses, and layered poses.

Body movement can be performed in unison, as sequential movement, or as random movement. Modern drill programs allow visual designers to incorporate body movement into the Real View or Perspective View rendering of the show. Such Real View options not only allow designers, teachers, and students the opportunity to preview a complete visual package, but can also serve as a tool palate for body movement options.

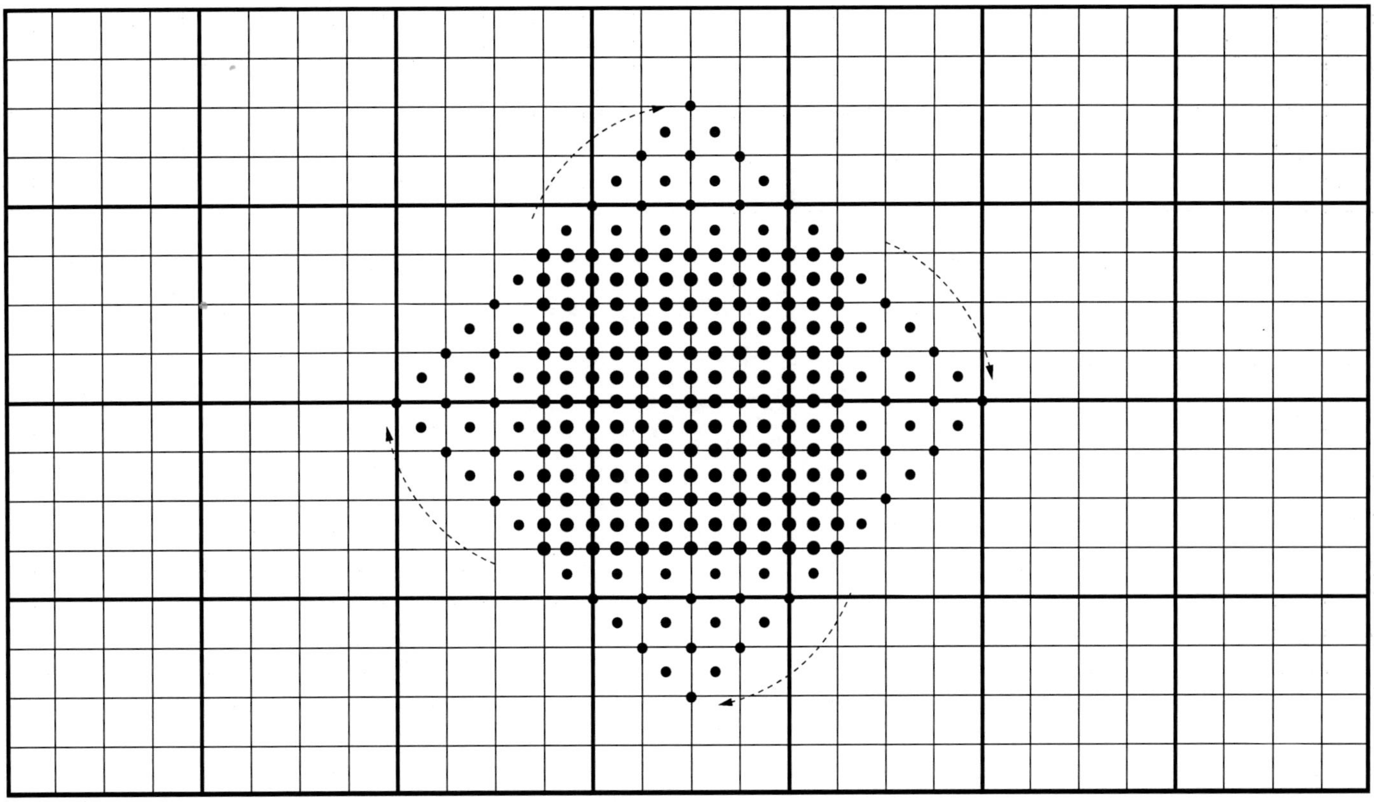

Combinations Example 1

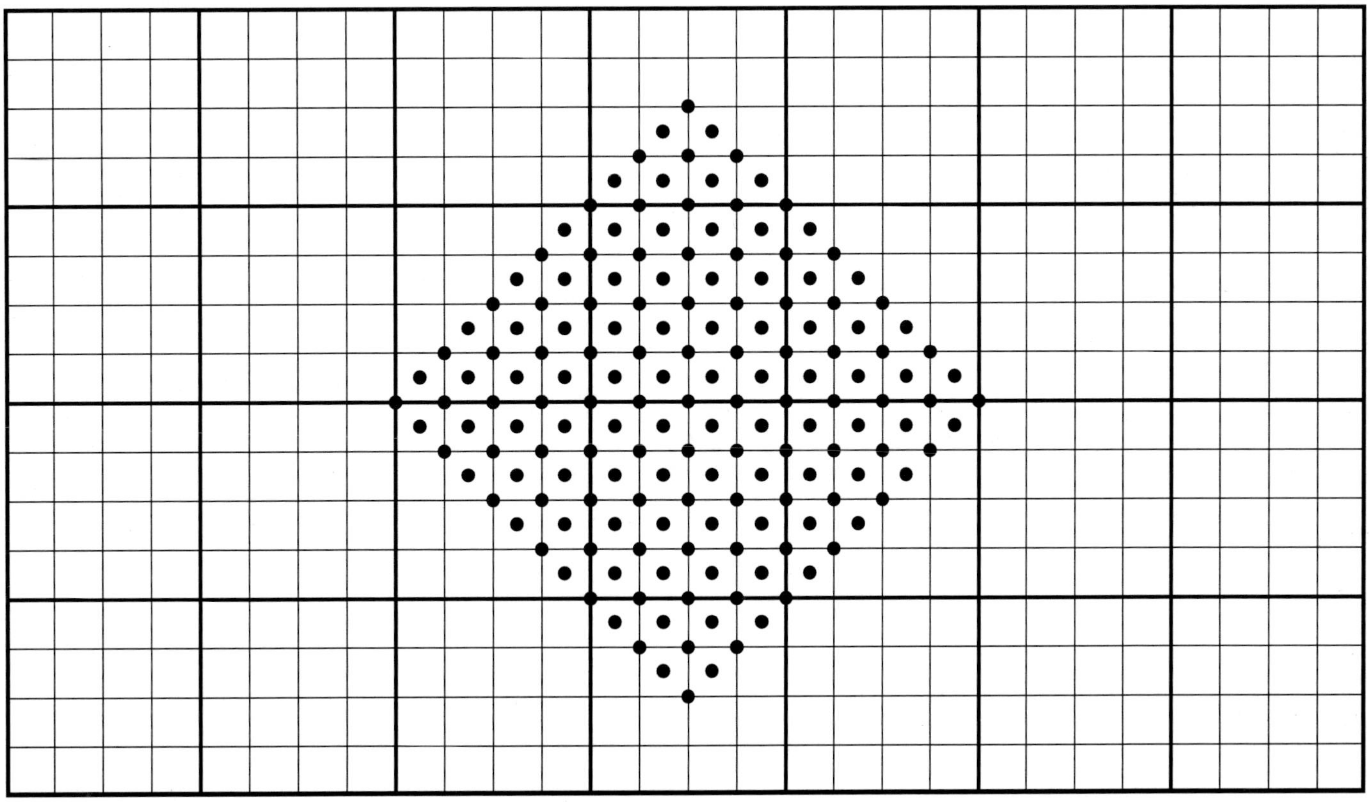

Combinations Example 2

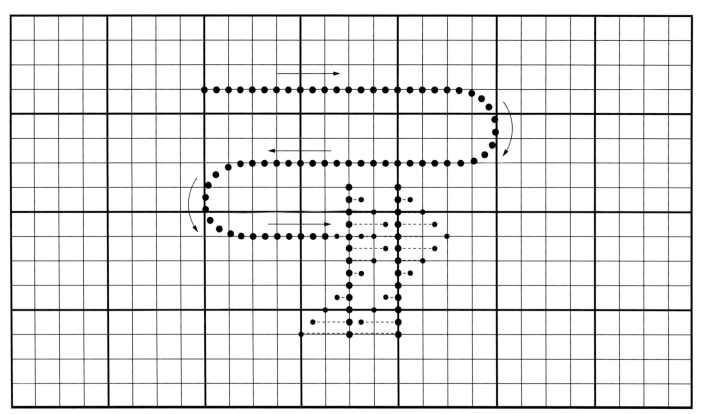

Combinations Example 3

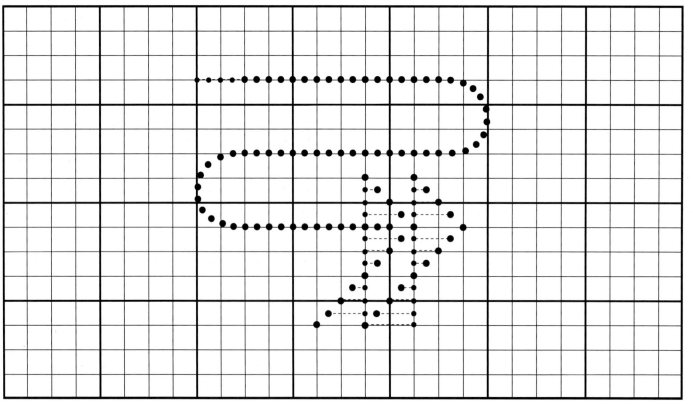

Combinations Example 4

Coordination Of Sound & Movement

The most important factor affecting the success of drill, beyond the basic principles of design, is the coordination of movement with sound. Sound includes all audible aspects of the show (music, narration, prerecorded samples, video, or other special effects). Movement includes drill, as well as instrumental, and auxiliary choreography.

TOPICS

- Style
- Orchestration & Form
- Impact Point
- Building Intensity
- Relaxing Intensity
- Maintaining Intensity
- Transition
- Dissonance & Consonance
- Tempo & Rhythm
- Coordinating Procedure

Style

Drill designers must consider the general style of the musical selection. Certain types of formations or movement are more appropriate for particular styles of music and/or particular segments of a given musical selection. Lyrical music with a relatively slow tempo is better represented by soft, continuous forms and flowing movement, achieved through floats/morphs to and from curvilinear sets. In general, segmented, angular forms and motion combined with movement concepts, produces contrary motion, and maximizes visual contrast. It's best represented detached by music with a fast tempo.

Orchestration & Form

Contemporary designers strive to produce drill that supports the form and orchestration of the musical selection. To accomplish this objective, they often create, for each section or voice in the ensemble, a distinctive visual plan that supports their musical function. This allows designers to isolate and spotlight instrumental sections presenting melodic material and then unite segments during major tutti sections. Designers can draw attention visually to certain musical lines simply by moving the featured section while keeping others still or vice versa. The same result is accomplished when melodic instruments move towards the audience, while accompanying voices move away. Both techniques are enhanced when melodic lines are given prominent staging.

To write drill that is supportive of the musical structure, designers must first analyze musical selections to determine the large form (major sections of the piece). This is followed by a more detailed phrasal analysis. A particular move should not only support the mood of the specific musical phrase (count sequence) for which it is conceived, but should also enhance other movement within the overall segment of the show. When combining movement concepts, designers should strive for a continuous visual idea just as the music arranger links phrases to complete a large formal section of music.

When analyzing musical phrases, designers must determine which of the following best describes the function of the phrase within the context of the complete section or piece: Impact Point, Maintaining Intensity, Building Intensity, Relaxing Intensity, or Transition to a new idea.

Impact Point

Musical impacts can occur at any point in a piece, including the opening and closing phrases. The relative importance of each impact often varies. Effective marching arrangements typically have one impact that serves as the major climax for a particular segment of the show or for the overall production. Impact points can be represented visually by static sets or motion. If it is determined that a static picture is most appropriate, it is best to use striking formations (elements with angles rather than curves).

Continuous sets (all elements that are connected) that incorporate recognizable shapes have more impact than disjunctive, abstract designs. If movement is used for impact points, expansion and shifts are the most effective. Also extremely effective, is the combined use of *follow-the-leader* movement, shifts, and/or rotations, especially that which creates contrary motion, or a "this causes that effect."

Building Intensity

To build intensity visually, designers can chose from a variety of movement concepts, but the desired movement or static formation for the upcoming impact point must be the determining factor. If an expansion is to be used for the impact, it is effective to build toward the maneuver by condensing the form in the phrases leading up to the impact. If a shift is to be used for impact, it is effective to rotate the form slightly as a building maneuver. Any type of predictable construction (*follow-the-leader* or *sequential movement*) is also effective for building towards a shift. If a continuous, static formation is designed for the impact, preceding random or sequential movement is often highly effective.

Relaxing Intensity

To visually represent relaxation of intensity, or movement from high to low states of energy, designers must consider the strategy for the preceding impact point so that the relaxation relates in some way to previous visual ideas. Or, the designer can consider the next impact point of the show and create a segment that is both a relaxation from the previous impact, and a transition to a new idea. If a static set, a shift of a large element, or an expansion of an element is used for impact, it is effective to employ—for relaxation—maneuvers that break down large forms, such as morphing, contraction, or random movement. For relaxation, it is also effective to move from angular forms to curvilinear forms. To alter the amount of field coverage, it is effective to move performers away from audience members.

Maintaining Intensity

Since impact points cannot exist without contrasting sections of relative repose, non-impact phrases are labeled according to their relationship to climactic moments: building towards, relaxing away, or maintaining the current energy level. Musical phrases can maintain any level of intensity, from complete relaxation to the climax of the show. However, extended maintenance of any particular level of intensity leads to boredom for audience members. To maintain intensity visually without remaining in a static formation, designers can simply continue movement (*shifts, follow-the-leader, rotation,* or *combination*) established in the previous phrase. Designers can also use morphing to change shapes. If the same field coverage is maintained, the perception of the intensity level will not change.

Transition

Though they are often not the most visually pleasing segments of drill, every visual design has segments that represent a transition from one train of thought to another. Careful planning ensures the designer that these visual transitions correlate with musical transitions, which must also exist in every work in order to provide the listener with sufficient contrast. Music transitions, and thus visual transitions, can occur immediately after impact points—either as relaxation, or as a build to another impact in a different style.

A transition can also follow a relaxation section or can serve as a false impact, if it immediately follows a build section. Transitions are typically executed using movement concepts that change the shape of previous forms, most commonly morph, sequential movement, curved paths, or random movement.

Dissonance & Consonance

Just as composers enhance the interest level of music through added tension and release, contemporary drill designers often incorporate various strategies to visually represent dissonance and consonance. For visual dissonance to consonance, it is common to create drill that moves from a scatter formation to a recognizable form or from a segmented to a unified set. Dissonance can also be created by combining, in a single move, double-time and/or half-time steps with quarter-note strides, or by mixing relaxed posture with strict attention. Meshing formations or *pass-throughs* are also highly effective for creating visual dissonance.

Tempo & Rhythm

Visual elements should also accurately depict the tempo and relative amount of rhythmic activity for the musical selection. In contemporary design, it is common for instrumental sections performing active rhythmic lines to execute drill with similar vigor, while those playing sustained lines move with less intensity. The number, pace, and size of steps for the individual performers is the primary factor determining the level of activity. The degree of contrast between the primary and secondary sets is also significant. Drill with large step sizes, executed at a fast tempo, and that creates significant visual contrast from one set to the next, is often described as having velocity.

Coordinating Procedure

The process of coordinating sound and movement begins with careful phrasal analysis of the various musical segments of the show, which, as previously stated, should occur after the order of selections is determined and before sketching begins. First for large sections and then individual phrases, designers determine the appropriate visual strategy (*curvilinear forms* or *angular forms*) and movement concepts as well as auxiliary equipment design and use. Designers must also determine the number of auxiliary members desired for each section of the musical selection.

It is sometimes effective to segment auxiliary members, which can be achieved one of two ways. First, is to have some auxiliary members perform while others change equipment. Second, is to divide the total unit into smaller groups that perform different choreography. Segmenting auxiliary members allows designers more opportunities to incorporate multiple colors and/or flag sizes, isolate and showcase the most talented performers, and/or combine dance with flag work.

Once scores are analyzed, coordination of sound and visual elements can be accomplished through the use of a flow chart and/or set planning sheets (a sample of each is included at the end of this chapter). The flow chart is used to develop the overall visual scheme for the entire show. It is a valuable tool for insuring that there is an appropriate amount of visual contrast, and that the best possible movement and formations represent musical phrases visually. Flow charts also enable the designer to determine the total number of sets before charting. Referring to the sample flow chart at the end of the chapter, the first column displays in order, the page numbers for the drill.

The second column lists the specific measure numbers that make up each segment, while the third lists the total number of counts per segment. With the fourth column, use descriptor terms (impact, maintain, build, relax, transition) to apply the most appropriate movement for the particular phrase of music. The fifth column indicates which instruments or groups of instruments present the primary musical material so designers can plan ahead to stage them properly. The sixth column should be used to add any other pertinent information, such as auxiliary features or equipment changes.

While flow charts assist with the continuity of the overall show design, set planning sheets provide more specific information about individual sets and moves. Like the flow chart, the set-planning sheet can be used to describe the music, define the counts, and make suggestions about effects and special ideas. Since there is a separate sheet dedicated to each move, there is additional space to include information about the style of the musical phrase, as well as movement type (*shift, follow-the-leader, rotation,* or *combination*). The sheet also includes two miniature fields, the first of which should be used to sketch the starting position of the move, and the second to sketch the ending position.

DRILL CHARTING SOFTWARE

- *Pyware 3D* by *Pygraphics, Inc.*
- *Envision* by *Box 5 Software, Inc.*

purchase from www.**swbandproducts.com**

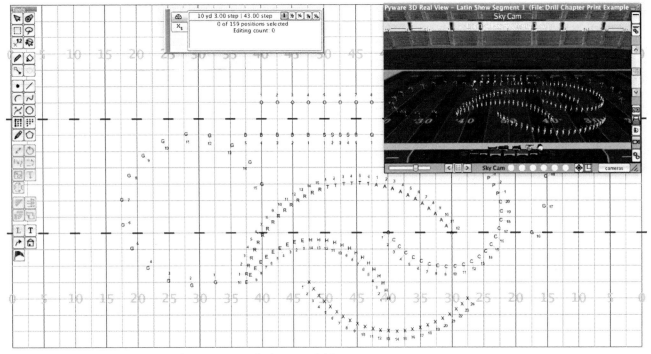

Screenshot of Pyware 3D user interface. Win/Mac platform available.

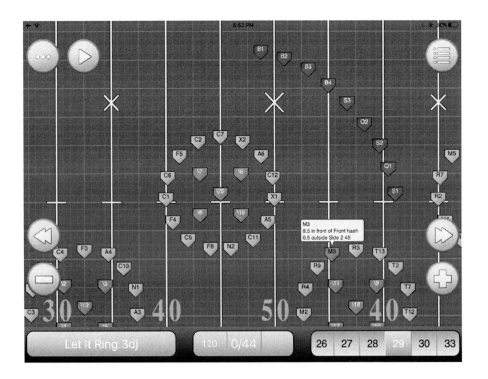

DrillbookNext is a versatile drill teaching and learning application available for *iOS*, *Android*, and *Kindle Fire* devices and is free for desktop browsers. It combines count by count, and set to set navigation, with a modest set of editing tools. Names, section colors, counts, tempo, and coordinates of performers are all editable within the application. Changes made to the show can be synced to all performers' devices following the show.

www.drillbooknext.com

Computer Charting

Much like modern composition and arranging, the actual notation or placement of performers in contemporary drill design is accomplished using computer software. The charting process varies with different computer programs. It is not the intent of this chapter to function as a manual for the use of any particular program, but to simply offer general instruction and guidance that will benefit designers regardless of what program is used. Computer software significantly enhances the drill writing process, by allowing the designer to chart multiple members at one time using a variety of easily adjustable shapes and maneuvers.

Programs also provide a multitude of information throughout the charting process (number of performers, interval, step size, etc.). Moreover, animating motion between sets allows designers to preview movement.

However, despite numerous advancements, designers must always consider the shortcomings of computer charting. First and foremost, a computer cannot duplicate creative thought processes; it is simply a tool to efficiently convert visual ideas to a graphic presentation that can be printed in vivid detail. As stated above, before sitting in front of a computer, drill designers should develop an overall visual plan and general design scheme by sketching ideas on paper.

TOPICS

- Preliminary Steps
- Creating Sets
- Labeling Performers
- Printing Charts

Preliminary Steps

Before charting a set on the computer, depending on the program, designers have the option of changing the appearance of the grid so that it closely matches the actual rehearsal field and/or primary performance field. Also before charting, designers may be required to enter the count structure of the music, and designate which counts represent the end of a phrase, and thus, the completion or start of a drill move. This type of program is optimal because it allows designers the flexibility to start the charting process with a musical count, other than the beginning.

As previously discussed, drill relates better to the music when the designer first charts the set for the biggest musical impact and then works backward and forward from that point. With this procedure, the musical climax, not the introduction, is the top priority and insures the designer that the visual representation of the impact point is exactly as envisioned.

Creating Sets

Most drill programs offer a palette of drawing tools that are used to create at least the first set of drill. Often there are specific tools for placing performers in each of the basic forms previously discussed (straight line, arc/circle, curve, or block). Once a page is complete, designers can create subsequent pages with drawing tools, or with some drill programs. Choose from a variety of editing or maneuvering tools that are used to alter existing forms and elements to create the next set. Editing and maneuvering tools are intended to expedite the drill writing process, the idea being that it is easier to redesign and relocate existing elements, than to redraw new formations for each successive page. Because maneuvering tools place greater emphasis on the type of motion used to get from one set to the next, and not the appearance of the actual set itself. There is a greater chance that design flaws will exist with the resulting picture, when maneuvering tools are used.

Such flaws may include: performers charted off the grid, angular forms lacking true corners, or arc or curve forms lacking proper depth. Once the first set is complete, designers often limit themselves to maneuvering tools and avoid drawing tools, which are sometimes the better choice to create sets without design flaws. One possible reason for the overuse of maneuvering tools is that most programs offer an animation function, which allows designers to see simulated motion. It is easier to create a true animation of each move if editing and maneuvering tools are used, particularly with any drill move that is not a float. The precision placement of performers on the grid, though, should be the designer's primary concern, not correct animation on the computer screen.

After all, the printed charts, or coordinate sheets, and not computer animation will be the primary instructional tool used during the teaching process. Type of movement is certainly a critical factor, but it is not essential that the computer animate the maneuver correctly, only that the students perform it correctly. However, it is essential that charts and/or coordinates provide students with the correct starting and ending position for each move.

With drill software, some concepts of movement are easier to implement than others. As previously mentioned, certain edit and maneuver tools exist for implementation of specific types of movement. Designers simply determine the count sequence for the move, select the performers involved, click the appropriate icon for the desired type of movement, and adjust the form or element accordingly. However, there is not a tool for every possible type of motion. It is important that designers not limit themselves to those movement concepts that have a command in the program tool palette. Even if no command exists for the maneuver, most drill programs can be manipulated to chart any desired formation, movement, or effect.

The aforementioned animation function is an important tool for calculating movement, especially for those concepts of movement where collisions or contraction of space is possible, or for those concepts for which it is difficult to visualize the true appearance of the motion. Animation should be used frequently as a checkpoint, but too often designers become dependent on the feature, and programs sometimes lack the capability to correctly animate obscure maneuvers. Effective visual ideas should not be avoided for this reason. Special maneuvers can be explained with added symbols and text, and designers should have the ability to visualize the final result without depending on the animation

capabilities of the computer. Even if extra effort is required, designers should select the type of movement that best represents the corresponding musical phrase.

Labeling Performers

Most programs offer designers a variety of choices for applying symbols and labels in order to easily distinguish sections and individual performers. Designers can label performers after the drill is complete or during the charting process. Designers should choose symbols and labels that best fit the desired system for teaching drill. The more traditional system, most closely resembling hand-written drill, is to chart all performers with the same symbol (usually a dot), and to label individuals by assigning each performer to one of a series of four-person squads.

A common approach in contemporary design is to assign each section a different symbol (either a letter or a small image of the instrument) and each individual performer within the section a different number. For example, an ensemble with *18 alto saxophones* and *12 horns* would have *18 "A"s* on the drill chart, each with a number *1-18*, and *12 "H"s*, each with a number *1-12*. It is advisable to choose letters or other symbols that center cleanly on the grid, eliminating any ambiguity as to the exact location of each position. Symmetrical letters with an obvious center (*X, A, H, O, M, Y*) are generally the most efficient. If a key is provided for students and staff, any letter can be assigned to an instrument; it is not necessary to use the first letter of the instrument as the symbol. The clarity and readability of the drill is the most important consideration.

Adjusting the font size of symbols and labels can also enhance the clarity of the drill. Smaller symbols and labels actually reduce ambiguity because they appear more centered on the position and, because there is more space between each symbol, the drill is less cluttered.

Printing Charts

Once all sets and movement are charted, computer programs offer designers a variety of print options to produce the final product. Charts can be printed with only the primary set on the page, which requires performers to flip back and forth between pages to calculate movement. Charts can also be printed with the previous or subsequent set included on the page as a background to the primary set, which, when charting for large groups, often leads to a cluttered appearance. Typically, it is easier and quicker for performers to flip back and forth between pages than it is for them to interpret a cluttered chart.

Designers also have a variety of print options for written instructions. Text can be placed anywhere on the grid where there is available space, but it can be hard to find ample space when charting for large ensembles. To alleviate the problem, designers can create a separate header for drill using a word processing program. With this approach, the actual grid must be extracted from the drill program and pasted on the header, digitally or manually.

This approach allows the designer to place text above the performers rather than taking up space on the grid with a text box. Whether creating text using the drill program or with a separate word processing program, designers can structure written instructions one of two ways. First, explain how to get to the page on which the text is included. Second, explain how to get to the next page. Both are effective and the best system depends on the preference of the director.

The following examples represent two opposing philosophies for printing charts. The drill page in the first example *(see example 1 on next page)* includes, on the grid itself, all possible information for performers (primary and secondary sets, lines showing paths, arrows, etc.)—as well as written instructions in a text box on the grid (created using the drill program). The written instructions, as well as symbols on the chart, tell the performer how to get to the next page of the drill.

The second example *(see example 2 on next page)* includes

only the primary drill set, and presents written instructions using a header created with a separate word processing program. Written instructions in the second example tell the performers how to get to the current page from the previous page. Notice that the second example still incorporates arrows when needed, to indicate movement type. But, contrary to the written instructions, the arrows indicate how to get to the next page, not to the current page.

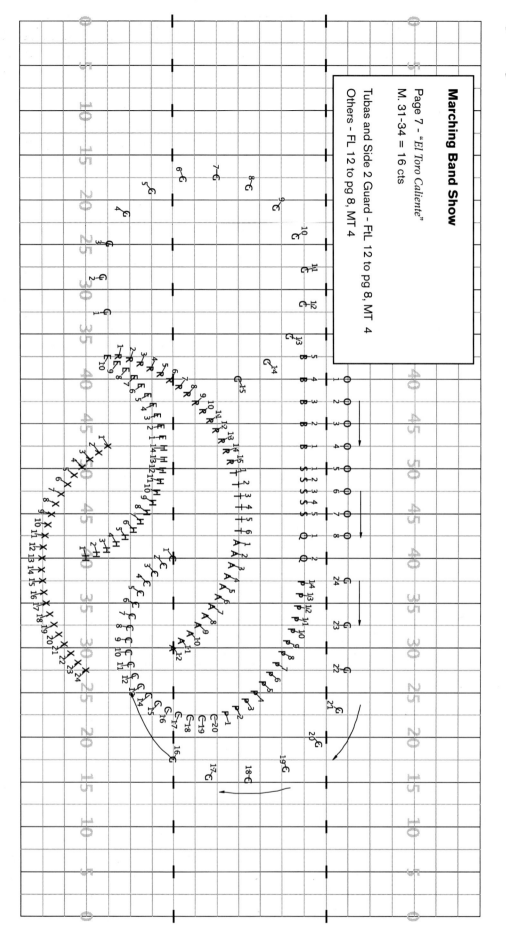

Marching Band Show

Page 7 - "*El Toro Caliente*"
M. 31-34 = 16 cts

Tubas and Side 2 Guard - FtL 12 to pg 8, MT 4
Others - FL 12 to pg 8, MT 4

Marching Band Show

Page 8 - *"El Toro Caliente"*
M. 31-34 = 16 cts

Tubas and Side 2 Guard - FTL 12 to pg 8, MT 4
Others - FL 12 to pg 8, MT 4

FLOW CHART & PLANNING SHEETS

SHOW SEGMENT _____   MUSIC TITLE _____

PAGE	MEASURE	COUNTS	MOVEMENT TYPE	INSTRUMENTATION	COMMENTS

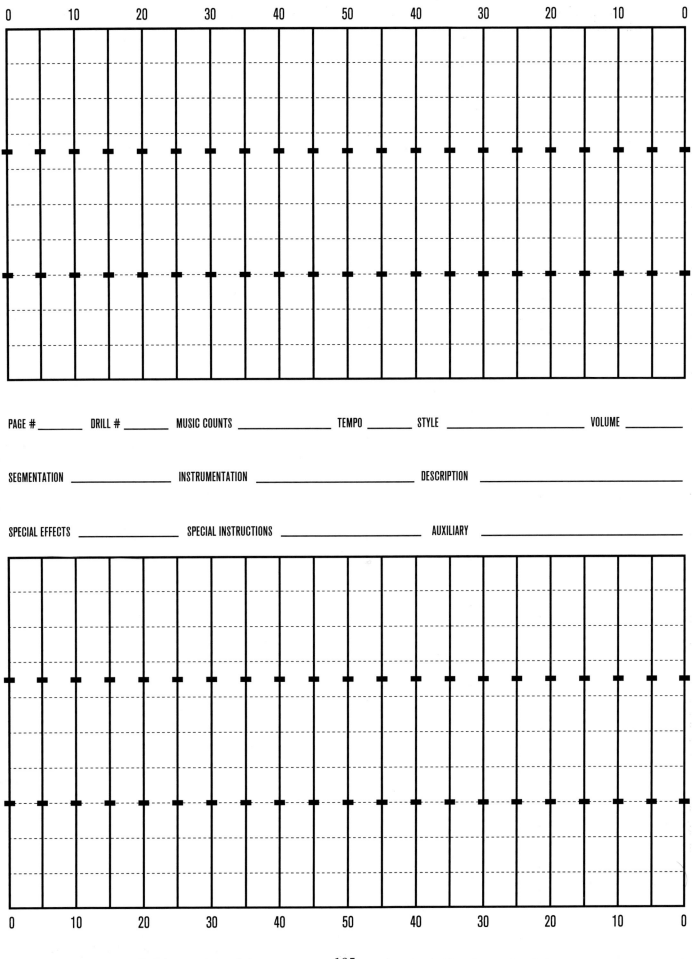

0   10   20   30   40   50   40   30   20   10   0

PAGE # _____ DRILL # _____ MUSIC COUNTS _____ TEMPO _____ STYLE _____ VOLUME _____

SEGMENTATION _____ INSTRUMENTATION _____ DESCRIPTION _____

SPECIAL EFFECTS _____ SPECIAL INSTRUCTIONS _____ AUXILIARY _____

0   10   20   30   40   50   40   30   20   10   0

VIII. CONCUCTING

CONDUCTING

Hand Positions & Posture

The conductor's role is to use meaningful gestures to convey to the ensemble the musical thoughts of the composer or arranger. Gestures convey basic musical characteristics such as tempo, style, mood, volume, meter, phrasing, releases, and entrances. Conducting is an artistic skill that requires many years of study and practice to develop, and begins with a disciplined approach to learning the fundamentals.

During a marching performance, the drum major serves as a conductor, while also adding a visual element to the presentation. Once the basic rudiments have been mastered, one can begin learning advanced conducting techniques. It is appropriate for drum majors to integrate their own conducting style, incorporating more showmanship, and enhancing the expressive qualities of the gestures.

Body Position

For conducting formal music, for example the "*Star Spangled Banner*," stand with the feet together in first position. For less formal music, the feet can be about shoulder-width apart with the body stretched upward and the head held high. Conducting is to be performed primarily with the arms and the hands, avoid excessive movement of the upper body.

Formal—feet together

Informal—feet apart

Traditional baton grip style one

Traditional baton grip style two

The Conducting Window

The "window" is the area in which the conducting patterns are executed. The size of the window is determined by the size of the beat patterns. For example, faster tempos or softer dynamics, should be conducted with a smaller size window and slower tempos or louder dynamics, conducted with a larger size window. When conducting with one hand, the window should be centered in front of the body. When conducting with both hands, there should be two windows placed symmetrically on each side of the body.

Arm and Hand Positions

As stated before, center the window in front of the body when conducting with one hand. The elbow should be **45 degrees** away from the side and slightly in front of the body. Conduct symmetrical patterns within the window. When conducting with both hands, the elbows should again be slightly in front of the body, and away from the sides. All movement with the arms and hands should be vertical or horizontal, and parallel to the body. The arm position for count 1 should be parallel with the ground, palms down, wrists straight, and the fingers slightly bent in a relaxed and natural position. The fingers should be spread slightly, but not excessively so.

Hand Positions with and Without Baton

This is the basic hand position when conducting without a baton. The wrist is straight, the palm is facing down, and the fingers are relaxed, slightly curved and apart (similar to the position used for a handshake).

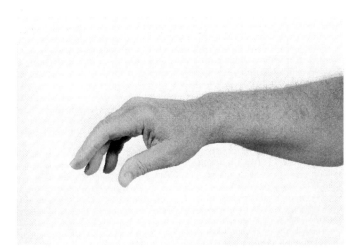

Here are side and bottom views of a basic grip with a baton. The baton is gripped between the first joint of the first finger and the ball of the thumb. The remaining fingers are lightly

curved around the base of the baton. The wrist should be kept straight without any tension in the arm and fingers, making the baton an extension of the arm.

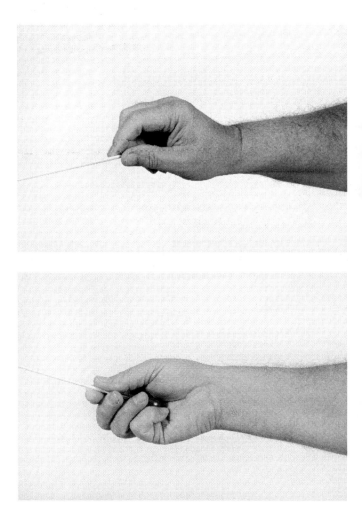

Right Hand Stylistic Gestures

Use this hand position with a tighter grip when conducting *accents*, or when conducting in a *marcato* style. To conduct in a *marcato* style, use a heavy ictus with a quick rebound to indicate a heavy attack with space between the notes. With both styles, keep the wrist straight and rigid at the point of the ictus. When conducting *accents*, use a heavy ictus (the exact point at which sound commences) with a slow rebound to encourage players to accent the attack and sustain the notes for full value. The hand position is either in a fist or with fingers together with a straight wrist. Most of the movement is from the forearm. The position of the hand is the same when conducting without a baton for both of these styles.

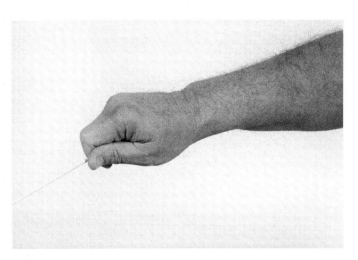

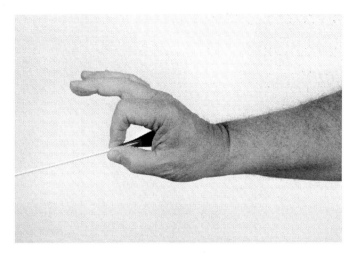

For *legato*, the fingers should be extended and slightly curved. The beat pattern should be rounded to encourage the players to play smoothly. When conducting legato, lead with the wrist for a smooth flowing action of the pattern. Use the same procedure when conducting without a baton. A *slurred pattern*, or moving smoothly from one note to the next without an articulation or break, is conducted in same manner as *legato*.

Left Hand Stylistic Gestures

The most common use of the left hand in a marching situation is to mirror the right hand beat patterns—a necessity since the players are continually moving and are spread around the field. In concert situations this is not desirable. Since the primary function of the right hand is to indicate the pulse, the left hand can be used to indicate other musical messages to the players. Some common gestures with the left hand include cues, dynamics, articulations, phrasing, attacks, and releases. In addition the left hand can be used to attract attention for special signals such as "watch me" for a change in the music or for sudden tempo or volume changes. There are also some traditional hand signals conductors use in commercial situations: take the first or second ending (use *1* or *2* fingers), go to the beginning of the piece (tapping the top of the head), or prepare for a sudden cutoff (clenched fist held up).

A misconception among some conductors is that the left hand should always be busy. This is not the case. When the left hand is not needed, place it in front of the body slightly above the waist, parallel to the ground, or let it hang naturally on the side of the body. Overuse of the left hand, such as constant mirroring (in concert situations), reduces its significance to the ensemble.

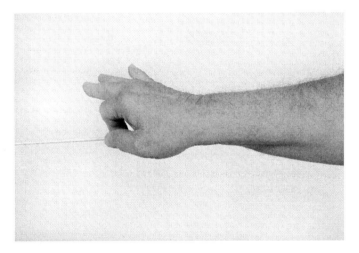

For *staccato*, the first finger and thumb should form the "O.K." sign. The remaining fingers should be curved and slightly apart. The wrist can be slightly bent. Conduct the patterns primarily with the wrists and fingers, with very little arm movement, and a "flick" of the wrist and fingers with little movement from the arms. *Staccato* conducting should always be crisp and light, think of flicking a drop of water off the tips of the fingers. This stylistic gesture encourages the players to play lightly with the notes detached.

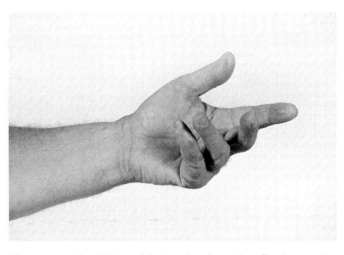

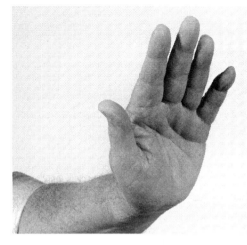

How to use the left hand for louder dynamics. For increasing volume, move the fingers repeatedly towards the body.

This indicates a softer volume level. For very soft dynamics, bring the left hand closer to the face. Turning the palm down also indicates a softer dynamic level.

Preparatory Beat Exercises

When executed properly, the preparatory beat not only indicates when the sound begins, but also the tempo, volume, and style of the music. In most cases, the preparatory beat is the count immediately preceding the beginning of the music.

For example, if the music has four beats per measure and the entrance is on the third count, the preparatory beat would be on count 2. The preparatory beat should be very clear, and in the proper style and tempo of the music being performed, in order to prevent a tentative entrance by the ensemble.

Good habits to establish in order to assure an appropriate and accurate gesture, are mentally "singing" the music before conducting, and breathing in tempo on the preparatory beat.

**Basic exercises in which the first entrance note occurs
on the beginning of a full beat:**

Preparation on count 3, play on count 4   *Preparation on count 2, play on count 3*

Preparation on count 1, play on count 2   *Preparation on count 2, play on count 3*

**Basic exercises in which the first entrance note occurs
after the beginning of a beat:**

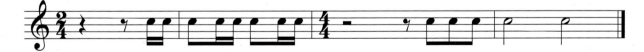

Preparation on count 2, play on the "and" of count 2   *Preparation is on count 3, play on the "and" of count 3*

A double preparatory beat can be used if the tempo is very fast, and/or if the first entrance note does not occur on the beginning of a count. When using a double beat preparation, the first gesture should be smaller, and with less emphasis than the primary preparatory beat. Using a double preparatory beat takes much practice. If not executed properly, it can cause false entrances. The double preparation should be used sparingly as a clarification for the players.

The next example at a faster tempo would be best conducted with a double preparation; practice making the first preparatory gesture smaller and lighter than the second gesture.

Preparation on counts 3 and 1, play on "ee" of count 1   *Preparation on counts 1 and 2; play on "and" of count 2*

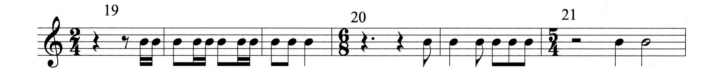

Practice the exercises above at various tempos:

Moderate tempos- Use a single preparatory gesture

Fast tempos- Examples with entrances not "ON" a count should be conducted with a double preparatory.

Slow Tempos- Practice using a subdivided (triple and duple) preparatory gestures

Beat Patterns

Basic

EACH BEAT WITHIN A PATTERN CONSISTS OF 3 BASIC ELEMENTS:

1. The preparatory movement
  (not to be confused with a preparatory beat)

2. Ictus

3. Rebound gestures

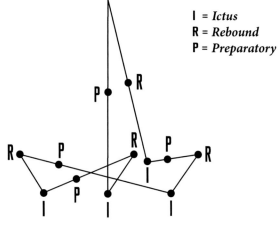

I = *Ictus*
R = *Rebound*
P = *Preparatory*

The *preparatory movement* precedes the *ictus*; it determines the tempo, style, and volume of the music, and it prepares the initiation of sound.

The *ictus* is the exact point at which sound commences. The *rebound* is the motion that occurs following the ictus. The intensity and timing of the *rebound,* partially determines the style and expression of the music.

When conducting, beat patterns must be consistently clear and precise. This is especially important when the ensemble is moving on the field, or spread apart in large formations. If the conductor loses control of the beat pattern in an attempt to hype the performance, the musicians will be confused and will seek alternate sources for the beat.

Practice the following *7 patterns* with both hands mirrored and then with each hand independently. Avoid excessive movement of the elbows and body. Keep the feet close together, about shoulder width apart, with the weight slightly forward and the body erect. Keep the elbows away from the side and forward from the body. For the starting position, the arms should be parallel to the ground, palms down, and wrists straight with fingers extended and slightly curved. Maintain relaxed shoulders.

When conducting with both hands in a marching environment, the patterns should be symmetrical. Once these basic patterns have been learned, practice them using *legato, staccato, accented,* and *marcato* beats. Since the size of the beat patterns is related to the volume and tempo of the music, practice all the patterns at varying dynamic levels and tempos. Use small-sized beat patterns for soft volume and fast tempos, and large patterns for loud and slow tempos.

Finally, practice accelerating and slowing down the tempos while gradually changing the size of the beat patterns.

7 Basic Patterns Every Beginning Conductor Should Master

*While learning these patterns, the primary focus should be **accuracy** and **consistency**, not style.*

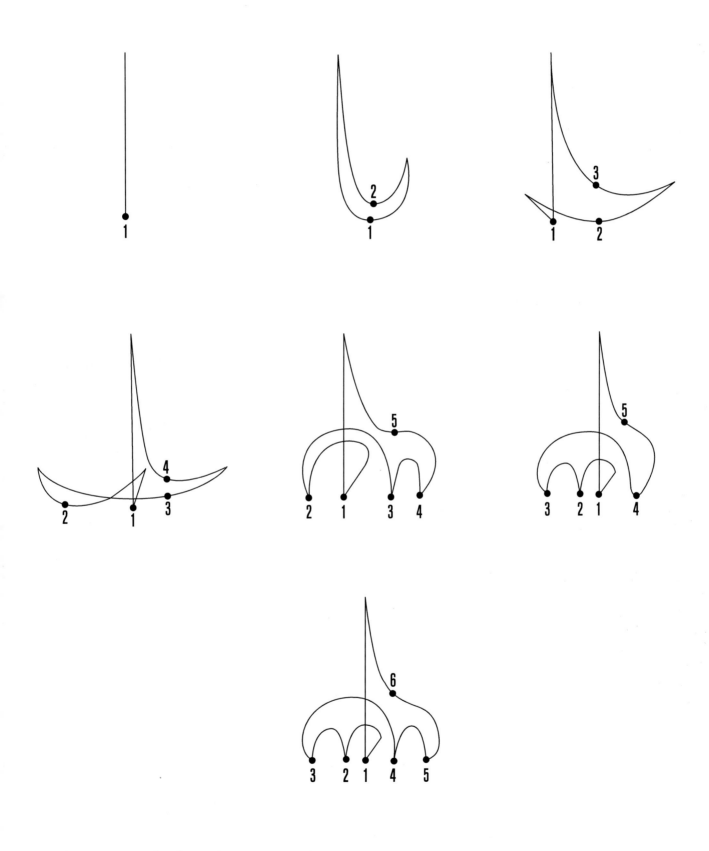

Stylistic

Every conductor should be able to conduct all **stylistic beat patterns** *neutral*, *slurred*, *legato*, *marcato*, *staccato*, and *accented*. The gestures should be obvious that the musicians will be able to determine the articulations and style, merely from observing the conductor's gestures.

Example 1: This is for conducting various styles on a 4 beat pattern. It is an appropriate pattern for conducting *staccato*, *marcato*, and *accented* articulations. Notice that the pattern consists of straight lines, with a distinctive *ictus* position.

Staccato: Conduct primarily with the wrist and fingers with very little arm movement. The ictus should be light with a quick rebound.

Marcato: Keep the wrist rigid with a heavy ictus and a quick rebound.

Accent: Keep the wrist rigid with a heavy ictus and a slow rebound.

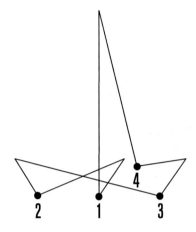

Example 2: This 4 beat pattern is appropriate for *legato* or *slurred* passages. Notice all lines are smooth and rounded. Conduct this pattern leading with the wrist for smoother flowing gestures. Although the pattern is rounded, there must be a clearly defined pulse at the *ictus* point, so the *tempo* is clear to the ensemble.

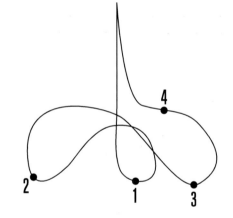

Practice the exercise below, incorporating appropriate gestures for the various articulations.

Subdivision

When the tempo becomes too slow to control with a regular pattern, individual beats can be subdivided into two or three parts, clarifying the timing between each pulse.

There are 3 basic types of subdivided beat patterns that can be used, depending on the style of the music:

1.) Repeat each count with a smaller sized beat on the *'and'* of each count. This is the easiest pattern to execute. Think of conducting a large beat, followed by a repeated small beat on each count (twice if in a triple *meter*). Mentally subdivide to maintain a steady pulse. The primary beat must be larger than the subdivided beat(s) to avoid the temptation for the ensemble to double the *tempo*.

2.) Conduct a pulsed rebound on the *'and'* of each beat. To accomplish this type of subdivision, alter the beat pattern by rebounding in the opposite direction of the next regular beat. This style does not work for triple meters.

3.) Double or triple the counts of the original meter and conduct a different meter. For example, a slow 2 beat pattern could be switched to a 4 beat pattern when the *tempo* slows down. A *waltz* conducted in one could be switched to a three pattern when the tempo becomes slower.

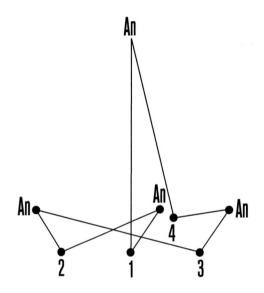

Hand Gestures

Left Hand Expressive Gestures

Soft Volume
Turn palm of left hand down, arm extended, or toward the players with the hand close to the face.

Loud Volume
Turn palm of the left hand up, arm extended toward the players.

Cues
Point with the left hand, emphasize a beat, or nod with the head. Use the eyes to reinforce the cue.

Releases
Use a circular beat with either or both hands.

Continuous Phrases
Use the left hand to smoothly connect two phrases. Use the eyes and face to convey the mood of the music.

Sustaining Long Notes
Use the left hand, gradually moving through the appropriate counts. Flex the knees and use body movements to exaggerate accents, or dramatize exciting rhythms. Create new beat patterns that visually complement the music.

The Cutoff Gestures

A cutoff indicates the end of a major musical phrase or a *fermata* (hold). This gesture must be clear and precise.

There are 3 parts to conducting a basic hold & cutoff:

1. A gesture moving smoothly through the note to encourage sustaining the hold.

2. A gesture that prepares the release.

3. The cutoff gesture is usually a circular movement indicating the cessation of sound. The direction of the cutoff is determined by the count on which the next phrase begins. The hand position following the release should conclude on the count which precedes the next preparatory (2 counts before the next entrance).

There are three basic types of cutoffs:

1. The complete cutoff is used when more than 1-count silence separates the hold and the beginning of the next entrance. Some examples include grand pauses, caesuras, and slight pauses at the end of a movement within a multi-part composition. A complete cutoff consists of two separate gestures. The first gesture is a cutoff to stop the sound. This is followed by a pause. The second gesture is a regular preparatory beat, to indicate the next entrance (the count preceding the entrance).

FIRST HOLD: Conduct 4 beats, hold on count 1 for at least 4 counts, then cutoff outward and pause.

SECOND HOLD: Preparatory beat is count 4. Conduct counts 1 and 2, and then hold again on count 3. Cutoff outward and pause. Prepare the next note with count 2, and play on count 3.

2. The semi-pause is used when more than 1-count silence separates the hold and the beginning of the next entrance. Some examples include grand pauses, caesuras, and slight pauses at the end of a movement within a multi-part composition. A complete cutoff consists of two separate gestures. The first gesture is a cutoff to stop the sound. This is followed by a pause. The second gesture is a regular preparatory beat to indicate the next entrance (the count preceding the entrance).

FIRST HOLD: Hold count 2 cutting off with an outside circle ending in the position of count 2. This cutoff also prepares the entrance on count 3.

SECOND HOLD: Hold count 3 cutting off with an outside circle ending in the position of count 3. This cutoff also prepares the entrance on count 4.

3. The continuous hold is used when the held note moves into the next phrase without a break. Accomplish this by slowly conducting through the last count of the hold (the preceding count to the next entrance) and then smoothly moving to the beginning of the next phrase. There needs to be a clear ictus on the first beat of the new phrase. A good exercise to master the technique of this gesture, is to practice conducting regular beat patterns and "stretching" various counts at different lengths. The left hand can help indicate the continuation of sound from one phrase to the next.

FIRST HOLD: Conduct slowly through count 2 leading with the wrist, then smoothly to count 3. Make a clear ictus on count 3.

SECOND HOLD: Conduct count 2 to the right, skip the 3rd beat and conduct the hold through count 4, leading smoothly to count 1 on the next phrase. It is the same as conducting this measure with a 3 pattern, and holding count 3.

Cut Off Exercises

Developing Style

Once you have mastered the fundamentals, individual style can be incorporated to enhance showmanship, and to encourage both a higher level of energy and an expressive musical performance from the ensemble. Stylistic conducting should always be in good taste, with the primary goal to present clear and concise movements that contain both meaning and purpose.

As stated in the beginning of this chapter, good conductors should be able to convey the emotional style of the music and their own musical thoughts to the ensemble through meaningful gestures. A conducting style should enhance, not detract from, the ensemble's performance. Maintaining eye contact with the players can also create an image of confidence and dignity.

Dynamic conductors use more than their hands and arms to convey their feelings. Eyes and facial expressions can also communicate mood. To intensify energy even further, utilize other parts of the body such as nodding the head, flexing the knees, or turning the shoulders. In addition, moving the beat pattern "window" to different locations can also draw attention to different sections of the ensemble.

The best conductors learn the score thoroughly so that they know how they want the music to sound before it is played. They are mentally able to process the performance of the music in four stages, in a split second.

- Hearing the music in their ear before it is played.
- Making the appropriate gestures to produce what is imagined.
- Listening to what musicians have played.
- Making a mental comparison between what was played and what was expected.

The ideal gestures are the ones that accurately produce the sounds from the ensemble that were conceived in the conductor's head. This is called "non-verbal communication". When the desired results are not achieved, most conductors clarify what they really wanted with "verbal communication". As both the ensemble and the conductor mature musically there should be more emphasis on "non-verbal" rather than "verbal" communication. Furthermore, when needed, always speak with confidence and a clearly projected voice.

Styles For Drum Majors

Since a marching ensemble performance conveys both visual and musical elements, a drum major therefore has more freedom to incorporate showmanship when conducting. They can contribute to the overall effect of the ensemble's performance by adding energy to the musical production by using choreography, exaggerated body movements, and more dynamic beat patterns. Good taste and musicianship should always prevail when incorporating showmanship into the conducting style. Never allow excessive emotion to gain control of musicality when conducting any ensemble. Flashy gestures should be created to inspire the players, not detract from the performance.

When the music is complex or when the ensemble is spread in larger formations, keep the conducting patterns simple and clear. Save dramatic gestures for high impact points in the show.

Drum majors should think of themselves as an integrated component of the entire ensemble when conducting, and not as a separate entity performing independently from the ensemble.

The conducting style should always be compatible with the musical style. If the music is formal, the gestures should be basic with the body tall and the feet together. When the music becomes more spirited, it is appropriate to loosen up and reflect the mood with more effective showmanship.

Music Terminology

—— Terms Relating to Tempo ——

(listed in order from very slow to very fast)

Grave—Very slow and solemn

Largo—Very slow and broad, with dignity

Adagio—Very slow and expressive

Larghetto—Not as slow as LARGO, but slower than *andante*

Andante—Rather slow, but with a flowing movement ("Walking tempo")

Andantino—A little quicker than *andante*

Moderato—Moderate speed- not fast, not slow

Allegretto—Light and cheerful, but not as fast as *allegro*

Allegro—"Merry", quick, lively, bright

Vivo—Lively, brisk (usually with *allegro*, as *allegro vivo*)

Vivace—Vivacious, faster than *allegro*

Presto—Very quick, faster than *vivace*

—— Terms Relating to Change of Tempo ——

Accelerando—abbr: *accel;* To increase the speed gradually

Stringendo—abbr: *string;* To increase intensity by increasing tempo

Affrettando— To increase the speed gradually

Allargando—abbr: *allarg* Slower and louder

Ritardando—abbr: *Ritard* or *Rit.* Gradually slackening the speed.

Rallentando—abbr: *Rall;* Slowing down, gradually.

Rubato—Literally means "Robbed"- a lingering on some notes and hurrying of others; free from strict tempo, but preserving the value of the rhythmic notation.

A Tempo— Return to original tempo after a *Ritard.*

Tempo I (Primo)—Return to original tempo after a *Ritard.*

—— Terms that Accompany Tempo Markings ——

Molto—Very much; e.g., **Molto Ritard** means to slow down exceedingly **Meno**—Less; e.g., **Meno Mosso** means less fast (slower)	**Piu**— More **Non Troppo**—Not too much, e.g., **Allegro Non Troppo** means fast, but not too fast	**Poco A Poco**—Literally "little by little". Used in combination with tempo markings. e.g., **Accel. Poco a Poco** means to increase the speed gradually over a span of measures.

—— Terms Relating to Dynamics ——

(listed in order from soft to loud)

Pianissimo—abbr: **pp** Very soft **Piano**—abbr: **p** soft **Mezzo**—Medium or moderately **Mezzo Piano**—abbr: **mp** Medium soft **Mezzo Forte**— abbr: **mf** Moderately loud **Forte**—abbr: **f** Loud **Fortissimo**—abbr: **ff** Very loud	**Diminuendo**—abbr: **dim** or the sign means gradually getting softer **Crescendo**—abbr: **cresc** or the sign means gradually getting louder **Poco A Poco**—"Little by little". Indicates a gradual increase or decrease in volume of sound.	**Accent**— A stress on notes so marked **Sforzando**—abbr: **sfz** A strongly accented note or chord. **Sforzato**—abbr: **sfp** strongly accented by then immediately **piano**. **Subito**—abbr: **sfp** Suddenly. Usually to indicate a dramatically sudden change in dynamic level of sound then immediately **piano**.

— Terms Relating to Style —

Agitato—With agitation, excitedly.

Alla—In the style of (always used with other words) e.g., *Alla Marcia*- in the style of a march.

Con—With (as a connecting word), e.g.,

Andante Con Amore—slowly, with tenderness.

Animato—With animation, in a spirited manner.

Appassionato—With intensity and depth of feeling.

Brillante—Bright, sparkling, brilliant.

Brio—Vigor, spirit.

Cantabile—In a singing style.

Dolce—Sweetly and softly.

Energico, Con—With expression.

Fuoco, Con—With fire or much energy.

Grandioso—In a noble, elevated style.

Grazia, Con—With a graceful, flowing style.

Legato—Smooth and connected, in a flowing manner. (opposite of *staccato*)

Maestoso—With majesty and grandeur.

Marcato—In a marked and emphatic style.

Pesante—Heavily, every note with marked emphasis.

Quasi—In the manner of; e.g.,

Quasi Una Fantasia—in the style of a fantasia.

Scherzando—In a light playful and sportive manner.

Scherzo—A jest, one of the movements of certain symphonies, a composition of light and playful character.

Secco—Dry, plain, without ornamentation.

Sempre—Always; e.g.

Staccato—to continue playing in a short and detached style.

Spirito, Con—With spirit, or animation.

Staccato—Short and detached, with distinct precision. The opposite of *legato*.

Tenuto—Sustained for the full time-value.

Tranquillo—With tranquility, quietly, restfully.

— Combinations of Terms —

tempo and style

Largo Ma Non Troppo—Slow, but not too slow. (ma = but)

Adagio Cantabile E Sostenuto—('e' = and) Very slow and in a sustained and singing style.

Andantino, Con Affetuoso—Faster than *andante*, with tender feeling.

Allegretto Con Grazia—A moving tempo with a graceful flowing style.

Allegro Agitato—Quick with agitation.

Poco Piu Mosso—A little quicker.

Allegro Con Molto Spirito—Fast with much spirit.

Andante Maestoso—Rather slow-moving tempo, majestic feeling.

Presto Con Leggierezza—Very fast with lightness and delicacy.

— Miscellaneous Terms —

Accidentals—Flats and double flats, naturals, sharps and double sharps.

Alla Breve—"Cut time" of the meter. ₵

Arpeggio—A broken chord. (Each note of the chord played in succession.)

Attacca—Begin the next movement immediately.

Cadence—The close or ending of a phrase.

Cadenza—An elaborate solo passage with fancy embellishments to display the proficiency of a performer.

Chromatic—Proceeding by semitones.

Coda—Literally "A tail"- the closing measures of a piece of music.

Con—With; e.g., **Con Sordino** means "with mute".

Da Capo—abbr: **D.C.** from the beginning.

Dal Segno—abbr: **D.S.** to the sign.

Divisi—Divided, one performer plays the upper notes, the other plays the lower notes.

Fermata— A pause, marked 𝄐

Fine—The end.

G.P.— General Pause; a dramatic moment of silence for the entire ensemble.

Segue—To the next piece without pause.

Senza—Without; e.g., **Senza Sordino** means without mute.

Sordino— A mute. (used by brass and string players)

Tacet—Rest for an extended period of time, without playing.

Tempo Primo—(sometimes **Tempo I**), means to return to the original tempo after a **Ritard** or **Accel**.

V.S.—Abbreviation found at the lower corner of a music page, which stands for **Volti-subito** and means to turn the page quickly.

Col Legno—Applies to string instruments. Bowing or tapping the string with the wood of the bow instead of the hair.

Glissando—To slide. Pulling or drawing the finger quickly up or down a series of adjacent notes. Also poss. on trombone and other inst.

Conducting Exercises

The following exercises are designed to improve conducting skills. Novice conductors should master the basics before developing individual stylistic variations. These skills take a great deal of time to develop at an advanced level.

1. DEVELOPING A CONSISTENT PULSE WITH VARIOUS SIZE BEATS AND TEMPOS

(use a metronome)

- Tap the baton on the back of a chair at 60 beats per minute while counting "one, one thousand two, one thousand".
- Practice with small size taps, flicking at the wrist only.
- Practice with a large rebound, flicking the wrist with a full arm rebound.
- Practice alternating with a small and large rebound.
- Practice one small and two large rebounds.
- Practice two large and one small.
- Practice same exercises at 120 beats per minute by doubling the speed, and 30 beats per minute by halving the speed.
- Make sure the volume of the taps remain the same, regardless of the size of the rebound.

2. LEARNING THE BASIC BEAT PATTERNS WITH VARIOUS STYLES, TEMPOS, AND DYNAMIC LEVELS

(use a metronome)

- Practice beating 1, 2, 3, 4, 5, and 6 patterns neutrally.
- Practice all patterns *staccato, legato, marcato,* and *accented.*
- Practice drawing all basic patterns on the blackboard to develop consistency, and symmetry.
- Practice all patterns conducting *crescendo* for 8 counts, then *decrescendo* for 8 counts using the right hand only.
- Smoothly and gradually increase and decrease the size of the beat with the dynamic changes.
- Practice all patterns conducting *accelerando* for 8 counts, followed by *ritardando* for 8 counts using the right hand only.
- Smoothly and gradually increase and decrease the size of the beat with the dynamic changes.

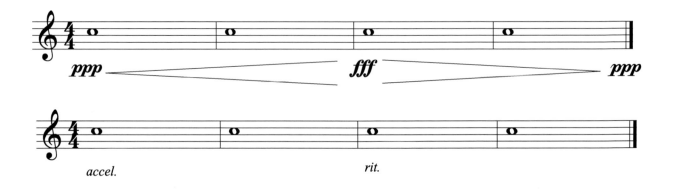

3. TO DEVELOP LEFT AND RIGHT HAND INDEPENDENCE

(use a metronome)

- Practice making smooth circles with both hands, vertically and horizontally and in a parallel motion.
- Circle both hands counterclockwise, clockwise, in opposite directions, then in opposite direction reversed.
- Do these same exercises in contrary motion (one hand on top, one on bottom)
- Do the first two exercises with vertical circles.
- Conduct all beat patterns while conducting dynamic changes with the left hand.
- Vary the number of counts for the dynamic changes. Do not change the size of the beat in the right hand.
- Practice a three pattern in the right hand, while conducting a two pattern in the left hand.
- Practice conducting a three pattern in the left hand, while conducting a four pattern in the right hand.
- With this exercise, conduct the dynamics with the left hand, and the *tempo* changes with the right hand.

4. LEARN HOW TO PREPARE ACCENTED BEATS.

(use a metronome)

- Practice a 4 beat pattern with an accent on count 1, then 2, then 3, and finally on count 4. Prepare the accent.
- Practice all the beat patterns, accenting various counts.

5. COMPOUND METER CONDUCTING

Practice conducting these meters maintaining an even eight note pulse throughout. The numbers under the staffs indicates the number of beats per measure. The slashes above the measures indicate when to use short and long strokes, while conducting the beat patterns.

Transposition Chart
From Sound to Sight

TO SCORE: WRITE:

Db Piccolo — down minor 9th

C Piccolo, Xylophone, Chimes, Celeste — down 8va

Bells, Glockenspiel — down 2 8vas

Flute, Oboe, C Trumpet, Violin, Marimba, Vibes, Chimes, Harp, Piano — same

Eb Soprano Clarinet, Eb Soprano Trumpet — down minor 3rd

Bb Clarinet, Bb Trumpet-Cornet-Flugelhorn, Bb Soprano Saxophone — up major 2nd

Eb Alto Clarinet, Eb Alto Saxophone, Eb Horn — up major 6th

Bb Bass Clarinet, Bb Tenor Saxophone, Euphonium-Baritone (T.C.) — up major 9th (treble clef)

Eb Contra Bass Clarinet, Eb Baritone Saxophone — up 8va + major 6th

BBb Contra Bass Clarinet, BBb Bass Saxophone — up 2 8vas + major 2nd (treble clef)

F Horn, English Horn, Basset Horn — up perfect 5th

All tubas, Trombone, Violincello, Baritone (B.C.), Timpani, Piano, Harp, Bassoon, Marimba, Vibes, Euphonium — same

Contra Bassoon, String Bass — up 8va

Transposition Chart
From Sight to Sound

WRITTEN   SOUNDS

D♭ Piccolo	up minor 9th
C Piccolo, Xylophone, Chimes, Celeste	up 8va
Bells, Glockenspiel	up 2 8va
Flute, Oboe, C Trumpet, Violin, Marimba, Vibes, Chimes, Harp, Piano	same
E♭ Soprano Clarinet, E♭ Soprano Trumpet	up minor 3rd
B♭ Clarinet, B♭ Trumpet-Cornet-Flugelhorn, B♭ Soprano Saxophone	down major 2nd
E♭ Alto Clarinet, E♭ Alto Saxophone, E♭ Horn	down major 6th
B♭ Bass Clarinet, B♭ Tenor Saxophone, Euphonium-Baritone (T.C.)	down major 9th
E♭ Contra Bass Clarinet, E♭ Baritone Saxophone	down 8va + major 6th
BB♭ Contra Bass Clarinet	down 2 8vas + major 2nd
F Horn, English Horn, Basset Horn	down perfect 5th
All Tubas, Trombone, Violoncello, Euphonium- Baritone (B.C.), Timpani, Piano, Marimba, Vibes, Bassoon	same
Contra Bassoon, String Bass	down 8va

Tests

by **Dr. David Waybright**

Conducting Test I
Basic Patterns, Preps and Cut-Offs

Conducting Test II
Basic Articulations and Dynamic Changes

Conducting Test III
Accents and Gesture of Syncopation

Conducting Test IV
Subdivision

1)

2)

3)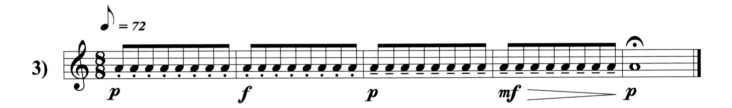

4)

Conducting Test V
Fermatas

1)

2)

3)

4)

5)

Conducting Test VI

Cues: CL-cue left CR-cue right CC-cue center

1)

2)

3)

4)

5)

6)

216

IV. THE DRUM MAJOR

by **Barry L. Houser**

Roles

BEFORE CHOOSING TO AUDITION FOR DRUM MAJOR

First and foremost, become proficient on your instrument, as this will enhance your musicianship, and ability to share with others. No one wants to listen to the worst player in the section when it comes to refining a musical excerpt. Play in a variety of ensembles to gain fantastic performance experiences, and take private lessons if possible.

Begin to develop your presence as a leader in the band. Do this by being a great band member first. When the opportunity arises, interview or audition for a position of section leader within the band. Volunteer for other leadership positions if you are not named a section leader or ask your director where you can assist the band most effectively. Some examples of these positions include: equipment manager, tracking and issuing of uniforms and equipment, music librarian, publicity, or public relations. This willingness to serve will show your director that you are serious about taking steps in becoming an integral part of the band in a leadership capacity, and may lead to future potential as a drum major candidate.

Learn the fundamentals of conducting from a current drum major or director or by attending a great summer camp. Start by learning the basic conducting patterns and techniques, and then proceed to conducting recordings of band or orchestral pieces. Continue to build upon the fundamentals by increasing the complexity of the music you are conducting. This will allow you to work on advanced conducting skills including instrument cues, dynamics, phrasing, and other musical and conducting nuances.

Let your director know you are interested in auditioning for the position of drum major. Ask your director for any advice he or she may be willing to share as you begin this wonderful journey. The more you work with your director and develop a rapport, the more you will trust each other, know how the other thinks, and know what is expected. This will make you a stronger and more committed member of the band.

Do not wait until a few months before the audition to start working. Baton, mace work, and conducting, takes a lot of practice that will not happen overnight. The more you practice prior to the audition, the more confident you will be. Most students start working towards the position of drum major during their freshman or sophomore year with the goal of becoming drum major the following year. The position of drum major requires intense training, and others that are better prepared, will have a definite advantage over you, so plan now.

A Musician

An effective drum major must have a good understanding of music. This includes possessing the ability to conduct with good coordination, count and read rhythms, read and analyze a musical score, understand terminology, and teach proper musical stylistic interpretations. A drum major must also be able to study, analyze, and make preparations to conduct all music scores to be performed by the band. This process includes knowledge of proper tempos, phrasing, balances, rhythms, dynamics, style, and articulations. The drum major's musicianship should be a resource for other students to utilize in their efforts to grow as musicians.

A Marching Specialist

A drum major must possess knowledge and exceptional marching technique related to the total science of marching including drill writing, grid systems, marching styles, teaching techniques for learning fundamentals, concepts of drill movements, acoustics of outdoor sound, methods for developing precision and style, and procedures for teaching and refining drills.

A Teacher

A drum major must be able to clearly communicate and convey their musical and marching knowledge to fellow band members by administering full band and sectional rehearsals, and providing assistance to individual participants. Knowledge of fundamental pedagogy is of the utmost importance in becoming a great pedagogue!

An Administrator

A drum major should be prepared and willing to accept administrative responsibilities such as taking attendance, passing out music, uniforms and instruments, preparing the field or band room for rehearsal, working with booster groups, serving on committees, writing handbooks, planning shows, working in the library, maintaining band records, promoting band performances, trips, and competitions, and other duties as defined by the director.

A Communicator

A drum major can be a liaison between the director and students. He or she must be well informed at all times, and be a resource of information for all students. The drum major can monitor and communicate the feelings between the students and director, to prevent potential problems from arising.

A Leader

A drum major should always lead by example. A drum major who is skillful, talented, and knowledgeable, can have an inspirational effect on participants in the band. This can cause individuals to motivate themselves to achieve excellence, elevating the success of the entire band. Your attitude will define your leadership abilities as well. Always lead from the focus of positive reinforcement.

A Performer

Ultimately an outstanding performance excites the audience and stimulates the band. The total process of developing a performance style is called showmanship. Showmanship is an extension and variation of the fundamentals. It is the essential ingredient of a performance, whether it be skill in conducting, handling equipment, choreography or playing an instrument in the band. The effectiveness of creative showmanship is limited only by the ability of the performer to extend, vary, and mold basic fundamentals into a dynamic performance. This creative process can be developed with proper instruction and practice over time.

A Friend

A drum major should be accessible to fellow students at all times. A drum major should be friendly and helpful, especially to new students and others having problems with any aspect of the program. Drum majors should be prepared to spend a lot of time outside of rehearsal, helping others find solutions to their problems.

Remember, Communication is the Key to Success.

Audition Process

The importance of the drum major audition is crucial because the wrong choice can lead to a plethora of negative situations that will make for a very unhappy marching season. Having a variety of people serving on the adjudication panel, will assist your program in making the right choice. In addition to a diverse panel, the content matter included in the audition is necessary.

SELECTING & PREPARING DRUM MAJOR CANDIDATES

The process for selecting drum majors is important, and should identify the most qualified candidates for the position. The process should be fair, and the evaluation of the most desired qualities appropriate to each band program's unique situation, should be included. When determining the content matter for the audition, consider what responsibilities the position of drum major will include for the band program. The director should make these decisions, which can vary from simple conducting duties, to an extensive involvement similar to that of an assistant director.

In addition, the director needs to make a decision of how many drum majors he/she would like. The total number of drum majors varies from program to program, and depends on what the needs of the marching program are.

Workshops can be held before the actual audition process in order to educate all candidates in the areas of marching, teaching and command ability, conducting, and showmanship. The director, band staff, or former drum majors can teach these workshops.

In addition, the workshops should be scheduled far in advance so the adjudicating panel can see the true potential of each candidate as drum major. Directors can send students interested in auditioning for drum major to camp as well. Evaluators for the adjudicating panel can include music faculty, band staff, student representatives, section leaders, or teachers from other academic disciplines.

The Evaluation Process

The evaluation process in this example includes six different sections. Each section is designed to demonstrate how well a student can perform the different roles of drum major. Drum major candidates are evaluated on posture, showmanship —including any mace or baton work—clarity of patterns, confidence, originality, creativity, and the ability to exhibit great marching technique. The director can use any combination of the six sections to suit his/her program. Finally, each of the sections can be divided into three different rounds, in order to eliminate candidates throughout the audition process. This works extremely well if you have a large number of students auditioning for the position of drum major.

Round 1—VERBAL COMMANDS

The purpose of this section is to demonstrate confidence, vocal projection, and memorization of a sequence. All candidates should participate in this section at the same time, with one person calling commands while the other candidates execute each command. This allows each candidate to demonstrate his/her knowledge and precision of marching technique. The voice should be clear, articulate, projected, and with good cadence and confidence. All commands should be given no faster than *120 beats* per minute. Each command is worth 1 point for a total of **10 points**.

Round 1—MARCHING FUNDAMENTALS

The purpose of this section is to demonstrate knowledge of basic marching fundamentals and technique. All candidates should participate in this section as the same time. It is important for the drum major to model these fundamentals as well as teach them. All candidates will execute the marching fundamental drill. Add conducting patterns where applicable while marching. Ideal posture, style, carriage, precision, rhythm, coordination and confidence should be demonstrated. This can be done with, or without a music recording. Each fundamental is worth 1 point for a total of **10 points**.

Round 1—CONDUCTING

The purpose of this section is to demonstrate fundamental and basic conducting patterns, knowledge of tempos, and showmanship. First, each candidate will conduct a 4 pattern to a variety of tempos without the use of a metronome. This will demonstrate their knowledge of basic tempos.

Secondly, each candidate will conduct *1,2,3,4,* and *5 patterns* to one tempo and one style consisting of *60, 90, 120, 144* and *staccato, marcato, accented,* and *legato* with the use of a metronome.

The final component is conducting a selected piece of music to a recording. The director should provide a recording and a score to each candidate at least two weeks before the audition. Each candidate is evaluated on posture and carriage, gestures, releases, clarity of patterns, and showmanship. This section is worth **20 points**.

Round 1—SHOWMANSHIP

Showmanship closes round 1 which includes the optional use of baton or mace. This section is worth **10 points**.

Round 2—INTERVIEW

The purpose of the interview is to determine skills, expertise, and attitudes each candidate has for performing as, and executing the responsibilities of drum major. The director and/or the entire adjudication panel conduct the interview. It is important that the same questions are asked of all candidates to insure that they are all being evaluated with the same criteria. Each candidate is evaluated on his/her leadership potential, communication skills, attitude, and knowledge of content matter. This section is worth **25 points**.

Round 3—TEACHING & CONDUCTING A LIVE ENSEMBLE

The purpose of this section is to see how well each candidate can teach and conduct the members of a live ensemble. Each candidate comes in one at a time. Part of this section is to see how well each person "thinks on their feet" in addition to communication skills in front of a live audience. The director chooses a marching fundamental for this section: an example would be the attention position. Each candidate teaches the same marching fundamental to the live ensemble. Students are evaluated on their confidence, clarity of instruction, content matter, and ability to work with the group.

The final portion of this section is conducting the live ensemble. Each candidate should start on the podium, calling the band to attention, horns up, and proceed with the piece selected by the director. This can be anything from the school song to a former marching band selection. Candidates are evaluated on their musicality, clarity of beat, confidence, command presence and showmanship. This section is worth **25 points**.

DRUM MAJOR
AUDITION

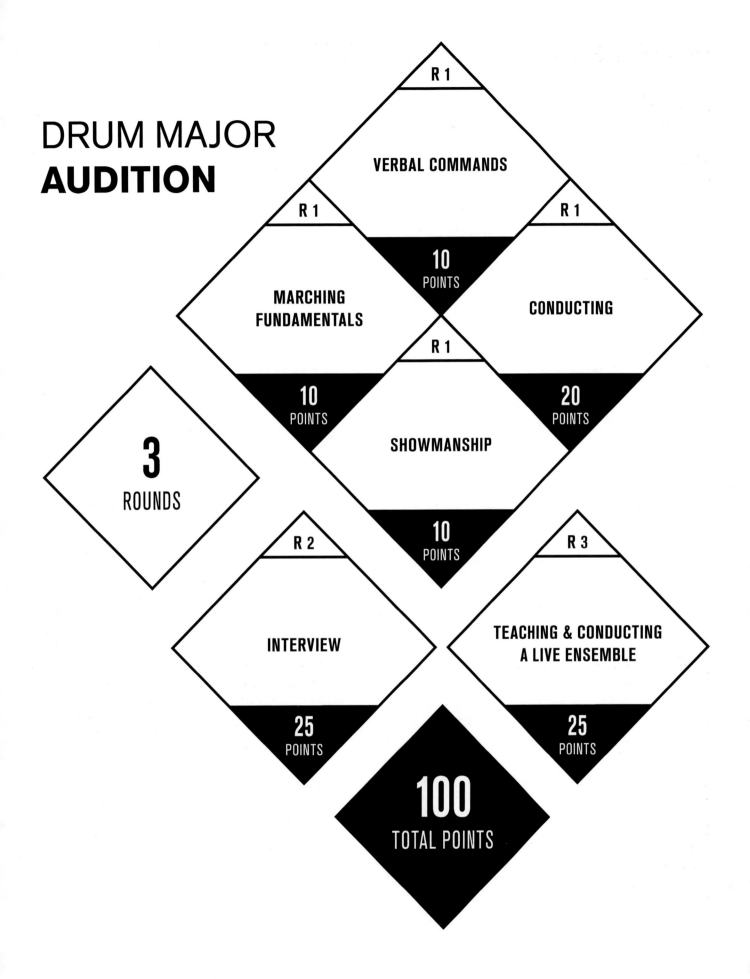

R 1

VERBAL COMMANDS

R 1

R 1

10
POINTS

MARCHING
FUNDAMENTALS

CONDUCTING

R 1

10
POINTS

20
POINTS

SHOWMANSHIP

3
ROUNDS

10
POINTS

R 2

R 3

INTERVIEW

TEACHING & CONDUCTING
A LIVE ENSEMBLE

25
POINTS

25
POINTS

100
TOTAL POINTS

DRUM MAJOR APPLICATION FORM

_____
First Name

_____
Last Name

FR   SO   JR   SR

_____
Instrument

_____
Years in Band   **School Grade next fall**

_____ _____ _____
Phone

_____
Email

_____
Street Address

_____
City, State Zip

Please attach your written responses for the following:

- List prior leadership experiences
- Briefly comment on your personal strengths and weaknesses
- State specific goals for future personal improvement
- List any volunteer activities in which you have participated this past year
- Outline your reasons why you are applying for the position of drum major

Be sure to sign-up for an interview/audition time when you turn in your application.

If I do not make the position of drum major this year, please consider me for the following:

_____ Section Leader/Student Staff

_____ Equipment Staff/Band Manager

_____ Uniform Staff

_____ Community Service

_____ Publicity

_____ Special Projects

_____ Senior Assistant

_____ Merchandise

_____ Show Planning/Concepts

_____ Other

I understand that the decision by the adjudicating panel is final, and will be accepted without question.

_____   _____
APPLICANT'S SIGNATURE   DATE

DRUM MAJOR AUDITION SCORE SHEET

_____
First Name

_____
Last Name

_____
Instrument

_____
Years In Band

FR　SO　JR　SR
School Grade Next Fall

_____
Date

_____
Evaluator

R 1

STANDING VERBAL COMMANDS

Each candidate gives these verbal commands while the other candidates execute each command. The voice should be clear, articulate, projected, with good cadence, and confidence.

1 point each

_____ Band Fall In

_____ Band Horns Up

_____ Band Dress Right Dress

_____ Band Ready Front

_____ Band Right Hace/Band Left Hace

_____ Band About Hace/Band About Hace

_____ Band Mark Time Mark/Band Halt

_____ Band Horns Down

_____ Band Parade Rest/Band Ten Hut

_____ Band Dismissed

_____ /10 TOTAL SCORE

MARCHING FUNDAMENTALS

Each candidate will execute the following marching fundamental drill while conducting a 4 pattern. Evaluate posture, style, carriage, precision, rhythm, coordination, and confidence. This can be done with, or without a music recording.

1 point each

_____ Mark Time 8

_____ Forward March 16

_____ Right Flank 16

_____ Right Slide 16

_____ Backwards 16

_____ Left Slide 16

_____ Forward March 8

_____ Backwards 8

_____ Mark Time 8/Halt (2 Points)

_____ /10 TOTAL SCORE

CONDUCTING

Candidates will be evaluated on style, precision, clarity, preparation beats, cut-offs, releases, and musicality.

1 point each

_____ q = 60　　_____ q = 144

_____ q = 90　　_____ q = 180

_____ q = 120

Each candidate will conduct 1,2,3,4, and 5 beat patterns using _staccato_, _marcato_, _legato_, or _accented_ styles to various tempos using a metronome. Pick 1 tempo and 1 style only for each beat pattern.

1 point each

q = 60　　q = 90　　q = 120　　q = 144

_____ _____ _____ _____ 1 Pattern

_____ _____ _____ _____ 2 Pattern

_____ _____ _____ _____ 3 Pattern

_____ _____ _____ _____ 4 Pattern

_____ _____ _____ _____ 5 Pattern

Each candidate will conduct a selected 2-3 minutes piece using a musical score and a recording.

5 points each

_____ Posture/Carriage

_____ Clarity of Beat/Use of Effective Cues & Patterns

_____ /20 TOTAL SCORE

SHOWMANSHIP

Each candidate will execute the following marching fundamental drill while conducting a 4 pattern. Evaluate posture, style, carriage, precision, rhythm, coordination, and confidence. This can be done with, or without a music recording.

_____ /10 TOTAL SCORE

DRUM MAJOR AUDITION SCORE SHEET

R 2

INTERVIEW

Each candidate will be interviewed by the adjudicating panel.

5 points each

_____ Attitude _(enthusiasm, positive, upbeat)_

_____ Communication Skills _(eye contact, clear and concise answers)_

_____ Emotional Maturity/Professionalism

_____ Knowledge of Related or Content Matter

_____ Confidence/Poise/Carriage

_____ /25 TOTAL SCORE

SAMPLE QUESTIONS

- Why do you want to be drum major?
- What is your definition of responsibilities for the role of drum major?
- What personal qualifications do you feel you possess that you would contribute to this position?
- Why do you think you are qualified to be drum major?
- Why are you more qualified for this position than the other candidates?
- As a leader, what do you feel your strengths and weaknesses are?
- In what areas of your life do you think you could improve?
- Describe a situation where you have demonstrated leadership
- What is your assessment of the band, and what suggestions can you offer to improve our band program?
- How would you implement these improvements?
- How would you handle a confrontation with a member of the band that took place during rehearsal?
- If there happened to be a conflict of interest between the director and yourself in dealing with a band situation, how would you address the issue?
- Describe a tense or crisis situation and how you dealt with it. Would you have done anything differently?
- What are your goals for the marching band next season?
- How will you plan on being instrumental in attaining these goals?
- If you had any advice for the director from the student perspective, what would it be, and why?

R 3

TEACHING & CONDUCTING A LIVE ENSEMBLE

Candidates will teach a marching fundamental, and conduct a piece with a live ensemble

1 lowest / 5 highest

1	2	3	4	5	Teaching Technique
1	2	3	4	5	Speaking Voice/Enunciation
1	2	3	4	5	Conducting Technique
1	2	3	4	5	Posture/Carriage/Confidence
1	2	3	4	5	Respect & Report with Band

FINAL SCORES

_____ Standing Verbal Commands (10 points)

_____ Marching Fundamentals (10 points)

_____ Conducting (20 points)

_____ Showmanship (10 points)

_____ Interview (25 points)

_____ Teaching & Conducting a Live Ensemble (25 points)

_____ /100 FINAL SCORE

_____ Ranking Out Of _____ Candidates

COMMENTS

Keys To Success

The drum major has a vital role as leader of the marching band during rehearsals, and in performance. His/her job is to carry out instructions of the band director, and other instructional staff, regarding what needs to be done with the band. In addition, you are the band's eyes and ears in communication with the director. You should meet with your director prior to the beginning of the season so you can discuss specific goals, responsibilities, and expectations as it pertains to the role of drum major and the band. It is important you keep all lines of communication open, and that you realize the director's word is final.

RESPONSIBILITIES - GENERAL

- Maintain communication with the director/staff about each rehearsal's game plan
- Organize meetings with the section leaders, so everyone is informed
- Be certain all equipment is set up; assign someone else if need be but be sure it is done
- Start and end each and every rehearsal on time
- Maintain discipline at all times
- Be prepared to rehearse in all kinds of weather
- Be certain rehearsals run smoothly, and productively
- Be attentive during announcements as you will be asked what they were by many of the band members
- If anyone is absent when announcements are given, be sure that person/section is aware of the announcements

RESPONSIBILITIES - MUSIC REHEARSALS

- Lead the band to the rehearsal area, into the proper formation, and ready to begin rehearsal on time
- Guide the band through a preplanned warm-up routine, both marching and musically and stretching exercises
- Teach marching fundamentals and drill to members of the band
- Maintain a steady pace when band is learning a drill
- Demonstrate marching maneuvers correctly, and with confidence
- Provide assistance when members are having technical issues by pulling them aside
- Always have a whistle on hand; keep an eye on the director, and be ready to stop the band if he/she requests
- Assist in making sure everyone is quiet when any staff member is giving instructions
- Quietly correct posture or any other problems you observe, if someone else is teaching

- Conduct and direct the band through rehearsal segments, and full run-throughs

RESPONSIBILITIES - PERFORMANCES

- Conduct the band in performance
- Add overall showmanship to the band with your own performance as drum major-strut, salutes, etc.
- Serve as the band's ambassador at award ceremonies and special functions
- Make sure the band is in proper formation in the stands during contests or football games
- Know the game of football; when the band can and cannot play, what to play and when, defense vs. offense
- Set the perfect example at all times in dress, behavior, and overall leadership

BEHAVIOR & ATTITUDE

- Be the first, never the last, to rehearsals.
- Always have the needed and required rehearsal equipment.
- Wear appropriate rehearsal attire: proper shoes, shorts, etc.
- Demonstrate desire, spirit and enthusiasm for learning, working, and contributing.
- Be one of those students who is always "there".
- Prepare and master your part of the performance in advance when possible.
- Believe that "Only your best is good enough".
- Refrain from making comments, or carrying on a conversation during a rehearsal.
- Maintain eye contact with Instructor or Section Leader in Charge.
- Use "High-Intensity Listening".

- Stop immediately when cut-off is given, or move is completed.
- Exhibit enthusiasm for practice, and understand the need for repetition.
- If you experience failure, analyze it, and make a plan to improve and succeed the next time.
- Turn work into play. Enjoy rehearsing: hot, cold, or rainy. Try to learn something new every day.
- Remember: "The Band will only be as good as my attitude and my contribution."
- Be humble in your success. Demonstrate class in all situations.
- Prepare for the next rehearsal.

CHARACTERISTICS TO EXHIBIT

- Develop an impressive level of skill of conducting or twirling a drum major baton or mace
- Project vocal commands with clarity and pacing
- Be responsible and reliable
- Convey your dedication to having the whole band succeed
- Develop interpersonal skills to provide leadership and aid to the band director
- Be patient and enthusiastic in order to effectively teach others
- Express your passion for excellence to inspire the band to perform at their best

THE ASSISTANT DRUM MAJOR(S)

The assistant drum major is the next-in-command behind the drum major. He/she assumes the drum major role whenever the drum major is not present or is unable to perform. He/she must be able to march as a regular member of the band, as well as step into the drum major's job at a moment's notice. He/she may also be asked to help during rehearsals.

Showmanship & Salutes

Showmanship is the visual contribution of the drum major to the band's performance. A drum major's showmanship is determined by conducting style, marching, and special skills such as twirling a baton or mace, playing an instrument, handling various equipment, gymnastics, dancing, arm swings, bows, and salutes. Showmanship is a creative outgrowth of the fundamentals and is the process that gives each drum major their individual style. Remember there are no shortcuts to success; fundamentals must come first!

Standard Military Salutes

The *SALUTE* has become one of the most significant aspects of showmanship for the drum major. Regardless of how involved or creative, there are three parts to every salute.

The *PRE-SALUTE* is any movement preceding the *SALUTE* position. It can be smooth or snappy, complex or simple, fast or slow, large or small. For a military style salute, a snappy movement to the *SALUTE* position, held for a period of *3–5* seconds, would be appropriate.

The *POST-SALUTE* is a conclusion to the *SALUTE*. This is done quickly by using a recoil from the original *SALUTE* position and then quickly snapping to the attention position. It is essential to have outstanding posture and presence at all times.

THE 3 DRUM MAJOR STYLES

Corps   Traditional   Mace & Signal Baton

Corps Salute

Notice that in the SALUTE position, the fingers on both hands are together, and the wrists are straight. The right elbow is at a *45-degree* angle from the body. The left hand is on the hip, with the elbow straight out to the side, the fingers together and straight, with the thumb in back of the hip. It would also be acceptable to extend the left arm straight down the left side, with the hand in a fist.

| *Position of attention* | *Pre-salute* | *Salute* | *Post-salute* | *Back to attention* |

Traditional Salute

| *Position of attention* | *Pre-salute* | *Salute* | *Post-salute* | *Back to attention* |

Mace & Signal Baton Salute

Position of attention

Shift before salute

Pre-salute

Salute

Post-salute

Reverse shift

Back to attention

Creating Original Salutes

An effective salute can be created by changing movements from fast to slow, snappy to smooth, big to small, simple to complex, or subtle to obvious. Also, by varying body positions with spins, kneeling, posing, incorporating marching, or character movements.

Good taste, effectiveness, practicality, and dignity should determine the type of *SALUTE*. It should reflect the drum major's competence, confidence, style, and pride. Remember that salutes should not distract from your marching band's performance, therefore, limit the salute. No one wants to watch a 5-minute salute. Watch and observe other drum majors for ideas on building your own salute vocabulary.

The following are techniques to help create original salutes that can be used with single or multiple drum majors.

PERFORM THE MILITARY SALUTE

- Be sure the motion is snappy and precise

VARY THE PRE-SALUTE MOTION

- Hands in blades, fists, incorporating rolls, or utilizing straight arms
- Smooth motion
- Fast or slow motion
- Vary the angle of the arms
- Vary the position of the arms (above head, parallel to ground)
- Vary the hand position (fist, fingers together, jazz hand)
- Use sequential movements for the arms (for multiple drum majors)
- Combine smooth, and snappy motion
- Add some type of lunge
- Vary head movement, and positions
- Add creative footwork
- Use dancing, gymnastics, etc. (in good taste)
- Start facing the opposite direction
- March (use different styles of marching)
- Use body spins
- Any combination of the above
- Create your own list of ways to vary the *pre-salute*

VARY THE SALUTE POSITION
- Hand position

- Arm position
- Lunge or pose
- Feet position
- Head position
- Create a list of ways to vary the *salute* position

VARY THE POST SALUTE MOTION

- Any of the variations from the *pre-salute* can be used for a completely new movement
- Reverse what you did for the *pre-salute*
- Vary the *pre-salute* in some way
- Use equipment (capes, hats, etc.)

MULTI-DRUM MAJOR SALUTES

- Perform in unison (everyone must match)
- Alternate starting the salute with sequential motion
- Alternate starting the salute but arrive at the *salute* position simultaneously
- Utilize symmetrical and asymmetrical poses
- Mirroring
- Use a variety of height levels for each drum major; two drum majors kneeling, one standing
- Staggered positioning
- Lunges
- Sequential moves, variations in speed, stark contrasts with large and small arm motions
- Variations in the *recoil* and *pre-salute* positions
- Incorporation of mace showmanship

OTHER CONSIDERATIONS WHEN CREATING A SALUTE

- Keep the length of salute within reason
- Do not make the moves too repetitious; the salute should have variety
- Look at the audience while in the *salute* position
- Use the *military salute* while saluting the flag or during the National Anthem
- Maintain good posture at all times
- Keep a list of ways to vary movement and poses, and refer to it
- The same concepts can be applied for baton or mace salutes

Arm Swings

The arm swings are basic, and can be used as a foundation from which to augment style.

Mace

The mace is held behind the right arm, perpendicular to the ground, with the head of the mace pointed down (*full tuck*). It stays in this position for both counts. The elbow should be naturally bent and does not move during the arm swing. On *count 1*, the left arm is straight and slightly behind the left leg, in a relaxed position. The hand is in a fist with the thumb on top. On *count 2*, the left arm follows the range of motion forward and reaches the point to which it is parallel to the ground.

Corps

The hands should be in fists—holding a roll of quarters with the thumbs on top with the arms relaxed and slightly bent. The arm motion is smooth and angled slightly, moving forward to the center of the body. Relax the arms and avoid jerky movements. Coordinate the arms as if walking.

Baton

The same as corps arm swing but with the baton in the bend of your elbow of the right arm, held between the thumb and forefinger. The left hand position is in a blade position with a straight wrist. Keep the movement smooth and flowing, without any jerking motions.

Showmanship Ideas

- Alternative arm swings
- Hesitation step: popping of the knee while executing flanks, turns, or halts
- 270 degree turn or ¾ turns
- Back bends
- Splits
- Front or back flips
- Run-on steps: MSU's drum major step, Illinois' fast chair step/kick step, Wisconsin snappy chair step)

Staging the Performance

Staging is the strategic placement of a drum major throughout the show and the maneuvering from one location to another.

The podium is not always the best position for a drum major. The basic considerations for staging positions for the drum majors, are the appearance of the band's drill, and the musical needs of the players.

There will be times during a show when the musicians desperately need a conductor, and other times when a conductor is not needed. When not needed, consider placing drum majors in different locations to perform special routines that showcase creative talents, and add interesting visuals to the show.

When creating specialized choreography or varying marching styles, certain qualities should prevail at all times.

Style

The drum major should be able to execute all marching styles. Choreography should be executed with good body control, in good taste, and in character with the music. The drum major's performance must exceed that of everyone else on the field, since the audience focuses much of its attention on the drum major.

Posture

During performances and rehearsals, the posture of a drum major must be a good example for all other band members. Think of stretching the body upward, as if suspended from above. Keep the head erect. Always remember the importance of composure, presence, confidence, posture and projection; including during transitions between salutes, and staging positions.

Poise

The dignity of a drum major is sacrificed by running to various locations on the field or the podium. Plan staging positions to avoid such awkward transitions. Either march, or use some special type of character step to move between various locations during the show.

Throwing one's hat or other uniform parts on the ground is another example of disrespect for the decorum of a drum major. Contrary to popular belief, it is possible to conduct with a hat when properly attired.

Signals

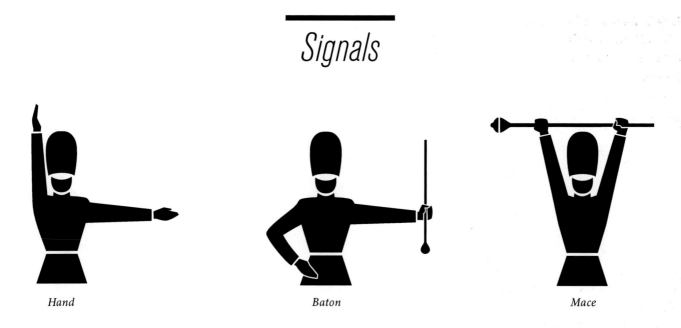

Hand   Baton   Mace

Hand Signals

Drum Major hand signals are usually given in 8 count sequences. However, when giving these signals it is not necessary to follow these count sequences, as long as the command of execution is given one count before the movement is executed. The purpose of using the 8 count sequence is to attain uniformity in class instruction, or to coordinate multiple drum major signals.

TERMINOLOGY TO HELP UNDERSTAND THE DIAGRAMS

Preparatory Position: The arms are straight with the hands eight inches from the leg. The fingers are together and the wrists are straight. This occurs on count 1 of the 8 count sequence.

Signal Position: The Signal Position defines the maneuver and usually occurs on count 2.

Recoil Position: The Recoil Position varies depending on the signal, and usually occurs on count 6.

Command of Execution Position: The same as Signal Position. It usually occurs on count 7.

FORWARD MARCH

Counts	1	2	3	4	5	6	7	8
Arms	*Prep Pos*	*Signal Pos*				*Recoil*	*Jab*	*Down*
Whistle	*Tweeeeeeet*				*Tweet*	*Tweet*	*Tweet*	*Tweet*

RIGHT FLANK

Counts	1	2	3	4	5	6	7	8
Arms	*Prep Pos*	*Signal Pos*				*Recoil*		*Exec*
Whistle	*Tweeeeeeet*						*Tweet*	

LEFT FLANK

Counts	1	2	3	4	5	6	7	8
Arms	*Prep Pos*	*Signal Pos*				*Recoil*		*Exec*
Whistle	*Tweeeeeeet*						*Tweet*	

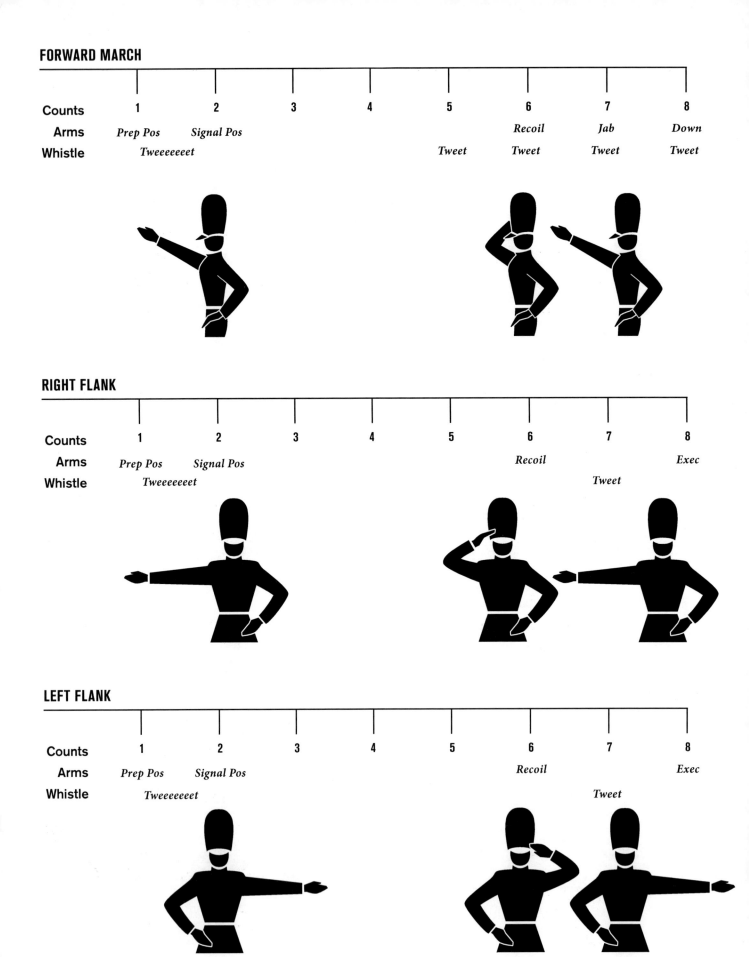

234

LEFT MINSTREL

Counts	1	2	3	4	5	6	7	8
Arms	*Prep Pos*	*Signal Pos*				*Recoil*		*Exec*
Whistle	*Tweeeeeeet*						*Tweet*	

RIGHT MINSTREL

Counts	1	2	3	4	5	6	7	8
Arms	*Prep Pos*	*Signal Pos*				*Recoil*		*Exec*
Whistle	*Tweeeeeeet*						*Tweet*	

LEFT OBLIQUE

Counts	1	2	3	4	5	6	7	8
Arms	*Prep Pos*	*Signal Pos*				*Recoil*		*Exec*
Whistle	*Tweeeeeeet*				*Tweet*	*Tweet*	*Tweet*	*Tweet*

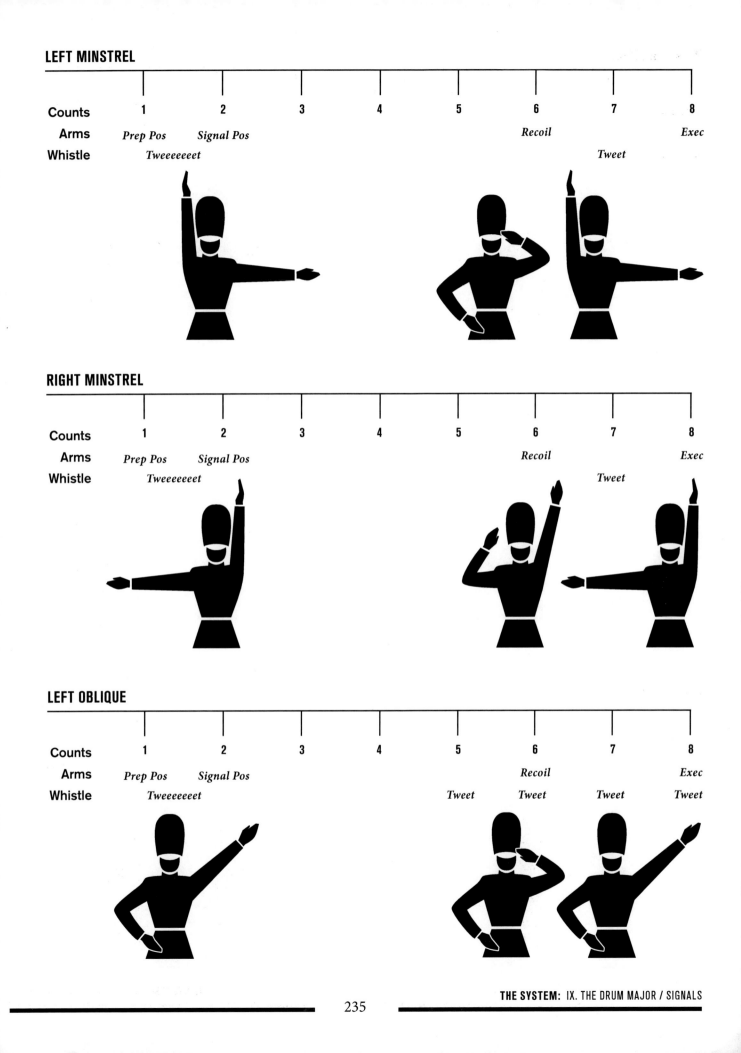

RIGHT OBLIQUE

Counts	1	2	3	4	5	6	7	8
Arms	*Prep Pos*	*Signal Pos*				*Recoil*		*Exec*
Whistle	*Tweeeeeeet*					*Tweet*		

LEFT FORWARD

Counts	1	2	3	4	5	6	7	8
Arms	*Prep Pos*	*Signal Pos*				*Recoil*		*Exec*
Whistle	*Tweeeeeeet*					*Tweet*		

RIGHT FORWARD

Counts	1	2	3	4	5	6	7	8
Arms	*Prep Pos*	*Signal Pos*				*Recoil*	*Jab*	*Exec*
Whistle	*Tweeeeeeet*						*Tweet*	

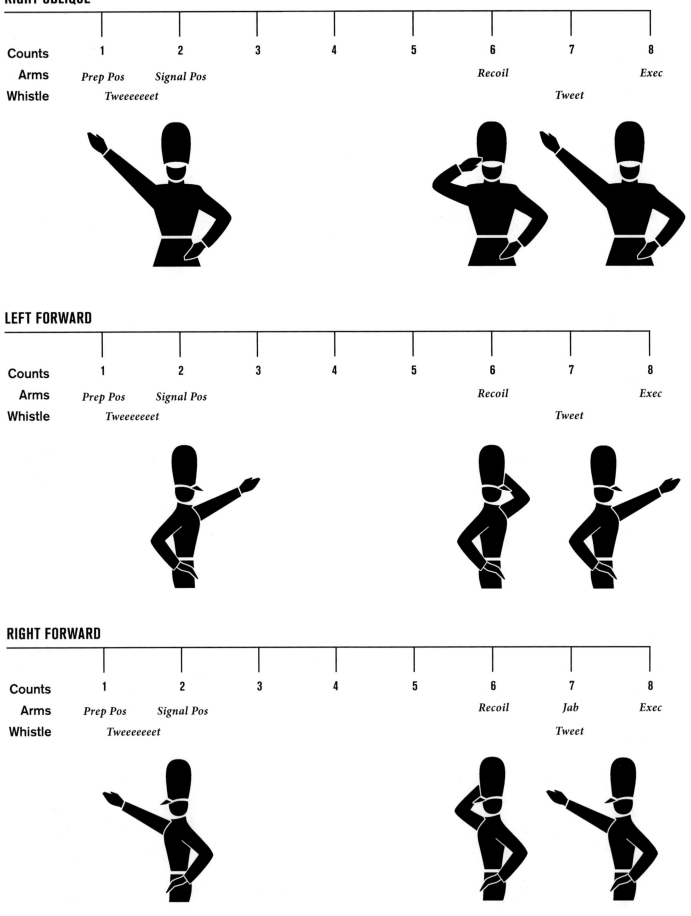

TO THE REAR

Counts	1	2	3	4	5	6	7	8
Arms	*Prep Pos*	*Signal Pos*				*Recoil*		*Exec*
Whistle	*Tweeeeeeet*						*Tweet*	

COUNTER MARCH

Counts	1	2	3	4	5	6	7	8	1	2
Baton	*Prep Pos*	*Signal Pos*						*Recoil*		*Down*
Whistle		*Tweeeeeeet*							*Tweet*	
March		*Turn*	*Step*	*Turn*	*Step*					

HALT

Counts	1	2	3	4	5	6	7	8	1	2
Arms	*Prep Pos*	*Signal Pos*					*Down*	*Sig. Pos*	*Down*	*Pos of Attn.*
Whistle		*Tweeeeeeet*					*Tweet*	*Tweet*	*Tweet*	
March	*TTR and B March*									

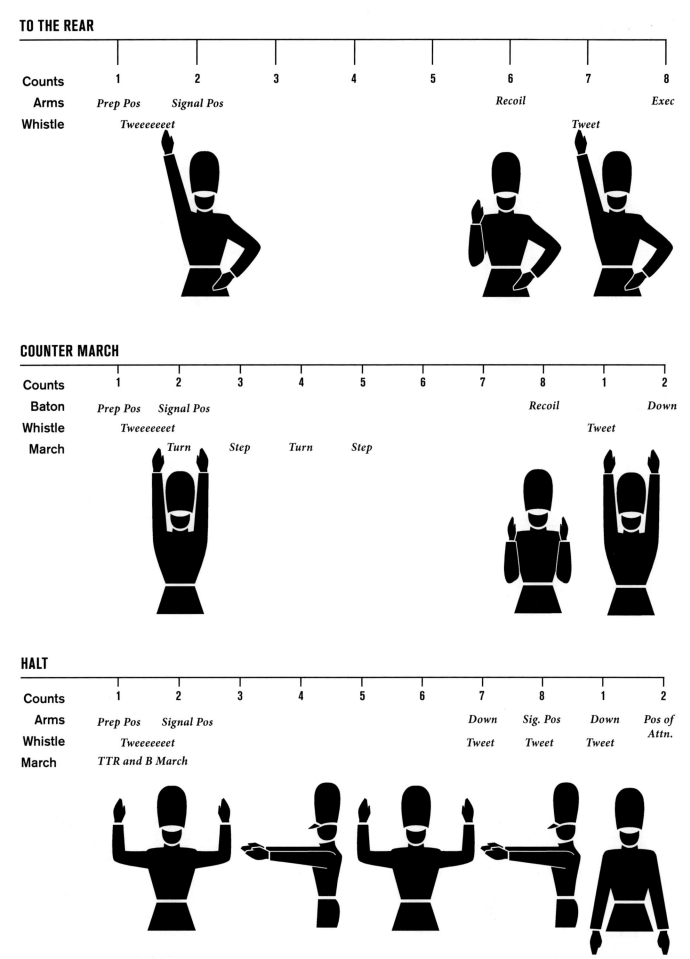

Baton Signals

Drum Major baton signals are usually given in 8 count sequences. However, when giving these signals it is not necessary to follow these count sequences as long as the command of execution is given one count before the movement is executed. The purpose of using the 8 count sequence is to attain uniformity in class instruction, or to coordinate multiple drum major signals.

TERMINOLOGY TO HELP UNDERSTAND THE DIAGRAMS

Flourish: This is done by making the baton spin forward for two or three spins during count 1. Grip the baton, in the crotch of the hand between the thumb and forefinger. Spin the baton forward with the ball rotating on the inside. Pivot from the wrist to avoid moving the arm.

Signal Position: The Signal Position defines the maneuver and usually occurs on count 2.

Recoil Position: The Recoil Position varies depending on the signal, and usually occurs on count 6.

Command of Execution Position: The same as Signal Position. It usually occurs on count 7.

FORWARD MARCH

Counts	1	2	3	4	5	6	7	8
Baton	*Prep Pos*	*Signal Pos*				*Recoil*	*Jab*	*Down*
Whistle	*Tweeeeeeet*				*Tweet*	*Tweet*	*Tweet*	*Tweet*

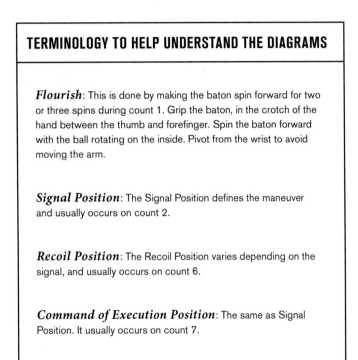

RIGHT FLANK

Counts	1	2	3	4	5	6	7	8
Baton	*Prep Pos*	*Signal Pos*				*Recoil*		*Exec*
Whistle	*Tweeeeeet*						*Tweet*	

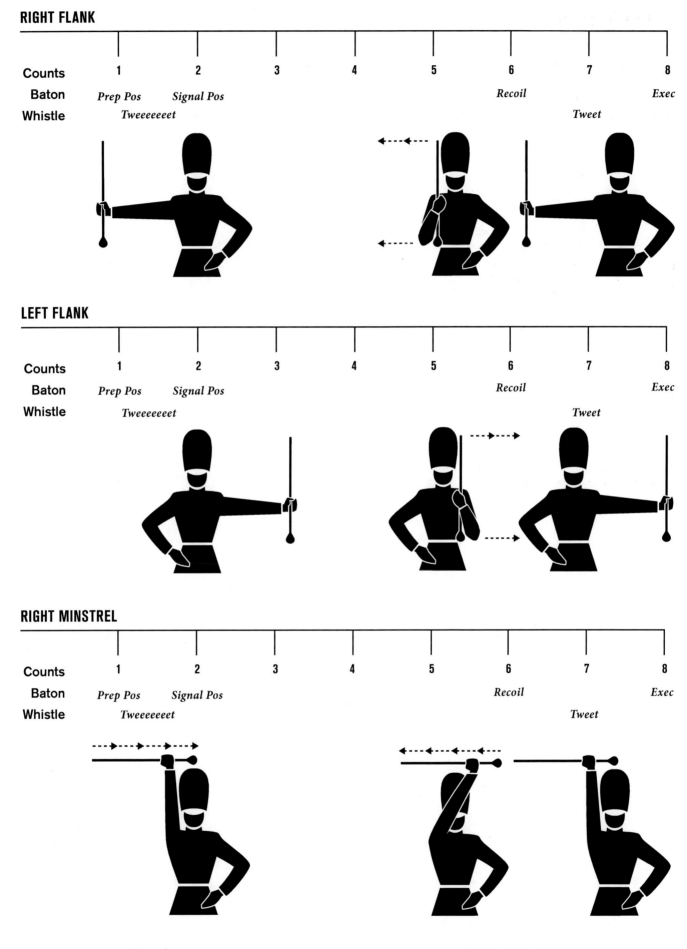

LEFT FLANK

Counts	1	2	3	4	5	6	7	8
Baton	*Prep Pos*	*Signal Pos*				*Recoil*		*Exec*
Whistle	*Tweeeeeet*						*Tweet*	

RIGHT MINSTREL

Counts	1	2	3	4	5	6	7	8
Baton	*Prep Pos*	*Signal Pos*				*Recoil*		*Exec*
Whistle	*Tweeeeeet*						*Tweet*	

LEFT MINSTREL

Counts	1	2	3	4	5	6	7	8
Arms	*Prep Pos*	*Signal Pos*				*Recoil*		*Exec*
Whistle	*Tweeeeeeet*						*Tweet*	

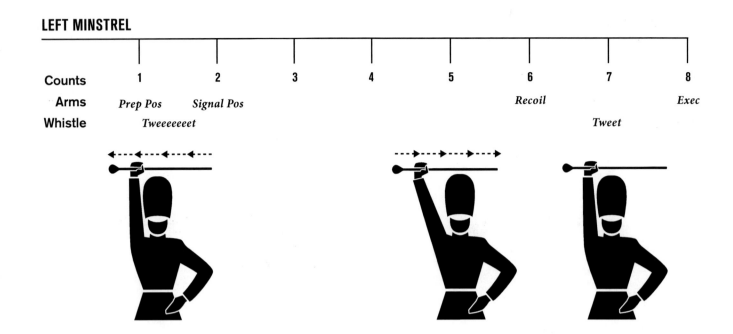

RIGHT OBLIQUE

Counts	1	2	3	4	5	6	7	8
Arms	*Prep Pos*	*Signal Pos*				*Recoil*		*Exec*
Whistle	*Tweeeeeeet*					*Tweet*		

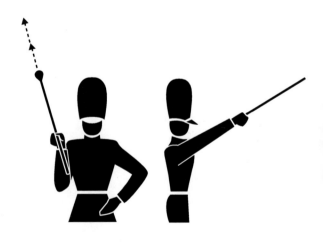

LEFT OBLIQUE

Counts	1	2	3	4	5	6	7	8
Arms	*Prep Pos*	*Signal Pos*				*Recoil*		*Exec*
Whistle	*Tweeeeeeet*					*Tweet*		

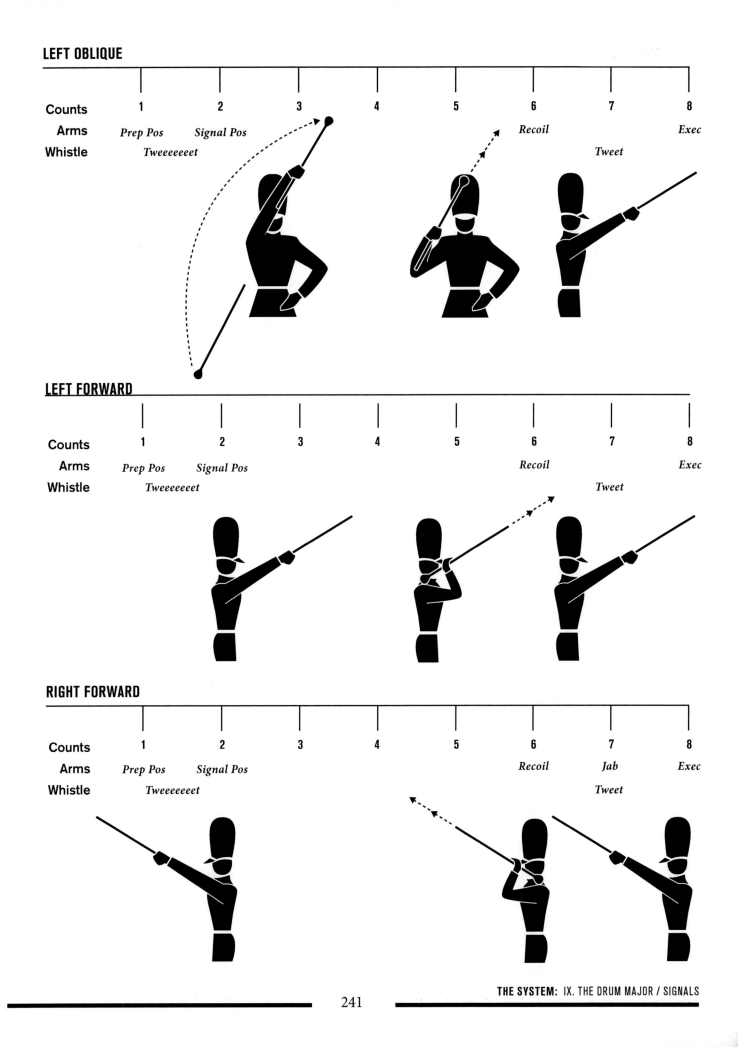

LEFT FORWARD

Counts	1	2	3	4	5	6	7	8
Arms	*Prep Pos*	*Signal Pos*				*Recoil*		*Exec*
Whistle	*Tweeeeeeet*					*Tweet*		

RIGHT FORWARD

Counts	1	2	3	4	5	6	7	8
Arms	*Prep Pos*	*Signal Pos*				*Recoil*	*Jab*	*Exec*
Whistle	*Tweeeeeeet*					*Tweet*		

THE SYSTEM: IX. THE DRUM MAJOR / SIGNALS

TO THE REAR

Counts	1	2	3	4	5	6	7	8
Baton	*Prep Pos*	*Signal Pos*				*Recoil*		*Exec*
Whistle	*Tweeeeeeet*					*Tweet*		
March			*Turn*					

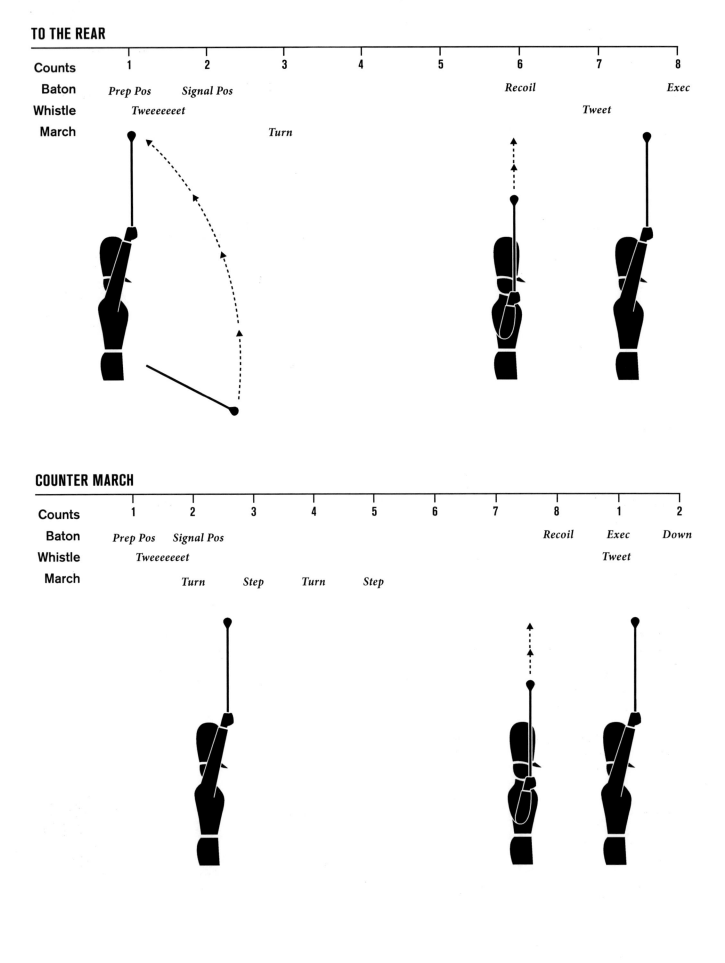

COUNTER MARCH

Counts	1	2	3	4	5	6	7	8	1	2
Baton	*Prep Pos*	*Signal Pos*						*Recoil*	*Exec*	*Down*
Whistle	*Tweeeeeeet*								*Tweet*	
March		*Turn*	*Step*	*Turn*	*Step*					

HALT

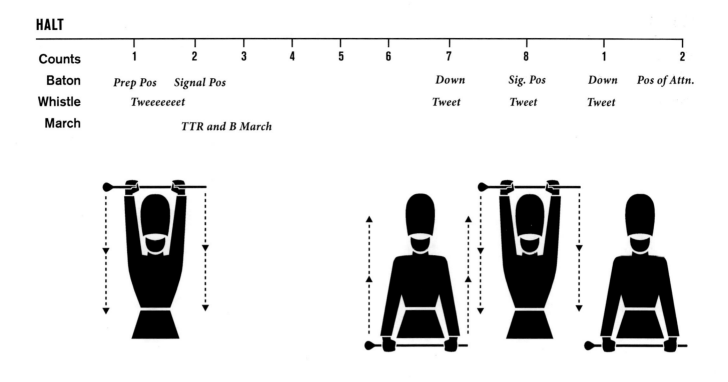

Counts	1	2	3	4	5	6	7	8	1	2
Baton	*Prep Pos*	*Signal Pos*					*Down*	*Sig. Pos*	*Down*	*Pos of Attn.*
Whistle	*Tweeeeeeet*						*Tweet*	*Tweet*	*Tweet*	
March		*TTR and B March*								

Mace Signals

Drum Major baton signals are usually given in *8-count* sequences. However, when giving these signals it is not necessary to follow these count sequences as long as the command of execution is given one count before the movement is executed. The purpose of using the 8 count sequence, is to attain uniformity in class instruction, or to coordinate multiple drum major signals.

TERMINOLOGY TO HELP UNDERSTAND THE DIAGRAMS

Home Position: This precedes every signal. The mace is at a 45 degree angle, with the head of the mace pointed to the right. The right hand is on the top and the left hand is on the bottom.

Right Hand Preparatory Position: The mace is in front of the body, perpendicular to the ground. The right hand is on top, left hand on the bottom, on count 1.

Left Hand Preparatory Position: Same as Right Hand Preparatory position, except the left hand is on top, and the right hand is on bottom.

Signal Position: The Signal Position defines the maneuver, and usually occurs on count 2.

Recoil Position: The Recoil Position varies depending on the signal, and usually occurs on count 6.

Command of Execution Position: The same as Signal Position, and usually occurs on count 7.

243

FORWARD MARCH

Counts	1	2	3	4	5	6	7	8
Mace	R. Hand	Prep	Signal Pos			Recoil	Jab	Hold
Whistle		Tweeeeeeet				Tweet	Tweet	Tweet

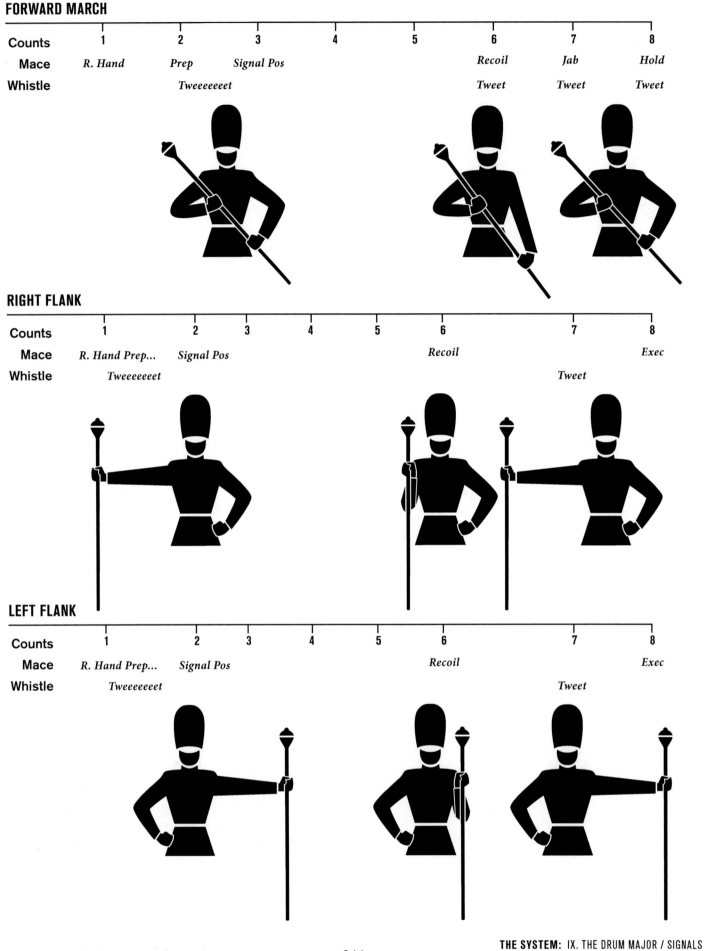

RIGHT FLANK

Counts	1	2	3	4	5	6	7	8
Mace	R. Hand Prep...	Signal Pos				Recoil		Exec
Whistle	Tweeeeeeet					Tweet		

LEFT FLANK

Counts	1	2	3	4	5	6	7	8
Mace	R. Hand Prep...	Signal Pos				Recoil		Exec
Whistle	Tweeeeeeet					Tweet		

RIGHT MINSTREL

Counts	1	2	3	4	5	6	7	8
Mace	*R. Hand Prep...*	*Signal Pos*				*Recoil*		*Exec*
Whistle	*Tweeeeeeet*						*Tweet*	

LEFT MINSTREL

Counts	1	2	3	4	5	6	7	8
Mace	*R. Hand Prep...*	*Signal Pos*				*Recoil*		*Exec*
Whistle	*Tweeeeeeet*						*Tweet*	

RIGHT OBLIQUE

Counts	1	2	3	4	5	6	7	8
Mace	*R. Hand Prep...*	*Signal Pos*				*Recoil*		*Exec*
Whistle	*Tweeeeeeet*						*Tweet*	

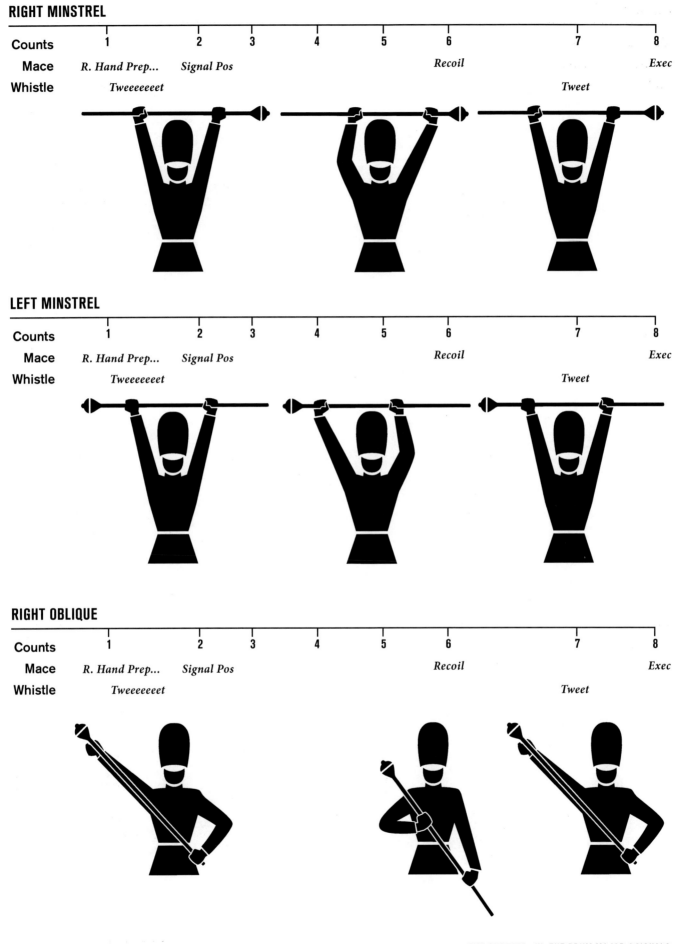

THE SYSTEM: IX. THE DRUM MAJOR / SIGNALS

LEFT OBLIQUE

Counts	1	2	3	4	5	6	7	8
Mace	*R. Hand Prep...*	*Signal Pos*				*Recoil*		*Exec*
Whistle	*Tweeeeeeet*						*Tweet*	

RIGHT FORWARD

Counts	1	2	3	4	5	6	7	8
Mace	*R. Hand Prep...*	*Signal Pos*				*Recoil*		*Exec*
Whistle	*Tweeeeeeet*						*Tweet*	

LEFT FORWARD

Counts	1	2	3	4	5	6	7	8
Mace	*R. Hand Prep...*	*Signal Pos*				*Recoil*		*Exec*
Whistle	*Tweeeeeeet*						*Tweet*	

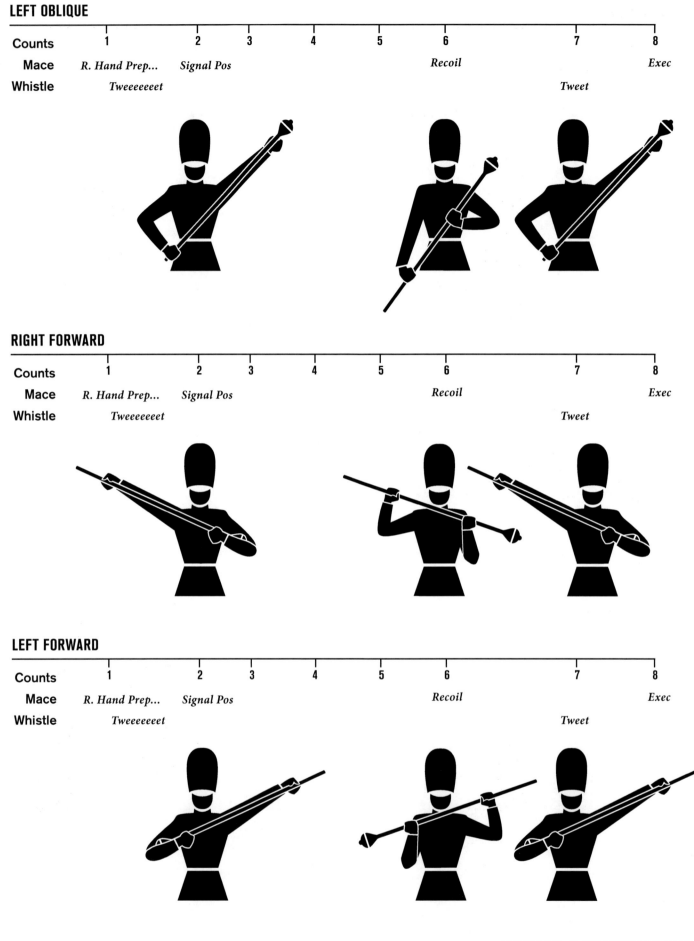

TO THE REAR

Counts	1	2	3	4	5	6	7	8
Baton	*Prep Pos*	*Signal Pos*				*Recoil*		*Exec*
Whistle	*Tweeeeeeet*						*Tweet*	
March			*Turn*					

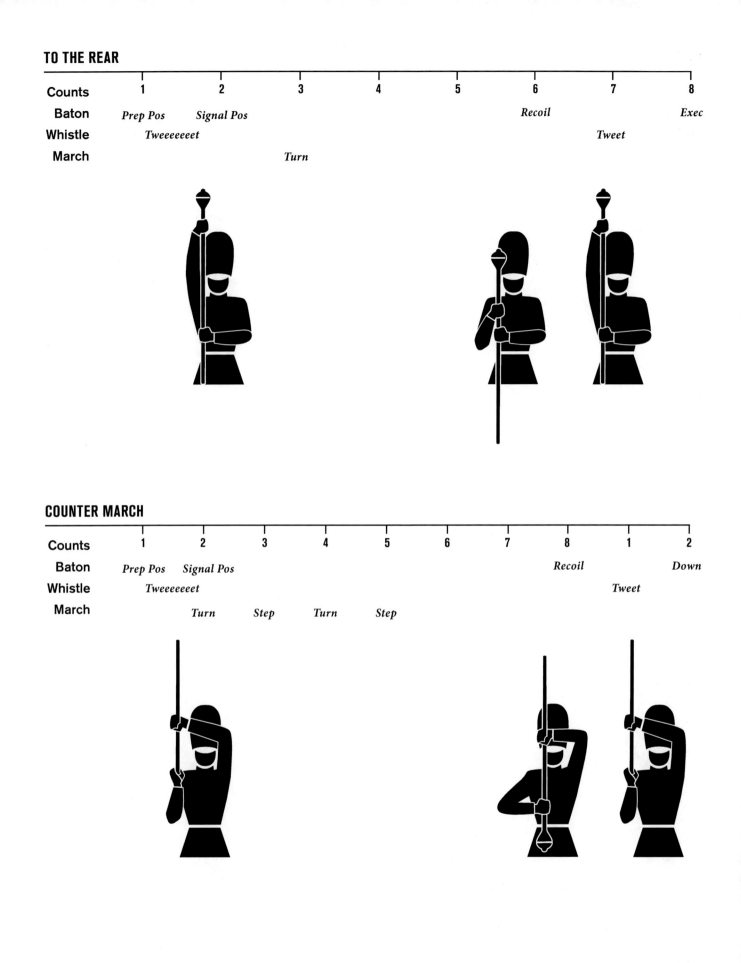

COUNTER MARCH

Counts	1	2	3	4	5	6	7	8	1	2
Baton	*Prep Pos*	*Signal Pos*						*Recoil*		*Down*
Whistle	*Tweeeeeeet*							*Tweet*		
March		*Turn*	*Step*	*Turn*	*Step*					

HALT

Counts	1	2	3	4	5	6	7	8	1	2
Baton	*Prep Pos*	*Signal Pos*					*Down*	*Sig. Pos*	*Down*	*Home Pos.*
Whistle	*Tweeeeeeet*						*Tweet*	*Tweet*	*Tweet*	
March		*TTR and B March*								

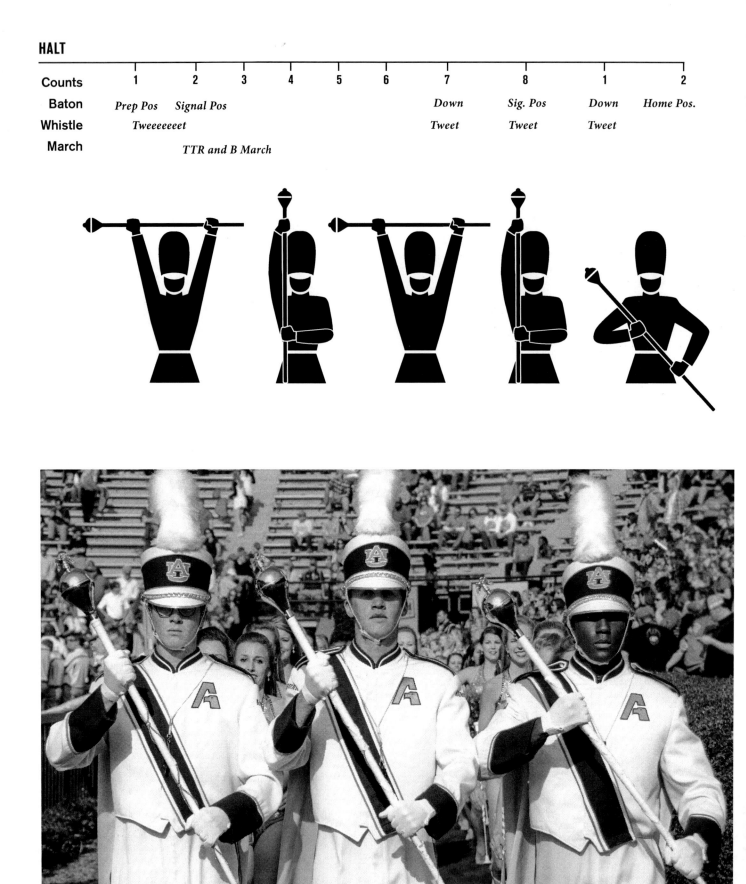

THE SYSTEM: IX. THE DRUM MAJOR / SIGNALS

X. MARCHING PERCUSSION

by **Tom Keck**

Grip Techniques

The major differences between concert and marching percussion playing styles stem from the differences in equipment, and the role of the player. For volume and clarity purposes, marching instruments are tuned much tighter (higher in pitch) than concert instruments, and therefore require more control of the rebound off the drum head after impact. Marching drums are deeper than concert drums, and marching drumsticks are longer and have a greater circumference. Because concert percussionists are solo players, and marching percussionists are typically *soli* players, a specific technique is recommended to unify their approach to playing.

Visual Guidelines

To begin, let your hands hang down at your sides, as if you are walking down the street. Bend at the elbows, and bring the forearms up slowly to a comfortable resting position, just above waist level, so that the shoulders are relaxed and the elbows have a slight downward angle. This is the basic arm position that should be maintained for most of the time while drumming. The right arm should be relaxed at your side, not forced out away from your body in a "teapot-like" position. The left arm is relaxed at your side as well, and not forced into your ribs.

The drum should be set at a height, near waist-level, so that when the player brings his/her arms to playing position, the "playing mechanism" is flat in relation to the drum and no adjustments from the wrist are necessary. The sticks should be held one-third of the way up from the butt-end so that the thumb and index finger create a fulcrum that is horizontally aligned (fulcrum will be discussed later). The sticks should be held parallel to the drum head (as horizontal as possible), to allow for the best response from the head and maximum bead impact. Some snare lines play with a downward angle to their sticks for visual reasons. This is acceptable, however not as much bead of the stick will impact the head, the rebound of

the sticks may be inhibited, and the tone will be characteristically different.

At the same time, the sticks are held **90 degrees** from each other so that the **45 degree** line bisecting them intercepts the player's navel. A common tendency among young percussionists, is to push the right arm out, and pull the left arm in simultaneously, so that the center of the angle is well to the left. It is important to resist this tendency, while remaining relaxed. The stick beads are to remain together in the middle of the head, just above the surface. Balance and relaxation are crucial.

The Right Hand

If one were to bring his/her right arm up from the side as described above, the hand would be perpendicular to the floor. This is the first natural bodily motion that must be altered through practice. The hand should be turned over so that the palm is flat to the floor, as if dribbling a basketball or holding bicycle handlebars. The arm remains in this position, and must stay relaxed.

The stick should be held diagonally in the hand so that when the fingers are gently curled around it, the wrist does not turn outward. It is imperative that the wrist remains straight with the forearm and not be angled. The thumb and index finger comprise the fulcrum, or the point at which the stick pivots. Presently a large gap exists between the thumb and index finger. Without changing the last three fingers, the thumb should be brought back and the space closed. The fulcrum is now between the fleshy part of the thumb, and the first joint of the index finger. The last three fingers wrap around the stick and stay in contact with the stick at all times. The second and third fingers have an active role in cradling the stick while the pinkie is more passive in its involvement.

The line of the drum stick should pass from the fulcrum, under

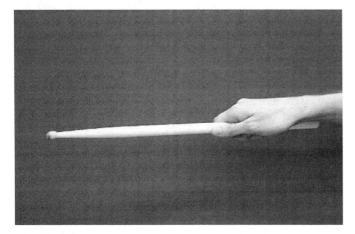

the palm, through the right side of the wrist making a 30 degree angle between the butt of the stick, and the wrist. The wrist should stay in the same horizontal plane as the forearm. This will enable the wrist to reach its fullest extension. If matched grip is used, simply mirror this procedure in the left hand. Both hands must look identical, or "matched." Refer to the photographs to the right and below, keeping in mind all the aspects of the right hand grip that were previously covered.

Traditional Grip—The Left Hand

As before, bring the left forearm up from your side. The hand is perpendicular to the floor, as if shaking someone else's hand. This position should remain intact while playing. The tendency to bend the wrist outward (counterclockwise) must be avoided. Perhaps most importantly, traditional grip players must avoid setting the grip with their left palm opened upward. Turning the palm upward is similar to rotating before actually playing; doing so causes a significant loss of potential wrist turn before the stroke is initiated.

The stick rests between the base of the thumb and index finger, and rests on the last joint (just below the fingernail) of the third finger, above the knuckle. The fingers should have a natural curve to them as if shaking hands; do not curl them into the palm. As with the right hand, motion generally will be initiated from the wrist. In the traditional grip, however, each finger has its own function in allowing the wrist to power the stick.

The Thumb and First Finger
Although the actual pivot point of the stick is the base of the thumb, these two fingers are the most important in keeping the grip intact. Therefore, they will be considered the fulcrum in the left hand. The fleshy part of the thumb and the first joint of the index finger should lightly touch at all times. The more stable the fulcrum is, the more consistent the sound quality and timing will be.

The Second Finger
The primary purpose of the second finger is to keep the stick from moving horizontally within the grip. This finger stays alongside the stick at all times. Do not let it come off the stick; it must remain relaxed and extended. Some rudimentary percussionists wrap this finger around the stick for more power and control. Both methods are acceptable, as long as contact is retained.

The Third Finger

This finger is the stabilizer of the grip. Since the stick rests on it at all times, it is responsible for holding the stick in place. In other words, it counteracts the fulcrum's power. This finger is most important for controlling the stick rebound height after each tap. Do not allow the stick to fall below the last joint of the finger. The stick should always rest beneath the fingernail yet above the knuckle. This may be painful at first, but after continued practice, any discomfort will subside.

The Pinkie

Like the second finger, the pinkie has a passive role in the grip. Simply, it supports the third finger in carrying the weight of the stick. It must be kept alongside the third finger in a relaxed position. As a guide, pull the pinkie back slightly until the first knuckle of the third finger is centered between the first and second knuckles of the pinkie. Be careful not to allow it to curl up too far behind the third finger or slip inside the hand; it will not perform any function in these cases. At first, keeping the pinkie in place will be challenging. However, with regular practice, one will develop the strength needed to keep it in place, and relaxed.

It is important, especially in the early stages, to keep the grip intact. Do not let the fingers come off the stick for any reason. Make all playing motions from the wrist. At first, this may seem limiting. However, if the grip is learned correctly from the beginning, it will save countless hours of future practice time.

Observe this photograph of proper left hand technique taken

> **TIP:** *A straight line should exist from the fulcrum through the drum stick to the third finger where the stick rests. Try to envision a needle running straight through these points.*

from above. Notice the connection between the thumb and index finger.

> **TIP:** *Do not let the fingers come off the stick for any reason. Make all playing motions from the wrist.*

> **TIP:** *While holding the left hand in the playing position, place the tip of the right stick in the palm of the left hand. The line established by the right stick should point horizontally without an upward angle. A second way to check this is to see that the thumb is directly on top of the grip.*

When beginning traditional grip, simply practice holding the sticks in the proper grip without playing. Since everything in the left hand is new and unnatural, getting the muscle memory used to the correct grip, will be time well spent.

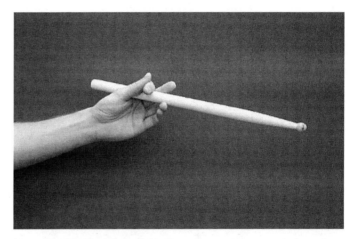

Learning bad habits will lead to discouragement later, when new levels of technique are required. The player should remain relaxed, and should never play faster than he/she can while keeping the proper grip intact.

Do not mindlessly practice bad habits that will take more time to correct later, that is the most ineffective thing for any aspiring percussionist to do. Mindful practice with a metronome, taking into consideration all the aspects of the grip, is the only road to improvement.

This photograph shows an inward view of the left hand traditional grip. Notice that the hand has not rotated, and the thumb is still on top. The stick is resting in the pocket between the thumb and index finger and extending to the last joint of the ring finger. The middle finger is holding the stick in place horizontally, and the pinkie is resting passively.

Battery Instruments

Playing Devices

The playing devices available to a percussionist can be broken down to the shoulders, the elbows, the wrists, and the fingers. If a person played by only turning at the shoulder, the sound would be too loud and the execution extremely slow. Playing from the elbow would be faster, yet not quite as loud. Strokes initiated from the wrists are faster still, almost as loud, and easier to control. Lastly, the fingers should be reserved for fast, single notes as they do not produce the volume that the wrist does; furthermore, they do not have endurance for continued playing. For these reasons, the wrist is the primary playing mechanism.

Developing wrist control is a difficult process that will ultimately pay tremendous dividends in speed and sound quality. It is difficult initially to get the feel of playing exclusively from the wrists. Consistent practice in front of a mirror is the only way to understand which playing mechanism is being used. In front of a mirror, it is easy to see if the arms are moving too much, or if the fingers are coming off the sticks.

Proper use of the wrists while drumming should feel like dribbling a basketball. It is possible to dribble by flicking the ball with just the fingers, and to dribble by locking up everything below the shoulder and bouncing the ball with the entire arm. Both of these methods are inefficient, though. Usually, a professional basketball player will dribble with a fluid wrist motion—as an efficient percussionist should do.

Moving down the arm from the shoulder to the fingers, the muscle groups that control each area become smaller. It is important to isolate which muscle group will be controlling the drum stick motions. This problem is paradoxical, as small muscle groups tire quickly and should be saved for rapid notes, but using too large of a group will be slow. In general, the wrist will propel most motions, with the fastest playing directed by the fingers, and possibly the arms in the unique case of hyper-speed rolls.

Stroke Types

There are three primary types of strokes that a percussionist uses: legato, staccato, and *marcato*. These terms correspond directly to their usages in other musical circumstances. Regardless of stroke type, the motions begin from just above the drum head and start with an upstroke lift. So, when not playing, the sticks must be controlled in the down position, 1.5 inches above the drum head.

A legato stroke is a smooth and continuous movement. The player can think of this as being much the same as dribbling a basketball with a fluid wrist motion. Legato strokes are used when playing consistent full strokes at one height. These strokes provide the most open sound and should be employed whenever possible. Most front ensemble playing (keyboards and timpani) is usually done with legato strokes.

Staccato strokes are shorter and more articulate. This style is necessary for rudimentary percussionists, but is employed more frequently than necessary. Staccato strokes involve stopping the stick at a low height, which is necessary for figures that combine grace notes and accented or unaccented notes. However, they should not be used as the default stroke as the sound quality can be pinched. In general, the player should think of playing strongly into the drum, driving the sound through the instrument. Staccato strokes can be thought of like a golf swing; the club starts inches from the ball, is drawn back to a maximum height, comes down and hits the ball, and follows through. In drumming, the stick rests above the head, is elevated to a predetermined height, comes down with a strong motion to the head, and follows through using the rebound of the head.

Marcato strokes are used for playing fortissimo dynamic levels. These are intense strokes which incorporate the arms. This stroke should be reserved for loud impact points in the music.

Stick Height

Every note needs to be played from the same height, with the same touch, and tone by each player. The player must concentrate on duplicating the exact height of each upstroke. For simplicity's sake, a system of defining stick heights by three inch increments has been established. These measurements do not hold exactly true to a ruler, so it would be unwise to tape rulers to the individual drums; the numbers merely serve as a reference. The common measurements used are three, six, nine, and twelve inches. These measurements correspond directly to traditional dynamic levels.

6 inches

Dynamic Level	Stick Height
p (and all grace notes)	1.5"
mp	3"
mf	6"
f	9"
ff	12"

Twelve inches can be thought of as a full vertical rotation, nine inches as a three-quarter turn, six-inches as a half-turn, three inches as a one-quarter turn, and an inch and one-half as the resting position. In other words, notes played from 1.5" are not lifted for, but rather are dropped. Once heights are defined, the player must watch to make sure that the sticks follow a straight up-and-down path without any "slicing." Compare the photographs below that illustrate different stick heights. Players must be able to automatically find these heights.

9 inches

3 inches

12 inches

Specific Techniques

SNARE DRUM

Specific issues that a snare drummer needs to understand, are the different playing areas, and available sounds of the drum.

There are three principal playing areas on a snare drum head:

- The center
- The opposite edge
- Halfway in between

The dynamics and timbre desired should determine which area to use, and often contemporary arrangers will specify which area, through their music notation. The responsive snare sound is located at the center of the drum, and halfway out, with the center being crisper and louder. The edge has more of a tom sound, with less snare response. This is important because piano-level playing at the edge will produce a significantly different tone quality, than piano-level playing in the center. Snare drummers need to continually develop their technique, including advanced flam, roll, and hybrid rudiments, as their parts tend to be more densely written, than other instruments of the battery.

Another sound available to the snare drummer is the rim shot, and there are three different types of rim shots commonly called for. First, the *cross shot* is executed by turning the left stick over (in the left hand), holding the bead against the drum head (on the left side of the head), and hitting the butt end of the stick against the rim (on the right side of the drum). This gives a "knock" sound, which is used in a lot of Latin style music. Second, the *stick shot* is performed by pressing the left stick into the drum head, and hitting the right stick against the left stick. The left stick can be held against the rim for a louder sound, or can be elevated to different angles for different resultant pitches. Notice how the stick shot is executed without changing the basic playing technique. Third, the *rim shot* is executed by striking the head and the rim at the same time. It is important to realize that rim shots are written for a timbrel difference, not volume. They should be played at the same dynamic level as the surrounding music. Experiment hitting the rim with different parts of the stick, the closer to the tip, the higher the pitch. In fact, high-pitched shots done near the tip of the stick have their own name, called *ping shots*.

Cross Shot

Stick Shot

Rim Shot

255

TENOR DRUMS

Tenor drums are the mid-voice of the battery percussion unit. What separates good tenor drummers from average ones, is their knowledge of playing areas and movement around the drums. The playing zone for each drum is about one-third of the way in from the edge, and definitely not in the center of the head. There is a *dead spot* in the center of each tenor head where it will not resonate as well (as with timpani).

If one were to look at the way most sets of tenors are put together, the edges of the drums closest to the player are in a straight line. This is to facilitate movement. Remember from geometry, *"the shortest distance between two points is a straight line."* Arcs and other non-linear motions will severely limit speed and consistency around the drums. The basic rule for motion is simple—the hands do the playing, and the arms do the moving. Never change grip or hand angles when moving around the drums; let the forearms make the motion. Make all motions as small as possible so as not to over-shoot the playing areas.

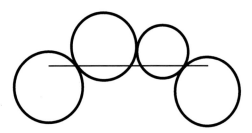

When first learning to play tenors, a good way to practice moving is to draw a straight line on a practice pad or table and try to play along the line without wavering. Get your muscle memory used to playing at different places along the line. When actually moving around the drums, continue thinking about playing straight down into the drums; do not concentrate on the moving aspect. Missed drums/clicked rims are usually the result of over-thinking. Specifically, hitting rims is a result of moving too fast or too slow; so just make a change next time, through the phrase.

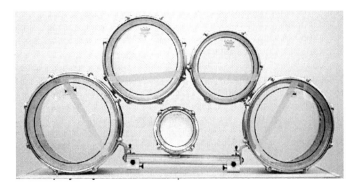

correct on one drum. The first few times through an exercise, play it on one drum; then, play it around after settling in. Nothing should change between playing a phrase on one drum, and playing it around the range of the instrument. If a passage is unclear on one drum, moving it around will not clean the phrase; it will only compound the problems. His photograph shows the proper playing zones for tenors. When practicing, players should repeatedly check to see that they are not moving outside the playing areas.

Tenor techniques and motion patterns have greatly evolved in recent years. Tenor players should be familiar with the techniques necessary to execute crosses (hand over hand playing) and sweeps (double bounces from one drum to an adjacent drum). As indicated earlier, these motions are no different than other motion patterns—the hands do the playing and the arms do the moving. When working on sweeps, the player must continue to think *straight down* about his/her playing. If the player starts thinking "outward" or circularly, chances are higher that the playing zone will be missed. Constantly think *down* and let the arms make the smallest motion necessary to complete the sweep.

Crosses are executed using the smallest motions necessary.

> **TIP:** *Practice towels are useful for practicing tenors while away from the drums. To make one, simply lay a beach towel over a set of tenors and trace the outline of each shell. With this, the exact sized drums can be practiced on at any time.*

When making a *one-drum cross* (i.e., drums *4* and *2*; drums *1* and *2*; drums *1* and *3*) only the mallets should be crossed. The hands should remain separated. When making a *two-drum cross* (i.e., drums *4* and *1*; drums *2* and *3*) the hands should be crossed. The wrists should remain separated. When making a *three-drum cross* (i.e., drums *3* and *4*) the wrists should be crossed. If these rules are followed, the motions will be efficient and will stay within the playing zones. Always cross as low as possible and keep the hands as close together as possible. This will prevent the mallets from striking each other. Players should be fluent crossing the left hand over the right and the right over the left. The motions should always be interpreted as crossing over, not crossing under.

Some of the rudiments that are useful for tenor drummers are to concentrate on including *paradiddle-diddles* and *hurtas*. Both of these rudiments provide a multitude of options for sticking patterns on the tenors that look very interesting to an audience.

BASS DRUM

The role of the bass drummer is much more involved and musically challenging with the use of multiple bass drums. To play in a bass drum line, each player must be aware of the overall musical phrase and how his/her part fits into the composite rhythm. However, a player cannot rely on the other bass drummers to "pull him/her through." If a bass drummer plays off of what he/she hears, his/her notes will be late due to the properties of sound delay. Bass drummers must have confidence that the other players will play their notes, and they must play their specific part right in time.

The playing area for the bass drum is the exact center of the

head, just like a snare drum. The grip used is the matched grip, with no difference from that of the matched grip used by snare drummers. The hands are turned perpendicular to the ground so that the thumb is on top and there is a *30-degree* angle forward slant. The mallet and hand angles must remain constant. To establish this, the player should start with their arms at their sides and then by bending at the elbows, bring the forearms up so there is a *90-degree* angle at the elbow. This is the arm angle that the player must memorize.

Then the drum carrier should be adjusted accordingly so that the player's mallets align with the center of the drum heads. Always bring the instrument to the player, not the player to the drum.

TIP: *A good first lesson on bass drum might be to play without mallets. By pointing the thumbs up and doing the forearm rotation as with this technique, the thumbs will follow the path of the mallets. This is an excellent way for beginners to learn the feel and path of these strokes.*

The motion of the wrist/arm during the stroke is similar to turning a doorknob. This mindset will allow the stick to travel in a straight line, perpendicular to the playing surface. The most significant playing difference between bass drummers and other members of the battery is their increased use of forearm for louder playing (it is quite challenging to play bass drum only with wrist and fingers).

Bass drummers should be concerned with stick heights, just like any other member of the battery. In general, assuming a *5-person* bass drum line, the "easier" drums to play are drums *3* and *5* (the largest). This is because when playing runs up and down the drums, basses *1, 3,* and *5* will more frequently fall on the downbeats while drums *2* and *4* tend to alter their patterns. The bass drummer with the best technical abilities probably should play drum 1 (the smallest) and the player with the best timing should probably play drum *2* (second smallest).

TIP: *In the beginning, place a piece of plastic tape in the center of each bass drum head. The players will be able to feel the tape with their mallet heads and can check their positioning on their own. After muscle memory develops for finding the center, take the tape away.*

THE SYSTEM: X. MARCHING PERCUSSION / BATTERY INSTRUMENTS

CYMBALS

The cymbal section represents the most visual portion of the marching band beyond the auxiliary groups. It is not only their job to accent the music through crashes and other effects, but to add color to the show through their visuals. Unfortunately, cymbal players are often ignored or treated as lesser musicians, which is grossly unfair. Cymbal players must appreciate that they are playing a musical instrument with a proper technique, and their contribution must be valued. When teaching and talking to cymbalists, make sure to talk about playing (not hitting) their instrument (not things). By showing them respect, they will develop confidence, and a sense of importance.

There are two standard methods of holding crash cymbals for the marching band:

    1. Garfield Grip
    2. Traditional Grip

In the *Garfield Grip*, the cymbals are gripped by putting the hand through the strap, turning the whole unit and re-gripping the strap in the pocket between the thumb and index finger. In this grip, the straps need to be lengthened to fit the hands.

In the traditional cymbal grip, the player tightens the straps so

Garfield Grip

that his/her hand fits snug into the opening and then pinches the strap between the thumb and first knuckle of the index finger.

In both grips, it is important to keep the finger tips off of the cymbal as this will dampen the vibrations of the cymbal. Pads should not be used on crash cymbals because they will get tiring. Cymbalists should rather wear leather gloves on both

hands. These can be purchased from marching band supply

Traditional Grip

companies as color guard gloves, sporting goods stores as baseball *batter's gloves,* or football receiver's gloves.

Crashes may be executed vertically or horizontally. The most important thing to do when executing a full crash is make sure that both cymbals *flam* with one edge hitting just before the other, as opposed to hitting the cymbals straight-on. Crashing straight-on will produce an air pocket and no sound. Dampening the cymbals can be done with either the forearms or the chest. Whichever method is chosen, make sure the sound is completely cut-off.

There are a variety of cymbal sounds available beyond the basic crash. Cymbals can be tapped by striking the edge of one cymbal against the inside of the other. Cymbals can be scraped by dragging the edge along the rings of the other cymbal. Cymbal *rolls* are done by stirring the edges of both cymbals together to produce a sustained sound. *Forte-piano* cymbal crashes are produced by making a full crash and immediately dampening one of the cymbals. *Fusion crashes* (or *slide-chokes*) are produced by dragging the top cymbal across the bottom cymbal after a crash, and quickly pulling it back dome to dome. They can be smashed together for a short sound effect. As far as visuals are concerned, your imagination is the limit; just follow the same rule as drumming. If a visual inhibits the music, remove it, because music is always more important than the visuals.

Along with developing your musicianship skills, you must also develop your physical forearm and upper arm strength because cymbals are much heavier than many people assume. Organize group stretches and strengthening activities such as push-ups, chin-ups, hanging time, and especially time spent holding the cymbals in an up-position.

The Ensemble

TOPICS

- Attacks
- Visual Aspects
- Balanced Instrumentation
- Drill Positioning

Attacks

The first note of each phrase is called the attack. It must be played precisely together like all other notes. To play clean attacks, every member should *dut*. *Dutting* is oral subdividing of the beat whereby each member vocalizes the syllable *dut* on the pulses. Any rest, quarter note or longer, should be *dutted* through. Also, sharp visuals and stick clicks that are inaudible to the audience, may be used just as effectively. For timing, when starting a phrase, remember to execute a clean, sharp, "sticks out" two beats, before the attack. Attacks should never be bad when the players adhere to the section leader tapping-off, the sticks-out visual, and group *dutting* to aid in establishing pulse. A bad attack is the sign of a lack of concentration from the members.

To maintain steady time and precision, everyone in the snare and tenor lines should listen in toward the center of their section. The center snare drummer is responsible for the time of the battery percussion section, when standing still. It is his/her job to play exactly in time. All other snare drummers need only be concerned about listening in, and playing together with the person inside of them. The center tenor drummer should listen to and watch the hands of the center snare drummer and play exactly in time with him/her. All other tenor drummers should be concerned only about the person inside of them. Non-center players are concerned only with themselves and playing precisely with the person inside of them.

Bass drummers each must watch the conductor; they share responsibility for the bass drum line. If ensemble problems exist in rehearsal, it is often a good idea to have only the center snare player, the center tenor player, and the bass drum line play to make sure they are together, and then add other players one at a time.

Due to the properties of sound, players should always listen backfield when playing together on the field. The center player positioned farthest back, (be it snare or tenor) watches and plays along with the conductor. Everyone in front of him/her should listen back. Listening far across the field can be dangerous; often, a phrase will sound misaligned on the field but will sound correct to the audience. It is essential for the director to listen from above during rehearsals. For larger bands, consider having multiple conductors spread around the field.

> **TIP:** *Percussionists should wear earplugs whenever playing rudimental percussion. The overwhelming volume can lead to long-term hearing damage. They should be worn during rehearsals and performances to allow players to adjust to hearing the sound in the same manner. For serious involvement in the endeavor, consider purchasing the best earplugs available.*

Visual Aspects

For the snare line and tenor line, try to keep all the drums at approximately the same height. This is difficult to do, as students will be of various heights and sizes. Nevertheless, few things look more bizarre in a marching band, than a line of uneven drums. The sticks should also be in line at rest position so that they look like one long rope across the *drum-line*.

When playing, always pick a point off in the distance, and stare at it with a look of determination. The players should appear neither entranced nor enraged; they should simply look and be relaxed, yet confident.

When in a form, align the form through the bodies of the players, not through their drums. Imagine what a line would look like if a snare drummer aligned his/her instrument with the largest bass drum, instead aligning his/her body with that player. There would be no sense of line to the form.

When dressing forms in parades, the best idea is to dress the snare, tenor, and cymbal lines center and have the bass drums dress off the smallest drum for front to back distance.

The purpose of visuals is to help with timing, and enhance the show. If a visual ever leads to a musical problem, remove it. Again, the music is always more important than the visuals.

Visuals should always be sharp and defined for a specific count. Their purpose is to fill rests, and aid in clean attacks. Remember that the most frequently seen visual is the sticks in/out; this should always be perfect.

The worst thing one can do to one's own body while drumming is to lean backwards while wearing his/her drum. This can lead to long-term back troubles for the musician. If players want to stretch, they should lean forward over the drums, letting gravity and their shoulders support the weight of the instrument. Never lean back, putting all of the weight on the small of the back.

Balanced Instrumentation

Try to avoid a section with one player. If this is unavoidable, have either one cymbal player or one tenor drummer; try to have multiple snares and basses. Five is the preferred number of bass drummers, and four or six are acceptable. A good rule for snares and tenors, is to have twice as many snares as tenors. For example, *9-10 snares* and *5 tenors*, *7-8 snares* and

4 tenors, *5-6 snares* and *3 tenors*, *3-4 snares* and *2 tenors*, *1-2 snares* and *1 tenor*. The drum line needs at least half as many cymbal players as snare drummers so they can ride on the cymbals and this can go all the way up to a *1:1 ratio*.

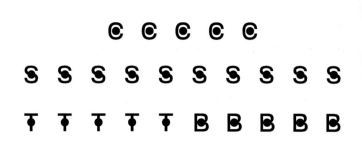

A trend in marching percussion, has been to eliminate the cymbal section and cover their parts in the front ensemble (assuming there is one). Disadvantages to this includes the loss of visual impact, by marching fewer members on the field. A major advantage is, that it permits more musical contributions and learning for the students, than crashing cymbals affords.

Drill Positioning

Within the drum line, it is important that the most consistent snare drummer stand in the middle of the snare line, and the most consistent tenor drummer stand in the middle of the tenor line. The order of players should progress outward in terms of ability. Even if the line does not look visually appealing, it is important to increase in talent as you move inward. This is for listening purposes (*see Attacks topic*). If there is an even number of players, decide who the "center player" is, and pair him/her with the next most talented percussionist.

For spacing, keep snare drummers in a one and one half or *2-step* interval, and the tenors and basses in a *3* or *4-step* interval. These intervals can be opened (never put snares farther apart than four steps), but they cannot be compacted, as the size of the equipment in use will not allow it. Cymbal players can stage as closely as two steps apart, or can be opened up to four steps, to accommodate visuals.

There are no absolute rules relating to drill formations for the percussion section, just suggested positions that make ensemble listening easier. Avoid putting the drum line in a vertical file. Not only will they have difficulty hearing each other, but they also cannot watch each other's sticks. Putting the entire drum line in a horizontal line should also be avoided, as the length of the spread could potentially reach twenty yards (enough room to cause the line to phase within itself).

Arcs and angular polygons are the best forms to use. It is easiest for a drum line to play together, when everyone can see and hear each other. When charting a form, try to put the snare line in the center, and the bass drums and tenors on either side. The cymbals can be at one end of the form, or in front of, or behind the snare drums. It is also a good idea to keep the bass drums to "stage left" of the snares, facing up the form. That way, when they play the drum with their right hand, (as they more often will) the sound will travel toward the audience.

Concave forms are preferred over convex forms. This is because it is easier for the players to look inward in a concave form. However, if charting a convex form, try not to position an inside member of one section as the point. Try to make the apex the interval between two sections, or the end player of one of the sections. Try to keep the drum line behind the front hash when

they are playing. Of course, during drum solos, stage the drum line on the front of the field.

Many inexperienced drill writers neglect to consider the importance of cymbal charting, when the snares will be playing ride figures on the cymbals during the music. Chart the cymbals in front of the snares during those phrases, and allow them time to get there and back. Another common mistake, is not recognizing that bass drums and tenors are heavy instruments, that cannot easily do sharp turns with the rest of the band. Quick turns look sloppy and usually lead to collisions. Slow turns are better ways for these players to change direction.

These guidelines describe marching percussion drill Utopia; in reality, an occasional horizontal form, or quick vertical pass through may be necessary. These are acceptable as long as they are not held for extended periods. Likewise, convex forms are acceptable (and better than horizontal/vertical lines), but a drill writer should not chart the drum line in such a position during a drum solo, or a difficult musical section.

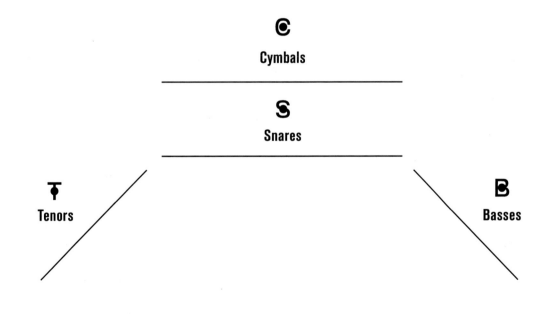

Equipment

Recommendations

Due to the rate of industry innovation, marching percussion equipment is adapted and "improved" faster than any other equipment in the band. Always consult with a rudimentary percussion expert before making a major purchase. In general, use equipment from reputable manufacturers. If their company spends significant money advertising in magazines, or if top drum corps/college bands use their instruments, you can probably rely on them.

Consider purchasing *14"* free-floating snare drums. These instruments are the current standard and can withstand the tension of contemporary articulate tuning. The smaller *13"* drums are also common, particularly for indoor percussion, but they do not project as well outside with a large number of wind players.

For high school tenors, buy quads sized *8"–10"–12"–14"* or quints sized *6"– 8"–10"–12"–14"*. Some college drum lines use quints with sizes *6"–10"–12"–13"–14"* or *8"–10"–12"–13"–14"* because the students are bigger and can carry the larger drums which will project better in large stadiums. Also, many bands/corps have two 6" shot drums instead of one, giving a total of six drums.

High school bass drums should be evenly distributed between *16"* and *26"*. You may occasionally encounter a high school student can carry a *28"* drum, but it is generally best not to exceed the *26"* size. *20"* cymbals are common for college ensembles, but most high school musicians cannot hold anything larger than *18"* cymbals for an extended time period.

There are specific cymbals intended for marching band/drum corps. Purchase these, as they are thicker and will have a more substantive sound outdoors.

Care & Maintenance

When storing or moving drums, always put them in cases. The storage area in the band room should have carpet to rest the drums on, even in each individual locker.

Every drum, cymbal, and carrier should be numbered and assigned to specific players, so as to eliminate confusion about whose instrument is whose.

All sticks should be taped with plastic tape at all times. This protects the sticks and unifies their color (eliminating the appearance of different shades of wood). Do not use cloth tape; it wears off too easily.

When taking breaks during rehearsal, always set the instruments down in an organized form. This is a major part of a line's discipline, it looks professional, and it helps protect the drums.

Never set a snare drum down on the snare side. Always put it on its shell, even if it comes equipped with "feet."

During rehearsals, bed sheets or commercially available drum covers should be wrapped around the drums to protect the shells from sun fading.

When changing drum heads, run paraffin (wax) around the bearing edge of the shell and put a dab of wheel bearing grease on each tension rod to lubricate the lugs and casings. Periodically throughout the year, tighten all the screws on the drums and carriers. They will loosen on their own due to the normal vibrations of playing.

Tuning Drums

by **Jim Bailey**

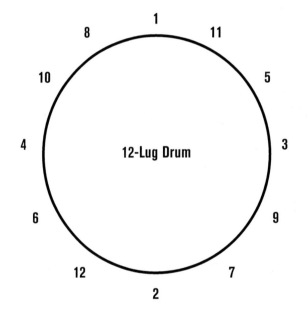

THE SNARE

1. Mount the top head, and finger-tighten all lugs to equal tension.

2. Using the appropriate sequential tuning method, continue tuning until the drum is within general marching snare tuning range.

3. Select a pitch for your top and bottom heads. I suggest using an "A" for the batter head, and a "D" for the snare-side head. Tune your top head up to pitch using a chromatic tuner.

4. Using the same techniques listed above in steps 1-3, tune the bottom head.

5. Disengage the snare strainer and turn the drum upside down as illustrated. Place a pen between the snares and the drumhead, so the snares can resonate freely.

6. Using a small screwdriver, tune the individual snares up until they resonate and produce the same pitch.

7. Remove the pen. Engage the snare strainer, turn the drum over, and rest on a stand.

8. Use the snare tension knob on the side of your drum to adjust the snare response, until you reach your desired sound.

TIP: *Beware of over-tightened snare drums. Aside from damage to the player's hands and the instrument, marching snares that are tuned too high do not have a lot of projection and don't blend well with other instruments.*

263

THE TENORS

1. Mount all heads and finger-tighten all lugs to equal tension.

2. Starting with the largest drum, use the appropriate sequential tuning method and use ½ turns on each lug, until the drum is within its general tuning range. As you bring the head up to range, use a stick to tap in front of each lug, to ensure that each lug produces an identical clear tone. Select a specific pitch and tune using a chromatic tuner

3. When selecting specific pitches, refer to the chart as a guideline.

4. Repeat steps 1-3 with the rest of your drums, tuning all drums in reverse order of size. Use a chromatic tuner to ensure the correct interval.

Size	Pitch
6"	F#
8"	C#
10"	A
12"	F#
13"	D
14"	B♭

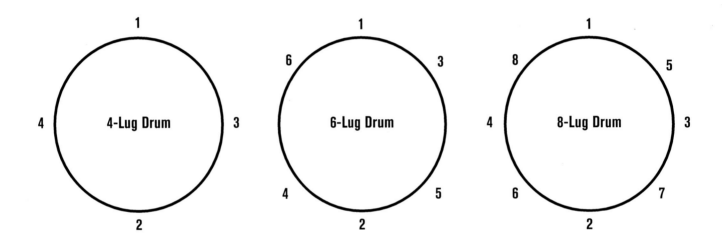

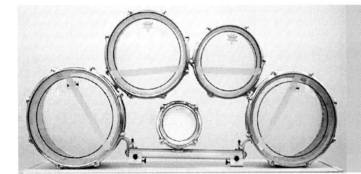

TIP: *Be sure to use a tuning device to ensure pitch accuracy. Tuning using this method will not only ensure proper tuning; it will decrease damage caused by over-tightening.*

THE BASS DRUM

1. Rest the drum on a table, so you can access both heads at the same time.

2. Before mounting heads, be sure to clean the rim and bearing edge of any debris.

3. Mount both heads and finger-tighten lugs to equal tension.

4. Starting with the largest drum, use the sequential tuning method to bring each head within its tuning range. Use a mallet to tap in front of each lug, to ensure that all lugs produce an identical clear tone.

5. Working between the two drum heads, bring both heads up to the desired pitch.

6. Recheck the pitch by tapping in front of each lug to ensure the head is clear of overtones; and in the center, to ensure both heads are at the same pitch.

7. Once you have the largest drum tuned, follow steps 2-6 for the remaining drums. Pitch intervals between drums depends on the size of the drums used. Experiment and select a tuning scheme that provides the best balance of articulation, and resonance.

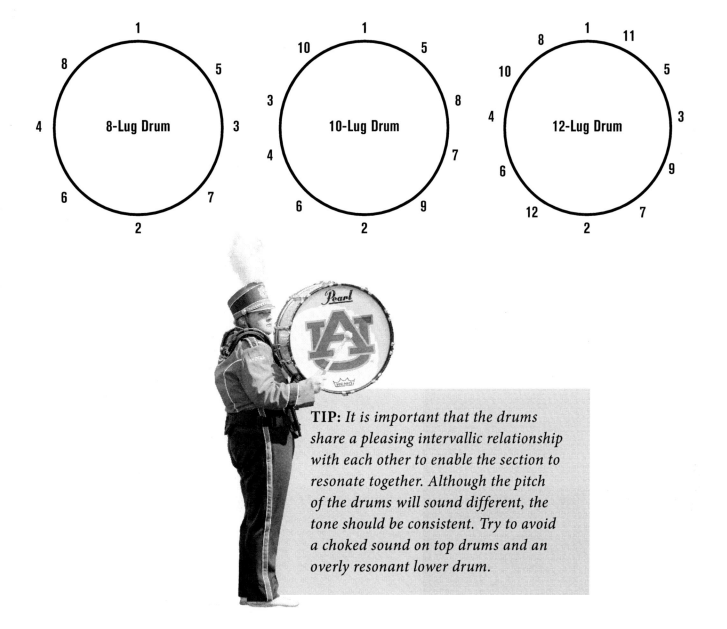

TIP: *It is important that the drums share a pleasing intervallic relationship with each other to enable the section to resonate together. Although the pitch of the drums will sound different, the tone should be consistent. Try to avoid a choked sound on top drums and an overly resonant lower drum.*

Technique Exercises

by **Tom Keck**

The following pages contain introductory technique exercises for the developing percussionist and drum line. These may be used for fundamental development until a percussion specialist can customize a warm-up program for your ensemble. At all times players should strive for relaxed motions that produce an open, resonant tone quality.

Eight on a Hand

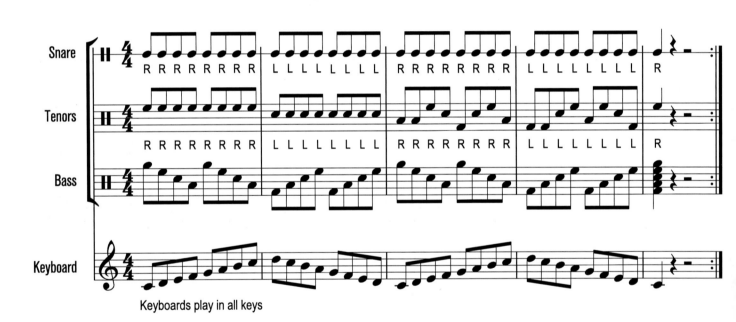

Keyboards play in all keys

Accent Tap

West Coast Singles

Subdivisions

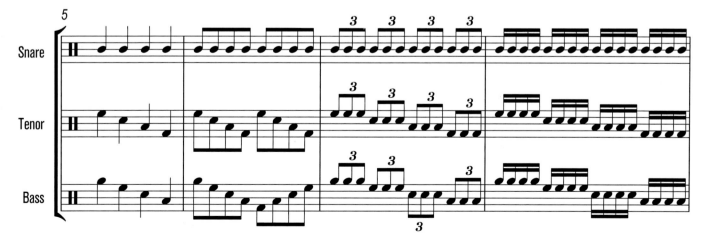

Two's and Three's

Stick Control

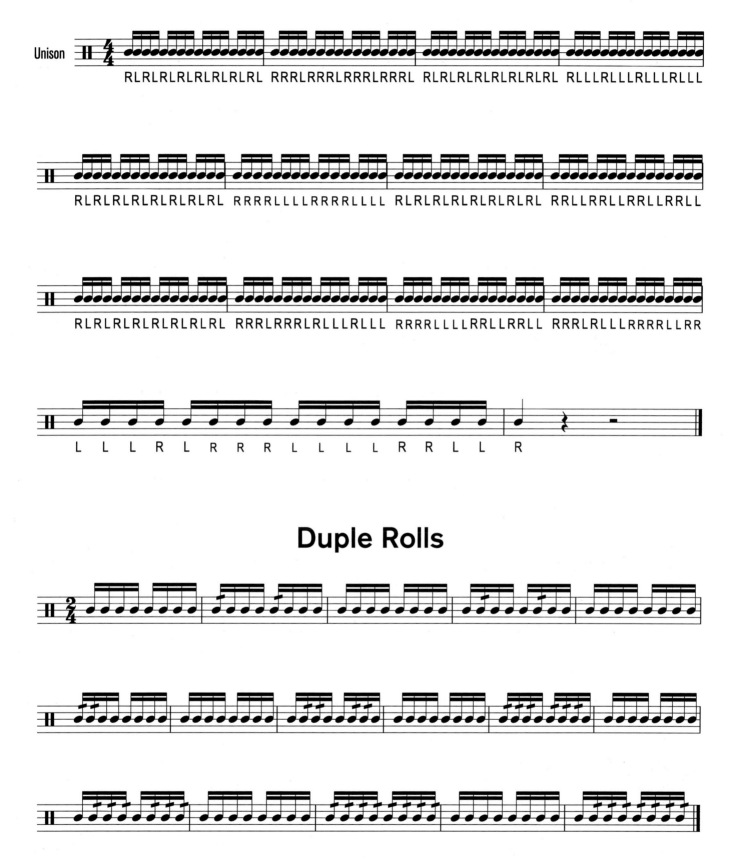

RLRLRLRLRLRLRLRL   RRRLRRRLRRRLRRRL   RLRLRLRLRLRLRLRL   RLLLRLLLRLLLRLLL

RLRLRLRLRLRLRLRL   RRRRLLLLRRRRLLLL   RLRLRLRLRLRLRLRL   RRLLRRLLRRLLRRLL

RLRLRLRLRLRLRLRL   RRRLRRRLRLLLRLLL   RRRRLLLLRRLLRRLL   RRRLRLLLRRRRLLRR

L L L R L R R R L L L L R R L L   R

Duple Rolls

THE SYSTEM: X. MARCHING PERCUSSION / EXERCISES

XI. THE COLORGUARD

by **Sara K. Clark Maccabee**

Getting Started

TOPICS

- Auditions
- Equipment & Supplies
- Staff
- Show Design
- Rehearsal Techniques
- Common Troubleshooting

An integral part of any successful marching program is the color guard. Flags provide the pageantry to enhance the musical program, by capturing the mood of the music, and adding visual interest for the audience. Ideally, the performers will reflect visually what the listener is hearing—both with colors that pop, and movement that expresses. Establishing a solid color guard program may seem daunting to someone who has not had any experience twirling, or teaching choreography, but this chapter should serve as a basic framework for what to do, and what to expect when setting up an auxiliary line.

Auditions

Auditions for your color guard will likely take place in the spring of the school year to allow for summer marching band rehearsals and camps. There are different thoughts regarding who should be included in a color guard. Some directors don't want to take away musicians from the field, so guard members are required to be non-band members. Other directors prefer to have musicians in their color guard, since they are already familiar with count structure, rhythm, melodic line, etc. The decision is often based on the size of the band program; if there are enough musicians to spare to the auxiliary unit, it is best to include as many band members as you can.

There are reasons for this beyond simple musical understanding. Band members tend to have an inherent loyalty to the marching band and understand their role as part of a "whole", rather than separating themselves into a detached unit. Oftentimes, directors will choose to limit guard membership to woodwind players, only to preserve the size of their brass and percussion lines. This makes good sense, and is an excellent compromise when possible. Both female and male students can be encouraged to participate in color guard.

A sign-up sheet for color guard auditions should be placed in the high school band room, as well as the middle school band room, if freshman will be accepted into the program. Announcements over the PA system are helpful to let band and non- band members know that auditions are being scheduled. The number of students auditioning will vary by the size of the program. A typical marching band with *120 musicians* will likely have a color guard numbering around *20*, but more is always better as long as the group performs well. Ideally, more students will audition than will be taken onto the squad.

There should be a level of competence expected during the process, and even if not everyone who signs up, makes the squad, a helpful standard is being set for the future. Also, students should wear proper attire for the clinics and auditions. Yoga pants and t-shirts are acceptable along with gym shoes. Absolutely no sandals, flip flops, or jeans should be allowed because these impede movement.

One way to conduct auditions is to hold instructional clinics for four days, either after school, or in the evenings on a Monday through Thursday. On the fifth day (Friday), students will be asked to perform a short routine, and go through some basics that were presented during the earlier clinic sessions.

THE FOLLOWING IS AN EXAMPLE OF WHAT THE CLINIC/ AUDITION WEEK CAN INCLUDE:

Monday

Distribute numbered practice flags to students (these will be collected at the end of auditions on the final day).

Put the students in a rehearsal block with returning members, distributed throughout the block. Returning seniors can be put in the front of each file so the new students have someone to watch, and learn technique from.

Begin with basic positions such as order arms, shoulder arms, presents, lances, and slams. Teach the positions, as well as commands, to move to those positions along with a clapped tempo. This will help the students achieve the right amount of precision and effort, from the outset of handling a flagpole.

The specific skills taught as basics, will vary from one color guard instructor to another. As long as skills are being built, it really doesn't matter which style the instructor embraces.

Teach a basic *dropspin* sequence of *8 counts*, with a hold at shoulder arms for 4 counts. Start slowly and build tempo as skills improve. Students can be asked to do *8 consecutive sets* of this sequence (or as many as necessary to exhibit competence).

Begin to teach a choreographed routine to recorded music. Be sure a decent amplification system is used so everyone can hear. A simple and efficient option is to teach the school song routine, since it will likely be used for parades and pre-game shows anyway. If that seems too humdrum, a choreographed routine to some popular music can be used, as that sometimes piques the group's interest and gets them excited. This routine should be no more than 64 counts because there is limited time to teach in four days. If a single rotation toss is included somewhere in this routine, be prepared to spend extra time teaching it. The ability level of the group can be gauged after seeing them work for a day or two. This may influence a decision about the need to simplify things, or challenge them further.

Tuesday-Thursday
Continue to work on basics to commands, *dropspins*, and the choreographed routine. You may not get through the latter until the Thursday clinic.

Teach marching basics, such as 16 counts of forward glide step and 16 counts of jazz step. Students may march in pairs so they don't feel so self-conscious.

Don't be concerned if you have some students who decide not to audition after attending a clinic or two. Color guard isn't for everybody. Do be sure they turn in their flag, though. Attendance can be taken for each clinic session, just as an indication of commitment and interest. Ultimately, however, it is the audition that counts.

During the clinic sessions, keep an eye on the returning members to begin to assess who might be assigned leadership roles for the upcoming season. Typically, these are strong seniors who have been in the group for a number of seasons, but sometimes it is nice to have juniors and seniors both as captains. This really depends on personalities and judgment.

It is helpful to break out into small groups to review skills, balancing each group with returning members, and new students. Small groups with a maximum of 5 or 6 is optimal.

Friday (Audition Day)
Be sure the students are dressed for auditions. Yoga pants and t-shirts are acceptable along with gym shoes. Alternatively, they can wear their gym uniforms, if that makes it easier to judge. Each student should be assigned a number to wear on their shirt for identification purposes.

Establish a panel of judges, and provide them with clipboards and a chart to write down their impressions as the audition progresses. The panel can include the band director(s), the guard instructor(s), any other member of the marching band staff that seems appropriate, and perhaps former color guard captains.

Predetermine groups of four to audition at a time, for the basic skills portion, and choreographed routine. For example, the numbers for the shirts; the first group can be called *#1-4*. This alleviates some of the pressure and enables the group to be arranged so there is at least one strong member in each. To assess their marching skills, have them go in pairs according to their number.

Allow time for call backs, since invariably there are a few people

who are borderline and will need to audition again. Often, students will ask for another chance regardless. Remember that one is looking for potential, not perfection.

It is also helpful if you know the background of the students. Some schools require signatures from all current teachers, before allowing students to audition for cheerleading, color guard, etc. This allows forewarning about potential problems with attendance, grades, attitudes, etc. Sometimes it tips the balance when faced with difficult choices.

The judging panel can confer after the students are dismissed and then post the results the following day. This is also when leaders of the group will be designated. Two captains per 20 members works well, but again this will vary from one guard to the next.

If rifles and/or sabers are being included in the color guard, hold separate auditions for these sections so the students are not overwhelmed trying to learn so much at one time. The weapons line should first and foremost be skilled with the flag; weapons can be added on after they have established proficiency.

Equipment & Supplies

Once the marching band show has been designed, the number of sets of flags and other equipment needed will be set. Try to have the same number of practice flags on hand as show flags. Requiring the guard to put practice flags on each of their poles will save wear and tear on the show flags.

The current trend is to have longer rather than shorter flag poles (6'-6.5') as the mainstay. Typically, one can choose from aluminum poles or fiberglass poles. The latter are a bit heavier but less prone to dents and bending. Poles come in many different colors so they can be adapted to the color scheme in the show. A basic supply of black, white, silver, and gold poles is a good start as they coordinate with many different colored flags. To branch out a bit, PVC piping can be incorporated for extra length or special effects. Inexpensive t-poles can be made with PVC and pipe joints, too. For example, swing flags can even be made using dowel rods and chain flags, with chain purchased at any home improvement/hardware center.

In addition to the poles, caps will be needed for each end of each pole. There are many different kinds on the market, but steer clear of the cheap plastic end caps that come with the poles and be certain to buy full sets of white, and black rubber end caps (they look larger in the catalogs and are shaped like

Apollo 13). Again, coordinate these with the colors of the flags and the poles. Have extras available as they tend to go missing. Some programs ask their guard members to purchase crutch tips for their own use, but the uniformity factor is missing when everyone is buying for themselves.

Flags themselves can be purchased ready-made or flag kits can be bought if willing band parents are available to sew them together. A word of warning: The kits are complicated and can be frustrating for band parents to complete. The last thing one wants is a group of frustrated band parents. Many companies offer the option to design original flags, too. All of these options come at a variety of costs. Another viable option for saving money and for sustainability efforts is to buy used flags from drum corps or other band programs. Most drum corps have an area on their website with used equipment for sale, and there are several online shops to locate full, and partial sets of flags, uniforms, and equipment.

As mentioned earlier, it's very helpful for guard members to have practice flags for each of the poles they will be using during the season. This will preserve the show flags from in-evitable wear and tear. Once students are assigned numbers for the drill, they should label each piece of equipment with their number and make sure this is kept readable all season. To label poles, they can put a piece of white electrical tape just above the bottom end cap and use a Sharpie to write the number. Flags can also be labeled discreetly with a Sharpie, if they have not already been numbered in past seasons. Obviously, rifles and sabers and other props can be numbered.

It's a great idea to distribute show flags in a *Ziploc* bag with the appropriately numbered flags inside the matching numbered bag. This makes the collection process at the end of the season easy too.

Groups have different methods of transporting equipment, often depending on the proximity of the practice field to the band room or the school. Some groups have fun with crafting flag bags out of old men's jeans from *Goodwill*. The pair of jeans can be cut in half, and then have the single leg stitched closed, fashioning a strap handle out of the discarded leg. Poles fit quite well inside the jean leg—the longer the inseam the better. Each member can personalize their flag bag with fabric paint, patches, etc. Some groups have the luxury of canvas flag bags provided by the school, or some students may opt to purchase zippered bags from a band supply retailer. Regardless, the items that each guard member should include in his or her flag bag are, electrical tape in both black and white, small scissors, and a *Sharpie* pen. Nothing slows down the process of changing out practice flags to show flags, than

having too much electrical tape and Sharpies from others. Guard members may also opt to store their gloves and drill books in the flag bag, so everything is always in one place.

The guard instructor will have a clear plan in terms of what color tape to use on each pole so the group has a consistent look. It is not necessary to use yards and yards of tape to attach each end of the flag to the pole nor is it necessary to elaborately tape on the end caps. If more weight is needed in the end caps, the guard instructor may choose to use carriage bolts or washers taped into the end caps. This will be very specific to each instructor and performer, as the students learn more complicated tosses that require finely balanced poles. Let it be noted, that carriage bolts can be extremely distracting in quiet portions of the show, if they are not taped in properly. Every band director has heard that tell-tale "rattle" in the midst of an otherwise beautiful pianissimo phrase on the marching field.

Rifles come with their own set of taping instructions to protect them from breakage. Be sure that guard members consult the instructor or the manufacturer guidelines regarding the use of strapping tape and electrical tape on new rifles.

Uniforms

Color guard uniforms can range from the simplest of designs, (jazz pants and tunic) to the most complex, and sometimes outlandish costumes imaginable. The choice will depend upon the show design and budget. As with flags, there are many companies out there with ready-made products to purchase or with custom designs to pre-order, with specific measurements for each student. Sometimes one piece, like stretch pants, can be purchased at a local department store then add a custom made tunic. The guard instructor should be included in the decision process, as he or she will have something in mind to coordinate with the show.

If a program doesn't have the budget or inclination to change uniforms each year, one should purchase something understated and tasteful in colors that coordinate with the band uniforms, without completely matching them. The most important thing to keep in mind regarding the color guard uniform, is that it should be as flattering as possible for all the body types out there on the field. This saves discomfort for the guard member and negative distraction for the band. Also keep weather conditions in mind. What works well for a winter guard program that performs solely indoors, may not adapt to all outdoor climates in the fall.

The guard uniform will also include shoes, gloves, and possibly headpieces. There are a variety of good jazz shoes on the market. Go for the sturdiest ones that match the style of the uniform. Most groups wear either tan or black jazz shoes. In terms of guard gloves, most suppliers carry the padded palm, fingerless style, in tan or black. These are wonderful for protection and gripping purposes for flag twirlers,, and rifle or saber spinners. They are a great investment, but the students should practice wearing them all the time to break them in and to get used to the feel of them.

Headpieces can be glitzy or understated, depending on the style of the marching band or the current show. Lately, more attention has been given to hairstyles and hair extensions than to headpieces. Both can be problematic with weather conditions, and varying hair styles, so choose with care.

Staff

Marching band programs may include a staff of technicians for each section, and a cadre of color guard specialists, along with two or three band directors. Most band programs have to be more streamlined. At the minimum, it is very helpful to have one color guard instructor who writes and teaches all of the guard work for the season, and who is available for continuity throughout the season (attends most of the rehearsals and all competitions).

In addition, it is beneficial to have one assistant to help with cleaning the guard work and running sectionals when the instructor is not available. That second pair of eyes is very helpful when trying to clean a show as one person can be on the field and one person can watch from a higher position (up in the bleachers, perhaps). Often the assistant can be a graduate of the program who went on to participate in their university marching band or drum corps. I would caution against employing or even utilizing as a volunteer any very recent graduates, as they tend to spend their time at rehearsals visiting with their old pals instead of digging into real teaching. Moreover, the current students will have less respect for somebody they just marched with a year ago, than for somebody who is more mature and experienced.

Compensation for the staff will obviously depend upon the budget. In general though, one can expect to pay an instructor a separate amount for writing the equipment work and choreography for the show. If a school purchases a show design that is already packaged with pre-written guard work, then they can simply pay the instructor a set amount of money for their teaching and time for the season. The assistant generally receives a bit less, depending on his or her time commitment and experience. Sometimes there may be competent volunteers to help. In general, these people typically fade away as the season progresses.

Show Design

Ideally, the lead guard instructor should be included in the decision-making process when choosing the musical program for the season. Collaboration with the drill writer and music arranger is crucial to create a unified show concept, even before the design process begins. Too many seasons are ruined before they start because the "theme" or "concept" has not been thought through, with several creative minds contributing to the discussion. The competitive marching band activity has become so sophisticated, that success will require careful planning in the winter or spring of the previous school year.

Themes, Concepts and Colors

Usually the theme of the show will be coupled with the music that is chosen, and in turn, the theme will dictate colors of flags, and choice of guard uniform. For example, if a band is performing *Stravinsky's Firebird*, one would expect to see brilliant hues of reds, oranges, and yellows, perhaps contrasted with blacks and purples. If the musical selection is more along the lines of Debussy, softer pastel hues would likely be incorporated. Also to be considered are make-up and hair styles to coordinate with the uniform and the theme. Keeping things simple makes preparation time shorter, and allows the guard to focus on the more important task of performing well for any given show or competition. Try to limit details to those that are visible to the audience, and to those that help the performers *get into character*.

Drill Integration

The importance of appropriate drill integration for the color guard cannot be emphasized enough. In this day and age, it is no longer sufficient to simply frame the band with an arc or files of flags. The drill writer needs to move the color guard through and among the musicians, to be sure there is visual variety and color, to emphasize musical phrasing. Think of the visual production as a kaleidoscope, with the color guard creating moving color elements among the uniformity of the band members. Judges and audiences alike will appreciate the creativity of what they are seeing and hearing.

It might be easier to describe proper drill integration in terms

of what not to do. First, don't stage your guard in one place, and leave them there for an entire piece, or (even worse) the entire show. Avoid staging the guard solely on one side of the band, because they look like an afterthought, tacked on by a novice drill writer. Furthermore, refrain from placing the guard members too close together, or too far apart. The former leads to collisions of equipment, and lots of negative space on the field; the latter leads to lack of visual cohesion, and lack of confidence in the younger performers. Think critically about how to incorporate equipment changes. There is nothing more aggravating from a judge's perspective, or more distracting for audience members, to have the music stop while watching untrained jogging guard members sloppily exchanging one flag for another, on a sideline or yard line, and then lope back to where they started and assume the position to begin the next piece. There are cases when someone runs the new piece of equipment out to the guard members on the field to make the exchange. Do not allow anything resembling this action, to avoid poor ratings from a judge.

What is the solution? The drill writer, in conjunction with the guard instructor, will literally write the equipment changes into the show. Ideally, they will occur organically within the musical construct (a fancy way of saying the exchange will be layered so not every guard member leaves the field at once). This will allow for some soloist opportunities to showcase stronger members, while the others drift out of center focus momentarily.

Deciding how many performers to include in any given portion of the show is also a design element to be considered carefully. There is no law that says everyone should play all the time. In fact, there is a great deal of benefit to creating visual variety by using smaller groups in various ways and then bring everyone together for a large visual and musical impact point. If rifles and/or sabers are incorporated, for example, they will generally travel as a separate unit from the flags until an impact point is required.

Choreography

The process of writing choreography is unique to every guard instructor. In general, it is tantamount that the guard instructor has in hand the drill, the musical score, and a recording of the musical arrangement. This recording can be an electronic version created by the music arranger's software as long as it is accurate in terms of tempos and includes a click track. The click track is especially helpful if the guard instructor intends to use the recording in rehearsals. The choreographer will look at the count structures of the drill and compare it to the score to create the visual phrases presented by the performers' bodies and equipment. On the most basic of levels, the choreographer will want to take into account any complicated pass-through involving guard members and musicians to avoid collisions.

The *choreographer* will also need to look at equipment changes to make sure that they are creative and don't interrupt the visual story. Most importantly, the choreographer will want to make sure the equipment work reflects the musical phrasing, creating highs and lows of intensity to match what the audience is hearing. The best color guards will always integrate the three key elements of body, form, and equipment into their performances—layering of dance work and footwork underneath the equipment while maintaining correct placement within the drill is the ultimate goal.

The *guard instructor*, therefore, will need a fair amount of lead time before they begin to teach the show to the color guard. This pushes the process back into the winter time in terms of planning, because he or she will need all completed elements before it is possible to write the choreography (music and drill). In many cases, the show will be taught in a separate color guard "camp" (perhaps lasting a week or two) prior to the actual band "camp" during the summer. If the guard members know their equipment work prior to starting rehearsals with the full band, they will be able to incorporate it AS they learn drill with everyone. It can be likened to the musicians knowing their music prior to the beginning of learning drill—everyone starts off more confidently and the likelihood of success is high.

It is really helpful if the *choreographer* can actually write out the routines to assist the guard members in retaining what they learn. This is usually done with the count structure of the drill in mind, so the routine sheets might look something like the following example.

To Set 15-20 counts: front arc continues to expand backfield

1-8	Right Butterfly ending at RP
9-10	Counterclockwise cone to RP
11-12	Continue rotation down to parallel at R waist (turning torso to R) —tip facing behind you
13-16	360 turn to left maintaining flag
17-18	Raise parallel pole to overhead, torso still to R
19-20	Turning torso to FSL, row tip down to L to end at RS

If the guard members can receive routine sheets and copies of the recording, they will be able to practice on their own time (and have no excuses as to why they did not do so). At the very least, there should be more consistency in what they remember if it is written down on paper, and it's a great reference for both the lead instructor and assistant(s).

Rehearsal Techniques

Summer Guard Camp

The structure of the summer guard camp will often revolve around the availability of the instructor and assistant(s). Some band programs send their color guards off-premise to a camp to learn an entire show in one week with morning, afternoon, and evening sessions, catered meals, and cabins. This is becoming rarer as students have increased work commitments of their own.

More commonly, the guard will have a morning session, break for lunch, and then have an afternoon session with the evenings off. If this is problematic, the guard can always meet in the morning and evening, or in the afternoon and evening.

Use caution if requiring students to be in session from 8 a.m. until 8 p.m. with only meal breaks. That is a long day and their bodies and brains will be "fried." Regardless, encourage or require the students to bring water jugs and sunscreen and to dress appropriately for sun exposure (tee shirts, shorts, socks, tennis shoes). They will want to wear tanks and sports bras, but by day three you will have students that are so sunburn they can barely function. Furthermore, it's a good idea to encourage **all** of the marching band members to stay active in the summer so the rigors of guard camp/percussion camp/band camp don't come as a shock to their couch potato systems.

The morning sessions can be half devoted to learning basics of equipment, body movement, and marching. The other half of the morning and much of the afternoon can be used to teach the guard work and choreography for the fall show. The last portion of the day's rehearsal can be spent reviewing the choreography. Breaking into small groups performing with the music in front of the rest of the guard works well as it puts students on the spot enough to make them try a little harder. Practically, it also serves as a conduit for constructive feedback as the camp goes along.

The instructor will have some ideas about number assignments prior to the start of guard camp because he/she will have analyzed the drill extensively while writing the show. However, waiting until the end of camp to assign permanent spots in the drill is wise. This allows for performers to develop throughout the camp and be placed in the most advantageous positions for the show. Some groups utilize an "alternate" system, so watching students throughout the week is imperative in assigning the weaker performers into the alternate spots. There are pros and cons to the alternate system.

The biggest pro is that if and when attrition happens due to injury, illness, or just plain dropping out—there are extra performers to fill in the holes so the visual production isn't marred for the season.

The biggest con is that the weaker members don't get stronger as quickly because they are not participating as much. The decision about this is really up to the band director and the guard instructor.

At the end of the summer guard camp, it is beneficial to have as much of the fall show learned as possible. However, sometimes it is better to *learn less and know it well than to very roughly learn more*. Retention is important at the beginning of the full band camp because you want the guard to be able to solidly combine the guard work and choreography to the new drill they will be learning.

Sectionals

It is necessary to have rehearsals for just the color guard outside of the full marching band rehearsals. A regular weekly sectional after school or in the evening is typical. Sometimes sectionals will happen concurrently to the band rehearsal if the band is reviewing drill that the guard knows cold or if they are having a music rehearsal. Don't let the guard go off on its own if new drill is being taught as this will put both groups behind when the guard has to come back and play catch-up.

The *instructor* should devise a standing rehearsal block for each sectional, usually 4-5 files with the same number of members in each file (this will depend on the size of your guard, naturally). *Captains* and strong upperclassmen should be placed at the front of these files so the members behind them can match to their timing and technique. The other members should be interspersed with newbies and returning members—it's nice to have a strong anchor person at the rear of each file, too, whenever possible.

Sectionals can be used to review previously taught guard work or to learn new work. Regardless, the rehearsal should always start with some warm-ups. This should include a stretching routine as well as some basic positions and drop-spins, preferably both regular and double fast. Specific tosses can also be reviewed or taught during sectionals.

The sectional rhythm should already have been established at the summer guard camp so the members will recognize the flow and be able to focus their attentions to the task at hand. These warm-ups will also be used prior to performances and competitions, again as an instrument to hone the focus of the performers. If rehearsals begin with unrestricted chaos, the guard will have scattered minds and will accomplish less.

If a weapons line is used within the color guard, they should likely have an additional sectional on their own during each week. This is a huge time commitment and the members who choose to take on that additional piece of equipment need to understand the added work required. A higher standard of expectations needs to be established from the outset for a weapons line, because if they are mediocre it brings down the performance of the entire guard and unfortunately the entire band.

Don't give in to a group of guard members who think it would be "cool" to have rifles in your show. They truly must commit to the extra skill set and have a certain *X-Games* mentality to make a weapons line successful. To provide for some basic training, there are a number of excellent summer guard camp organizations that aspiring sword and gun throwers can attend. It is highly recommended they do so.

Movement Exercises

Begin each rehearsal in the assigned rehearsal block as described above in Sectionals. Often there will be a stretching routine established to music that will help the students warm up their muscles to increase flexibility and prevent injury. This may include some basic choreography with ballet elements (*tendus, frappes, plies,* movement through all five ballet positions) or it could be a simpler routine to counts lead by the captains. Additionally, lower body warm-ups can be layered under equipment basics (such as including plies in all five foot positions performed sequentially during a drop spin warm-up).

Equipment Exercises

After the stretching and movement warm-up, the group should move on to the equipment warm-up.

Guard work is always built upon recognizable basic positions such as presents, lances, and slams (which can also be broken down further and called "points in space"). Without getting into too much detail, it is ideal to warm up by moving through an exercise that involves these points in space to a clapped rhythm or to music. This helps the performer become aware of equipment angles and placement which is essential to making the guard work precise and clean.

After this exercise is complete, basic spin sequences can be addressed. Exercises for both drop spins and double fast spins are common and are usually a cornerstone to measure improvement. As the guard's overall ability and focus develops, these spins become more synchronized and downright impressive.

Finally, the guard instructor will want to create an exercise to practice basic release work that may be included in the show. A single toss is the simplest, but other common tosses include the parallel, the cross toss, and other additional rotation tosses that have nicknames of the instructor's devising. Again, the shrieking and ducking that took place during summer camp will slowly be replaced by remarkable feats of precision and ease as the season progresses.

Marching Exercises

Contrary to popular belief, marching skills are just as important to the success of a color guard as to the rest of the band. Uniformity of style and understanding of rhythm are just two reasons to include the color guard in any and all marching basic blocks. Understanding of basic marching commands used during rehearsals is also key so the guard members know when and how to step off in a manner consistent with the rest of the group.

To that end, the color guard should learn the basic *glide step* that is utilized by the marching band as outlined in the other chapters. During the first rehearsals in the summer months the guard can begin to work on marching basics within their sectionals. One rehearsal technique that is helpful is to put the guard into two long files and ask the pair at the head of the files to lead off and forward march *16 equal steps* and hit close at the end of the *16 count* phrase (flag at shoulder arms). Then the next lead pair can do the same, continuing down the files until everyone has run the exercise. When each pair finishes, they simply rotate back to the end of the files so the exercise can be run continuously as many times as necessary. It is helpful to have the assistant or the captains watching the exercise and pulling aside the members who need some helpful hints.

Once the basic forward marching style is solidified, you can begin to add left slide and right slide positions with the guard marching at shoulder arms. Then the instructor can switch to backwards marching technique using the same basic exercise (*16 counts*, adding slides).

As skills are built, keep the guard members challenged by mixing up the *16 count* marching assignment. For example, an exercise can ask for *8 counts* forward march with a right slide, immediately adding *8 counts* backward marching with a left slide. Once they have learned pivot turns to march backwards from forward steps, the patterns can get even longer and more fun. Increasing tempo can also keep the guard interested and alert. Most will rise to the challenge and be thoroughly entertained.

One such challenge might be to *forward march 8* with no slide, pivot turn to *backward march 8* with no slide, add another *forward march 8* with right slide, and add another backward march 8 (no pivot) with left slide. These exercises can accurately represent drill they may encounter on the field and encourages them to think about the orientation of their upper bodies with equipment in hand.

Once the *glide step* and backwards marching have been covered, the next style to be taught is the *jazz step*. An extremely simplified description of the *jazz step* is that it is the opposite of the glide step; rather than landing on your heel with toes up and rolling through the foot, they will absorb the initial impact of the foot with toes outstretched and roll gently down through the heel. Think of a gymnast walking on a balance beam, knees slightly bent, shoulders and back in a vertical line.

Many guard members who have had dance training will take to the *jazz step* naturally; others will struggle at first. Having good examples set by the upperclassmen will make it easier for the new members to understand and envision the style. The purpose of the *jazz step* is to enable the guard to move with grace and ease when they need to be pretty and expressive in their performance, perhaps during a ballad or slower tempos. It is easiest to learn the *jazz step* with flags stripped and the pole tucked under the right arm at a lower *V position*.

Another important purpose of the *jazz step* is to allow the color guard to cover large distances across the field gracefully via the *jazz run*. Remember those equipment changes? A color guard is always on stage from the moment they step onto the field to set their equipment to the moment they march off the field after gathering their equipment.

The *jazz run* can be practiced with the same *16-24* count exercise as the glide and *jazz step*, increasing the speed and distance traveled as the style is solidified. The *jazz run* is very similar to the *jazz step* in terms of foot placement (toe first), but the key is **not** to turn into a gazelle creating lots of airborne space between the feet and the ground. *Jazz run*ning is about gliding across the grass with no extraneous motion of the arms, poised and silent, lightly landing on the balls of the feet.

The last marching basics exercise to consider is simply adding some flag work to the *16 count* exercise. Start with something easy like presents, lances, or slams. Then start asking them to twirl parts of the school song routine with the exercise- excellent practice for any upcoming parades. Throw in some slides and some pivot turns and *voila!* An increasingly adept color guard!

Full Ensemble

When the full marching band is rehearsing, the guard should adhere to the rehearsal etiquette established by the band director and staff. It should always be assumed that the color guard is just another section in the marching band, not a separate entity with separate rules. The color guard staff should continue to teach and clean, but they should not interrupt instruction from the podium because this will distract everyone.

As far as providing guidance on the field, it is best left to the color guard staff who may also occasionally ask the guard captains to take care of some drill details or re-teach someone who is lagging behind. Other members of the color guard should rehearse attentively to the directing staff and should not offer comments to their peers. It is imperative that all guard members learn to read their coordinates or drill charts just like everyone else in the band. As well, they should learn to pay attention to the "form" as they move through space. A flag in hand is not an excuse to ignore a curvilinear or a diagonal.

Common Troubleshooting

Choosing Leaders

Choosing color guard section leaders or captains can be a nerve-wracking process, as sometimes it is a fine line between organizational skills and charisma. Most groups will appoint two or more captains to help attain a balance of leadership qualities.

Clearly the ideal candidate will be able to model proficiency in movement and equipment skills to the rest of the group. They will also need to be able to communicate well with their peers without being condescending. Guard section leaders typically keep track of a myriad of student-led initiatives such as t-shirt orders, rehearsal treats, secret pals, scavenger hunts, guard parties, etc. The main trait to strive for in the leadership, however, is maturity.

These students will have to put the kibosh on bad behavior behind the scenes and on the field in a calm way without taking things personally. It is a stretch to maintain a positive attitude throughout the ups and downs of a marching season, so try to designate the students deemed most capable of doing so. In addition, choose leaders that get along with each other and form a natural team. They will need each other's support and positive energy.

Integrating New Members & Veterans

Part of the student leaders' responsibilities will be the pleasant integration of new members with veterans. In all actuality, it is a responsibility of **all** returning members to welcome the new members with encouragement and enthusiasm.

Each group is only as strong as its weakest member, so it benefits everyone to instill a love for the activity across the membership. Second year members have the most difficulty putting away their pride in having developed skills that the beginners can only hope to achieve. Gentle reminders that everyone was a beginner once can help get over the hump. A mentoring system should also be put into place so that each new member has a big sister or brother to assist him or her in

getting started. It also gives upperclassmen a sense of ownership and responsibility if they are allowed to teach some basic skills to small groups of younger students as long as the group session is productive.

Attendance

Regular attendance by all members of the color guard at all rehearsals is vital to its success. As with any group activity that requires precision, improvement can only be achieved through repetition with everyone involved. Therefore, it is important to set expectations for attendance right from the beginning.

To assist with this, a contract should be signed by the student and parent/guardian before the student is even allowed to participate in auditions. The contract can spell out the entire schedule for rehearsals and performances for the season (including summer activities), and can allow for the family to respond if there is a previously scheduled vacation, wedding, family reunion, church trip etc. that will conflict with any of these dates.

The *Instructor* and *Band Director* should take any of these conflicts into account when selecting the group at the end of audition week. The contract can also explain what absences are considered "excused" and "unexcused". In general, you will not excuse your guard members for work (these conflicts can be resolved by pro-actively informing work managers of the student's school commitments), or for any number of various doctor/dentist/hair/senior photo appointments. The contract should also convey who has the authority to excuse absences (i.e. the band director and the parent only—often the guard instructor is not technically an employee of the school district). In other words, students cannot simply text the guard captain that they will not be at practice because they are sick. The parent must contact the band director to let him or her know the situation directly.

Please note that students **and** parents will push back on this. Every band director must decide what will be deemed an "excused" absence and use common sense as situations arise. If absences are increasing and a student continues to fall farther and farther behind, termination from the group is warranted. It only takes one weak member to make the performance look sloppy, and this can become a detriment to the group's attitude towards teamwork.

Equipment Management

As noted in an earlier section of this chapter, there are many ways to label equipment to keep track of everyone's flags, poles, end caps, etc. Equipment management can still become a huge challenge and needs to be constantly monitored. The guard captains can do weekly "bag checks" to make sure that poles are legibly labeled and each student has all of the flags they have been assigned. This may seem like a hassle but it will ward off the inevitable anguished cries of *"Somebody stole my flag!"*

The other issue that often arises is performers not having the appropriate piece of equipment during a performance. They will raise a hue and cry that they set the flag in the right place along the sideline for an equipment change and "somebody moved it" or "so and so took MY flag by mistake so I didn't have one." This happens even to the best of the color guards. The best way to prevent this is to allow for a lot of practice in setting equipment prior to run-through of your show.

It usually only takes one instance of someone setting a flag incorrectly to solve that particular mistake. Be prepared, however, for the rage and threats of retribution that may arise. Nothing seems to promote unrest in a group more than this particular issue. To this end, it is best to require each performer to set each of their own flags and gear. Then there is nobody to blame but himself or herself if they are not set correctly.

Finally, discourage your guard members from allowing non-guard members to attempt to spin their flags or weapons. Just as your band members should not hand a saxophone over to a non-musician during a rehearsal break, guard members should not hand potential concussions over to hapless band members.

Competition Results

If you take your marching band to competitions, there will often be awards for best guard in class along with best percussion, best winds, etc. While using competitions as a natural way to help students get excited about the season, it is definitely a problem if winning becomes the main objective because it can truly backfire. For example, a guard that is improving steadily and has solid performances might go an entire season without being recognized with a trophy, and some students take this to mean that they are "terrible." The truth of the matter is that judging at marching competitions is a subjective process. Even though there are numbers and "boxes" to try to calculate how groups compare to each other, it truly comes down to personal preference in many cases.

Therefore, the result that should be emphasized to the group is how much growth they have seen in their own skills throughout the season and the positive reinforcement they receive from audiences and the occasional helpful judge's tape. With regards to the latter, I strongly encourage the *band director* and *instructor* to listen to the applicable judge's tapes (auxiliary judge, GE judges) **before** sharing them with the guard. Sometimes there are comments that are too pointed for individuals to hear; other times the comments are so generic and sparse it would be a waste of rehearsal time to sit the group down and listen.

So, what is a judge looking for in a competitive setting in terms of your auxiliary unit?

- Guard work should be synchronized (clean) and appropriate to the musical program
- Guard uniforms should be thematic and appropriate for every body type represented in the group
- Guard design (flags and props) should be thematic and represent nuances of the musical program
- Guard members should be an integral part of the visual program and complete drill formations meaningfully
- Guard members should be poised and professional performers at all times (even during equipment changes)
- Guard members should perform "up" to the audience, not down to the front sideline
- Guard members should recover from mistakes smoothly
- Guard work should include dance and body movement layered underneath spinning the equipment

Different states will have different judging templates that may reward these areas in different ratios, but this represents the key traits that mark successful guard programs.

Winter Guard

Winter guard can mean different levels of commitment to different band programs. A big factor will be the availability of rehearsal space and instructional staff. One might consider continuing basic guard training throughout the off-season to maintain or build on basic skills with flags and weapons.

Some schools train for one performance at the halftime of a basketball game, for example. If staffing and budgets permit, a group might consider competing in one or two shows at the state organization level (again, this varies widely from state to state). If the group is looking for another truly competitive season, you will want to explore regional shows sponsored by *Winter Guard International*. The latter is a very sophisticated organization that is closely linked to *Drum Corps International* and comprises its own system of requirements and adjudication.

Examine the goals you have for the particular color guard to decide which course of action is best during the off-season. While continuing the activity during the winter months can be advantageous, there is also something to be said about the "burnout factor" from staff and performer perspectives. In the end, only the director will know what the right decision is for the group based on their enthusiasm and energy level.

XII. ADMINISTRATION

Music Library

An efficient music library functions solely on information received from others and operates ahead of the organization to ensure that the music is prepared properly for the first rehearsal. Last minute changes and additions not only create an immediate stress on the library, but more importantly, it has a ripple effect on future concerts, as preparations for that concert must be halted to address the immediate need. To ensure the best possible music preparation, make every effort to give the library accurate information in a timely manner. Meticulous and efficient preparation of music is the first step in assuring a successful and productive first rehearsal and concert cycle. Poorly prepared music, or music prepared hastily, can stop a rehearsal and halt the overall progress of a performing ensemble.

THERE ARE 5 BASIC TASKS IN LIBRARY ORGANIZATION:

1. Cataloging

All music should be cataloged. There are many different library systems that can be used to organize the library. Information can be recorded on filing cards or in a computer database program that can generate various reports on the library's holdings, such as performance records. Commercially published forms can be purchased, or customized ones can be economically created in-house.

Meta Data Fields

- Title
- Composer / Arranger
- Publisher
- Type and style
- Instrumentation (including unusual instrumentation)
- Music size (march, concert, octavo, etc.)
- File location (file/drawer number etc.)
- Duration
- Difficulty level
- Performance dates
- Miscellaneous/Notes

After cataloging, each piece in the set should be stamped with the school's name and individual catalog number; which will assist in putting away any stray sheets, and keep them more organized. Custom-made stamps can be purchased from a print shop at a minimal cost, and should be stamped in a color other than black, to easily identify originals.

An inventory sheet set up in score order is incredibly useful to keep track of the number of parts for each instrument. A pre-determined numbering system for each individual sheet of music, (is also helpful when recollecting music, to easily ascertain if anything is missing) numbered either as a whole set or by section.

In addition, a skeleton set of one of each part, bundled separately, can ensure that if any sheet is lost, the work can continue to be performed until replacements are ordered. This skeleton set should remain in the library, and should never be distributed. If the music needs to be cut, use a high quality paper cutter so the music is cut precisely to the same size.

Next, place the music in an envelope or storage box that is labeled with the title, composer/arranger, and catalogue number. This information should be visible when the music is filed.

Finally, file the music in the storage unit. The two basic methods for filing music are, chronologically by acquisition, and alphabetically by composer or title. The disadvantage of the alphabetical system, is that it requires a constant reorganization as music is added. The advantage is that it is faster to locate the music by title.

3. Distribution

Ideally, marching music should be issued at the beginning of the season, with all the music needed for that season included. The first step to creating a set for distribution, is to determine how many of each part the set contains. An inventory sheet with a space for notes that is included within each set can be very helpful in this process. (i.e. errata corrected and by whom). It should include information about previously missing parts, so a student is not billed incorrectly for a part that was missing prior to this distribution, or any notes that might be helpful for the next performance of the piece of music.

Then, each piece should be cleaned of any stray pencil markings or notes specific to a past performance, to avoid confusion during rehearsal. A high-quality rubber eraser or an electric

eraser is useful for this process. This is also the time to make any page-turn amendments needed for concert size music, repair damaged music, mark cuts, notate measure numbers/ or rehearsal letters that match the conductor's score, and correct errata to ensure a successful first rehearsal.

If there is an audition process, the library should be the first informed of part assignments or rosters, as booking folders is a time-consuming process. Booking folders is easier with two students, one to record each inventory number on an inventory card, one to book the folders and also assist in preventing mistakes, when there is a large amount of folders going out.

When passing out folders, it is helpful to have either a spreadsheet or an inventory card, notating the parts each individual is receiving, that they can initial, so that they thoroughly understand that they are responsible for these sheets. This is especially important if the music needs to be returned at the end of the season, or if an individual piece of music is lost, and can be returned quickly to the correct student. This information should be kept on file in the library for future music distribution.

Keeping neat and accurate records saves time and money, so that charges can be issued for lost or damaged music. When the students are aware that accurate records are kept, and that they are responsible for lost or damaged music, they are more likely to take care of the music during the season.

Furthermore, any part changes that have occurred throughout the season should be reported to the library. Students should also understand that a specific sheet of music has been assigned to them, so that if part changes do occur, they must go through the library to receive a new part. This helps to maintain accurate records, and ensure that if a sheet of music is lost, that the correct student is billed.

4. Extra Sets

If rehearsals or performances are performed with music, it is always a good idea to have a set of extra parts on hand for emergencies, in case a student has forgotten their music, or lost a sheet to ensure that a rehearsal or performance can continue on uninterrupted. If they have merely forgotten it that day, a note can be taken of which parts and inventory numbers are taken and the music can be returned after the rehearsal or performance. In cases of losing their music, a new set can be issued to them quickly.

5. Collection & Refiling

At the end of the season, music needs to be collected, sorted, and re-filed. Set specific times for students to return music and sign releases indicating that all music has been returned. It is best to collect music immediately after the last performance, as the student will be less likely to forget to turn it in, and to save the library the time and hassle of tracking students down.

This entire collection process should be done as close as possible to the final concert for several reasons:

- Prevent music from piling up in the library
- Tracking down missing folders before the students disperse, and locating them becomes difficult
- It sets a precedent of a quick return of folders, and the issuing of bills for the next cycle

When this whole procedure is performed efficiently, and the students understand that they are responsible for every sheet of music and folder, they will be more likely to return their folders promptly in the future. De-booking should be performed with the original inventory used when the music was issued, to insure that every piece has returned. The librarian should then sort the folders into score order (this can also help ascertain precisely which folders are missing before any folders are opened), and begin removing the pieces and placing them in separate piles face down.

When the de-booking is complete, each pile should be in score order facing down. Once the music has been collected, repair damaged music, and clean the parts again from pencil markings. List the missing music on the note section on the set's inventory sheet, and order any replacement parts from a music dealer. It is recommended to record all performance records for future knowledge.

REMINDER—*It is against the law to photocopy music without the written permission from the publisher.*

Attendance Records

Maintaining attendance records can be time-consuming. However, accurate information is important as many directors use this data in determining grades, awards, promotions, etc. There are many different procedures and forms that can be used. Also several important factors to consider when establishing an attendance record-keeping policy. It should be accurate, consistent, and easy to manage.

MANUAL RECORD KEEPING

The attendance record-keeping method should not waste valuable rehearsal time. For example, a "tag board" system is an efficient method, which is easy to build and use. Make a tag board by inserting a grid of hooks into a sheet of plywood. The board can be constructed so that it can be folded for storage and transporting. Apply a different color to each side of the tag with highlighters. Print the names and sections of the members on both sides of the tags, and hang them on the hooks in alphabetical order (by name or by section) with the same color showing. On top of the board put one extra tag with the words "**COLOR FOR TODAY**" printed on both sides, so that everyone will know which color should be facing out for that day's attendance.

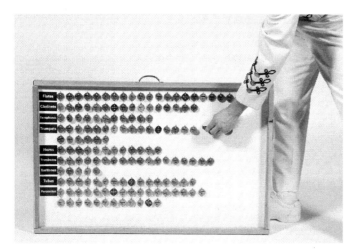

Whenever there is an event that requires attendance, set the board up in a location near the entrance. As students arrive they should flip their tags to indicate that they are present. It is best if someone is present to monitor this procedure. The tag board system is fast, accurate, and ideal for quickly identifying anyone who is missing or late.

Once a procedure is established, good record keeping is easier. Attendance records should be kept in a three-ring binder containing a summary sheet for each event. Each sheet should include the date, event, and a list of absentees and tardies. Be sure to use a symbol for absentees that can be easily converted to a tardy for late arrivals (e.g., a check mark can easily be changed to an "X"). Use another symbol to indicate whether the tardy or absentee was excused (e.g., a circle could be drawn around the "X" or check mark for an excused tardy). Include an explanation of these symbols on the top of the form. This method is effective because individual sheets are organized in the notebook in chronological order, making it easy to view attendance records for each activity throughout the entire season.

DIGITAL RECORD KEEPING

MyAT attendance software[4] is the closest to ideal for maintaining all types of tracking records for marching and concert bands digitally—on desktop and mobile devices. The reporting is easily accessible to everyone in your organization's network. The basic application (by the time of this writing) is free with a voluntary donation. However, it requires a paid upgrade to access more advanced and automated features.

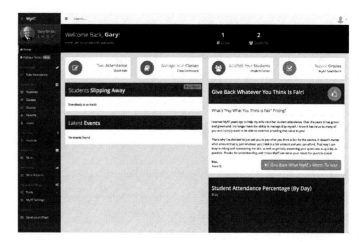

---

4 Website address: www.myattendancetracker.com

Organizing Trips

The director should be responsible for the majority of a trip's organizational duties; however, student leaders can easily assist in several ways. Here are some organizing tips to help with organization. Prepare the trip itineraries that include the following.

Before The Trip

- Departure and arrival times
- Emergency phone numbers
- Locations of all destinations
- Events schedule, including meal times, rehearsals, performances, and special occasions
- Dress for each event, including times and locations of changing facilities
- Bus lists, room assignments, and total trip personnel
- Rules, policies, and school regulations regarding proper behavior
- Directions and maps to all major trip locations
- A checklist of items for students to bring
- A checklist of school equipment needed for trip
- Submit copies of itineraries to school officials, parents, and students
- Load equipment truck and take inventory
- Collect and file insurance and health reports

After The Trip

- Check buses for lost and found items.
- Secure school facilities.
- Put away equipment and supplies and straighten the rehearsal room.
- Send thank-you notes to those who assisted during the trip.
- Thank the director for the extra work spent organizing the trip.

During The Trip

- Supervise loading of luggage, instruments, and personnel on buses, and equipment vehicle.
- Take attendance.
- Assist with setting up and tearing down equipment used in rehearsals and performances.
- Make announcements regarding schedule changes, either on the buses or during group meetings.
- Collect names and addresses of people who should be sent "thank you" notes.

Rehearsal Planning

The most important role of the director during rehearsal, is to supervise the marching and musical accomplishments of the ensemble. This leaves the director little time to emphasize specific aspects of the ensemble's execution of the music, and marching basics. The most valuable contribution a student leader can make for the success of the marching ensemble, is to focus attention on the specifics of music and marching fundamentals. This permits the director to concentrate on the overall progress of the ensemble.

A well-organized, productive rehearsal has a positive psychological effect on students. Student leaders should meet with the director to discuss their roles related to achieving defined goals. The director needs to be specific about the student leader's responsibilities. The following are a few examples of what a student leader might do to assist the director.

Before Rehearsal

- Set up chairs, stands, and equipment.
- Write announcements, schedule, and goals on the blackboard.
- Line the football field and install grid or drill markings.
- Set up ladders, podiums, and sound system.
- Arrange percussion equipment or other special equipment used in the show.
- Straighten rehearsal room or pick up trash on field.
- Take attendance.

During Rehearsal

- Help individuals with marching or music execution problems.
- Support the instructor by displaying a positive attitude.
- Set a good example with exemplary behavior and meticulous performance.
- Look for and correct spacing, alignment, or execution problems during drill rehearsals.

After Rehearsal

- Put equipment and supplies away.
- Communicate with the director and peers for suggestions on how to improve student leadership roles.
- Encourage and assist struggling students.
- Be a positive influence on those with discipline problems.

Publicity & Promotions

Seldom do marching ensemble directors find the time required to promote the ensemble's various activities. In this age of social media, encouraging enthusiastic students to help promote the band through various channels, will help enliven active interest for the organization.

RESPONSIBILITIES THAT CAN BE DONE BY STUDENT PERSONNEL:

- Print and distribute posters advertising ensemble events.
- Post events on your organization's Social Media official page.
- Prepare and have PR releases about ensemble events.
- Work with middle school ensemble programs to recruit new students.
- Establish a welcome program for new, or transfer students.
- Organize ensemble social events such as picnics, banquets, parties, sporting events, and field trips.
- Invite special guests and local celebrities to performances.
- Create and maintain a creative and informative page, group or profile, on various social media networks such as *Facebook, Twitter, Instagram, YouTube* and *Snapchat.*

INVOLVEMENT WITH PROMOTING EDUCATIONAL OPPORTUNITIES:

- Invite guest artists or clinicians for clinics, master classes, and/or performances.
- Search school faculty for former college musicians who could conduct section rehearsals or give lessons.
- Call extra sectional rehearsals when needed to prepare for performances or competitions.
- Organize a private lesson program of experienced players teaching younger players.
- Obtain and display valuable teaching aids such as videotapes, recordings, charts, posters, or books.
- Share videos on your official *YouTube* channel.

Property Management

Keeping records, storing, distributing, and collecting school property is a time-consuming job. Equipment includes uniforms, instruments, auxiliary equipment, accessory items, and props. Maintain descriptive records of inventory. Moreover, whenever equipment is issued to members, they should sign a contract.

CONTRACT INFORMATION SHOULD INCLUDE:

- Inventory number assigned to each item
- Date, ensemble name, record number, and storage location
- A detailed description of item being issued, including any previous damage
- Name and address of individual receiving items
- A clear policy regarding financial responsibility for lost or damaged equipment
- Deadline for returning music, uniforms, instruments, and equipment
- A place for a signature agreeing to contract conditions

Set specific times to distribute and collect supplies. Have extra people available to assist with uniform fitting problems, equipment testing, filling out contracts, and answering questions. When collecting equipment or uniforms, make sure everything is cleaned and repaired before returning it to storage. Work in coordination with music parents, dry cleaners, and music dealers to assist with the process of inspecting, cleaning, and repairing uniforms and equipment at the end of the season.

ABOUT THE AUTHOR

Gary E. Smith

Associate Director of Bands, Emeritus—
University of Illinois, Urbana-Champaign
President of the American Bandmasters
Association (ABA), 2017

Gary Smith received his B.A. degree from *Butler University* and his M.A. degree from *Ball State University*. He started his career as *Director of Bands* at *Northside High School* in Fort Wayne, Indiana in 1964–68. Following, he became the *Director of Bands* at *Saint Joseph's College* in Rensselaer, Indiana, from 1968–72. Next, Gary served as *Assistant Director of Bands* and *Marching Band Director* in 1972–76 at *Indiana State University* in Terre Haute, Indiana.

From 1976 to 1998 and again in 2004, Gary was the *Associate Director of Bands* at the *University of Illinois* in Urbana-Champaign, where he conducted the nationally renown *Marching Illini, Basketball Band*, and *Symphonic Band II*. He also taught marching band procedures, and band arranging in the *School of Music*.

In 1988 Gary was elected to be a member of the prestigious *American Bandmasters Association*. In 2015, he was elected to serve as the president in 2018. In addition, he is a member of *Phi Beta Mu, Phi Mu Alpha*, and *Kappa Kappa Psi* music honorary fraternities, and participates in the *College Band Director's National Association, National Band Association*, and the *Florida Music Educators Association*.

In 2005, he assisted with the production of the *Orange Bowl Halftime*. In 2007, Gary served as co-director of the *Oklahoma Centennial All State Marching Band*, which was featured during the 2007 *Rose Bowl Parade* opening ceremonies.

In 2015 Gary designed and produced the *Singapore Youth Honor Marching Band* for the finale performance for Singapore's *50th Anniversary of Independence Youth Celebration*.

Gary is the former owner of the *Smith Walbridge Clinics, a summer camp* for drum majors, colorguard, marching percussion, marching band student leaders, and band directors, where he continues to serve as a clinician. Since 1949, these clinics have attracted thousands of high school and college students from across the United States, and several foreign countries.

Over his entire career, Gary has served as a consultant, guest conductor and clinician throughout the United States, Singapore, China, Australia, Japan, Canada, Ireland, and France.

Presently, he serves as the producer of the annual *Disney Thanksgiving Parade of Bands* held at *Walt Disney World* in Orlando, FL. Since 1987 he has served as the coordinator of the band festivities for the *Chick-fil-A Peach Bowl*. In addition, he serves as the conductor of the

Bonita Springs Concert Band in Bonita Springs, FL. Alongside, he is an adjunct faculty member at the *Florida Gulf Coast University,* where he teaches marching band procedures.

His self-published textbook, *The System– Marching Band Methods*, was acquired by the music publishing company *GIA Publications, Inc.*, in 2016.

Awards:

The University of Illinois Alumni Association Outstanding Educator

The Mary Hoffman Outstanding Music Educator

The Spirit of the Illini from the University of Illinois Athletic Association

The Kappa Kappa Psi Distinguished Service to Music Medal

The 2015 Outstanding Alumni Award in the School of Music at Ball State University.

Phi Beta Mu Bandmasters Hall of Fame— Inducted 2017

Featured Publications:

The Instrumentalist
The School Musician
Band Director's Guide

CONTRIBUTING AUTHORS & EDITORS

Dr. Corey Spurlin
Associate Director of Bands
Auburn University
—Chapter XII. Drill Design

Dr. David Waybright
Director of Bands
University of Florida
—Chapter XIII. Conducting/Tests

Dr. Tim Lautzenheiser
Conn–Selmer
—Chapter I. Leadership /The Selection &
Development of Student Leaders

Barry L. Houser
Associate Director of Bands
University of Illinois,
President of Smith Walbridge, Inc.
—Chapter IV. The Drum Major

Tom Keck
Director of Bands
Utah Valley University
—Chapter X. Marching Percussion

Scott Casagrande
Director of Bands
Hersey HS, IL

Steve Scherer
Director of Bands
Geneseo HS, IL

David Maccabee
Director of Bands
United Township HS, IL

Alfred Watkins
Director of Bands, Emeritus
Lassiter HS

Roland Barrett
Composer/Arranger
University of Oklahoma
—Chapter II. Music / Editing Existing
Arrangements - Examples

Mark Greenburg
Managing Director at Tresóna
—Chapter II. Music / Copyright Laws

Chris Borgard
M.S., CSCS
Certified Strength & Conditioning Specialist
Cal Poly State University

Jim Bailey
D'Addario & Company / Evans Percussion
—Chapter X. Marching Percussion /
Tuning Drums

Sara K. Clark Maccabee
Colorguard Specialist
—Chapter XI. Colorguard

Stuart Smith
Book Designer/Editor
University of Illinois

PHOTOS COURTESY OF
Auburn University Marching Band
University of Illinois Marching Illini
University of Kentucky Marching Wildcats
University of Akron
Florida Gulf Coast University
Colts Drum & Bugle Corps
Terry Shuck (Parades)